SURGEON
KOOP

THE GRAND ROUNDS PRESS

SURGEON
KOOP

GREGG
EASTERBROOK

WHITTLE DIRECT BOOKS

Photographs: Young C. Everett Koop: courtesy of the Medical Archives, New York Hospital-Cornell Medical Center, page 6; Dr. William Ladd: courtesy of Harvard Medical Archives, the Francis A. Countway Library of Medicine, Boston, page 7; Koop's hands: Ed Eckstein, page 13; Koop with Isolette: courtesy of Children's Hospital of Philadelphia, page 15; Koop with baby: Ed Eckstein, page 21; Koop with Karen Kelso: courtesy of Children's Hospital of Philadelphia, page 28; Rodriguez twins separation: Ed Eckstein, pages 34-36; Koop with Clara Rodriguez: AP/Wide World, page 36; Editorial cartoon: ©Bill Day/*The Bulletin*, page 43; Koop at confirmation hearings: AP/Wide World, page 45; Surgeon General Luther Terry: AP/Wide World, page 50; Portrait of Surgeon General C. Everett Koop: ©the estate of Robert Mapplethorpe, page 52; Koop with AIDS pamphlet: AP/Wide World, page 55; Koop and Senator Edward Kennedy: AP/Wide World, page 59; Koop with wife, Elizabeth: Linda L. Creighton/*U.S. News & World Report*, page 63; Koop with portrait of son David: Linda L. Creighton/*U.S. News & World Report*, page 66; Koop with children: Linda L. Creighton/*U.S. News & World Report*, page 71.

Library of Congress Catalog Card Number: 91-65577
Easterbrook, Gregg
Surgeon Koop
ISBN 1-879736-02-0
ISSN 1053-6620

The Grand Rounds Press

The Grand Rounds Press presents original short books by distinguished authors on subjects of importance to the medical profession.

The series is edited and published by Whittle Books, a business unit of Whittle Communications L.P. A new book will be published approximately every three months. The series will reflect a broad spectrum of responsible opinions. In each book the opinions expressed are those of the author, not the publisher or advertiser.

I welcome your comments on this unique endeavor.

William S. Rukeyser
Editor in Chief

CONTENTS

This generation has witnessed an information explosion in the fields of biology and medicine. Although the resulting advances have brought about important technological breakthroughs, the primary goals of medical research remain the same: the treatment and care of patients, and the amelioration of disease.

At Syntex, our research and development efforts are directed not only toward the diseases treated, but also toward the needs of patients that can interfere with their ability to lead full and productive lives. Physicians who prescribe our products, and patients who use our medications on a daily basis, look to us to provide effective, safe, and convenient treatment options. We take our responsibilities seriously, realizing that the patients treated include neighbors, friends, and family.

In this age of advanced medical technology, and in our enthusiasm to treat diseases with sophisticated new therapies, it is easy to lose sight of the human factors associated with illness. What helps to keep our efforts in focus at Syntex is the realization that the needs of people lie at the heart of all we do.

Timothy P. Spiro

TIMOTHY P. SPIRO, MD
VICE PRESIDENT
MEDICAL AFFAIRS DIVISION
SYNTEX LABORATORIES, INC.

A

INDEPENDENCE.

RESTORING THE INDEPENDENCE THAT ARTHRITIS CAN DIMINISH.
A FIFTEEN-YEAR HISTORY OF HELPING PATIENTS REALIZE THE FULL
POTENTIAL OF INDEPENDENT LIFE.

NAPROSYN®
(NAPROXEN) 500 MG TABLETS.

THE MOST FREQUENT COMPLAINTS ARE GASTROINTESTINAL.
SEE "WARNINGS," "PRECAUTIONS," AND "ADVERSE REACTIONS"
SECTIONS OF PRESCRIBING INFORMATION.

SYNTEX IS MAKING PROFOUND CONTRIBUTIONS TO MEDICINE.

YOU CAN LOCATE THE PRESCRIBING INFORMATION FOR **NAPROSYN** ON PAGES I-IV OF THE APPENDIX.

PROLOGUE

If the setting dials of your time machine were broken, you might not be sure where in time you had landed: Around you, children are suffering and dying in what is supposed to be a place of healing. Through stuffy hallways, nurses move from one small patient to the next, aware that many of their charges are doomed. In the wards, young children may be strapped down to prevent them from moving while formidable surgical gashes labor to mend. Some children stagger along on crutches or in braces, their ability to move declining rather than improving. The place reeks of mothballs because children's chests are swabbed with camphorated oil to fend off respiratory infection. It is stiflingly hot in summer; nurses spend many of their working hours sponging down feverish children with wet cloths. Families are kept away except for brief visits, which means that many children live out the most desperate moments of their lives, up to the last, terrified and alone.

Recovery rates are sadly low for many patients in this place; of the serious surgical admissions, especially the youngest, more depart through the morgue than through the front door. Often surgery is staged at night, the surgeons having spent their business hours operating on older patients with better prospects. Often surgeons come to this place glumly, to stage operations they expect will fail. Most are fatalistic, believing the outcome cannot be otherwise.

Where are you? Not in Dickensian London, nor Europe during the plague, nor Calcutta at the turn of the century. You're in the United States, and the year is 1946. You are in the Children's Hospital of Philadelphia, then as now one of the country's top centers for the treatment of the young.

How rapidly it has been forgotten that during the lifetimes of many men and women in the United States, it was a common event for little children's bodies to burn themselves out with bacterial diseases or to become hopelessly crippled with polio. Even after

1

sulfa drugs, antibiotics, and vaccines had begun to change that picture, it continued to be common for the very young to die during procedures now done in a few minutes on an outpatient basis. In the late 1940s, even in the best pediatric hospitals in the United States, pediatric operations had mortality rates ranging from 50 percent for removal of a simple tumor to 100 percent for an emergency such as a blocked esophagus in a newborn. The surgical establishment regretted this, but saw nothing out of the ordinary in the situation. Few really expected children to survive serious illness.

Some physicians felt otherwise. In the post-Depression years they began the push for improved pediatric surgery that led to today's system of children's hospitals, in which preventable deaths have become such a rarity that medicine's very proficiency at keeping the seriously ill child alive is itself controversial. No one was more important to this transition than a pediatric surgeon now known for other things entirely: Charles Everett Koop.

In current public discourse, Koop's name is associated with the political turmoil surrounding abortion, AIDS, "Baby Doe" cases, the role of religion in public policy, and the other issues that marked his eight years as surgeon general. Yet for all the highly publicized commotion regarding his opinions, it was as a practicing physician that Koop made his greatest mark on society.

Koop arrived at Children's of Philadelphia in 1946 at age 30, and he became its chief of surgery in 1948—"chief" over no one, since he was the only pediatric surgeon in the city, and one of but a handful in the country. In time he would become one of the leading innovators in the theory and practice of pediatric surgery. He would also become the profession's top advocate, tirelessly arguing within the medical establishment that children needed specialized care—the kind of care they now receive routinely. His achievements in pediatric surgery are a reminder of how far this discipline has come in a very short time, with surprisingly little public recognition.

"During my lifetime pediatric surgery went through, at a highly accelerated pace, what all of American medicine went through roughly from the founding of the Colonies to the present day," Koop says. "We were an instant microcosm of the development of scientific medicine."

Those who know Koop's professional background will also know that his so-called astonishing conversion from conservative to liberal hero while he was surgeon general was neither a conversion nor out of character. Defying conventional wisdom has been Koop's lifelong stock in trade, as this story will show.

CHAPTER ONE

NOT BUNNY RABBITS

The first important facility dedicated to the treatment of the young in the English-speaking world was the Hospital for Sick Children, established in London in 1852. Though the facility, founded with the aid of Charles Dickens, alleviated some of the extreme disparities in care between children and adults, Tiny Tim stood about as much chance of being cured there as he did of learning to fly. The second major pediatric hospital, the Children's Hospital of Philadelphia, was founded three years later. Children's Hospital in Boston followed in 1869. Until the turn of the century these institutions were a small, dim candle in the darkness of pediatric medicine.

It wasn't until almost 100 years after these hospitals were founded—long past the point at which a hospital stay had ceased to be terrifying for most adults—that pediatric institutions became places parents could take children without dread. Nearly a century would pass before pediatric care improved to the point that common but calamitous childhood illnesses became either preventable through vaccination or curable through medical management. And a century would pass before a sick child would be as likely to be treated by a pediatric surgeon as by a general surgeon.

The slow development of pediatric surgery may have been due to the unpredictable timing of research and technological break-throughs, whose arrival in all medical fields has proved highly resistant to logical expectations. But an equally likely explanation is that the medical world was reflecting society's values in considering children less fully human than adults, and therefore less worthy of attention and resources.

Until this century, infant deaths were routine events. The large families typical of old-world cultures of the past (and third-world cultures today) prevailed at least partly because parents who wanted children to take care of them in old age had to bear many offspring so that several would survive to adulthood. Traditional Jewish law, dating back at least 1,000 years, holds that a baby does not acquire a soul until 30 days after birth. Because stillbirths and deaths immediately following birth were so common in biblical times, perhaps such beliefs helped ease parents' grief at the loss of a child.

In *A Distant Mirror*, a study of the 14th century, historian Barbara Tuchman noted that art from that period rarely depicts infants or children, except for the baby Jesus, who is shown as a kind of miniature adult. In cases where mother and youngster are depicted together, the adult stares at her child with blank abstraction, as if wondering whether she should care about this arrival. Such attitudes, Tuchman wrote, stem from the fact that in the Middle Ages, more than half of all children died before reaching adolescence.

Because little could be done until this century to lower infant mortality, most societies came to accept childhood death as the way of the world. The mere custom of calling a baby "it," a term never used for adults even when gender is uncertain, betrays this attitude. Limitations on legal rights for children arose from such premises, as did the notion—subconscious or otherwise—of concentrating medical resources on society's productive members, adults.

By the start of the 20th century, however, the young began to acquire improved standing in Western society: child labor laws, beginning in 1916, granted them some protection; child abusers were occasionally prosecuted; and education was beginning to be considered every child's right. But even upper-class children continued to receive surgical care of a quality that seems shocking today. For whatever reasons—cultural programming, the now-discarded theory that children are too weak for most surgical interventions, the simple fact that infants cannot speak for themselves—the surgical establishment did not question the status quo.

The first clear indicator of change came in 1941, when Harvard Medical School established the first chair in child surgery. That same year, Dr. William E. Ladd, the man for whom the chair was named, gave a lecture in which he criticized general surgeons for the care they afforded pediatric patients. Only by making pediatric surgery a specialty, Ladd declared, could the welfare of the young be safeguarded.

His audience, which included members of the Boston Surgical Society, a citadel of medical prestige, was unimpressed by Ladd's ideas. Surgical specialization by body area or organ was just becoming common, and general surgeons were fighting the encroachment at every turn. Now Ladd was proposing that an age group become a specialty, a powerful assault on the generalists' turf.

In response, Dr. Edward Churchill, a nationally famous surgeon who practiced at Massachusetts General, "the world's greatest hospital," informed Ladd that the surgical residents of Mass General were quite proficient at operating on rabbits; if they could do animals smaller than infants, said Churchill, pediatric surgery was not a problem. It happened that later a pathologist at Mass General asked Ladd to come to the morgue and help him autopsy some children whose deaths had baffled Churchill's residents. "What Dr. Ladd found there," Everett Koop later wrote, "were three cases of volvulus of the midgut caused by malrotation of the colon. In two, the abdomen had been closed because the lesion was not understood, while one had been operated on incorrectly—all by residents who well understood the surgery of bunny rabbits."

Against this backdrop of poor surgical care for infants and establishment resistance to pediatric specialization, Koop arrived on the scene in the late 1940s.

Born in Brooklyn in 1916 and brought up as a strict Baptist, Koop exhibited a precocious fixation on surgery; as a teenager, he sometimes sneaked into Columbia-Presbyterian Hospital to watch operations staged in the old surgical theaters. He was admitted to Dartmouth at the age of 17, and at 25 he graduated from Cornell Medical School. He then enrolled at the University of Pennsylvania for postgraduate study.

One day in 1946, Koop was admitted to the Penn hospital for treatment of a strep infection. A favorite medical-school professor, Dr. I. S. Ravdin, dropped by to see him and asked what he planned to do with his life. Koop replied that his aspiration was to run the Penn tumor clinic. When Ravdin asked the young physician what he thought about establishing a surgery department at Children's of Philadelphia, Koop rapidly ad libbed that, of course, that was his second choice.

Koop departed for Boston that same year to train for seven months at Children's Hospital under Dr. Robert Gross. Where to send him had not been a difficult decision: Children's in Boston was at that time the only hospital in the United States known for advancing the art of pediatric surgery. While there, Koop spent many hours listening to Ladd, who had by then retired, hold forth during visits with residents at the hospital. Koop has said that he learned as much from Ladd's talks as from his formal training. Once Koop decided to take the post at Children's of Philadelphia, he vowed to make that institution the rival of Children's in Boston—and to

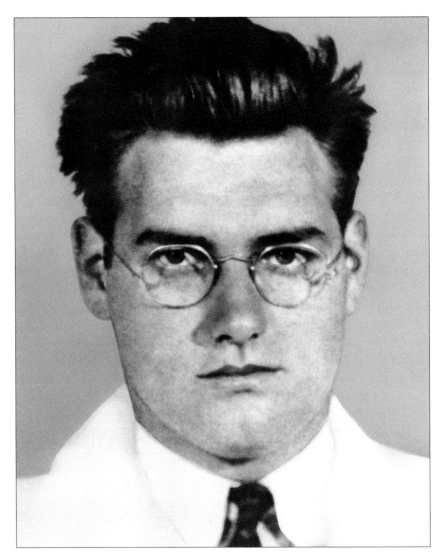

This photograph of C. Everett Koop appeared in the Cornell Medical School yearbook for 1941. The future surgeon was 25.

make himself the first great modern pediatric surgeon.

In the late '40s pediatric medicine was just beginning to rival medical care for adults. Koop was sharp enough to realize that the backward state of pediatric surgery created a tremendous opening for whoever could bring the subspecialty into the modern era. He was not dismayed that nearly everyone else thought children would never be able to withstand surgery as well as adults. Koop had been taught to believe he could do anything he set his mind to, including revolutionize an entire specialty. And he had the right characteristics for the attempt: intellect, vision, dedication, physical skill, and, from the start, an astonishing case of surgeon's ego.

Koop would later be accused of many things, but never of being paralyzed by self-doubt. On his very first day as a surgeon at Children's of Philadelphia in 1946, he clashed with Dr. Joseph Stokes, the hospital's physician in chief. When Stokes informed the new surgeon that all surgical admissions would be routed through the office of the physician in chief, Koop, then 30, brassily declared that he and he alone would set his own admitting procedures. He won the argument.

"We were all flabbergasted by how quickly this young fireball knocked our senior doctor down several pegs," says Richard D. Wood Sr., who was president of Children's Hospital through most of Koop's tenure there.

Wood also knew that one reason Koop had gotten the position was that nobody else wanted it. Although Koop was hardly the only young physician to notice the opening for dramatic improvements in pediatric surgery, others decided to play it safe, choosing careers with better odds for success. Pediatric surgery seemed a professional deadend, more like a job for a glorified mortician than a healer. And pediatric hospitals were at the bottom of the totem pole in prestige: they were poorly equipped, ill endowed, and lightly regarded academically. "Back then some of the places calling themselves children's hospitals might as well have been veterinary clinics for chimpanzees," Wood says. "When you told someone in medicine you worked at a children's hospital they looked away, embarrassed for you."

Koop's mentor, Dr. William E. Ladd, a professor of child surgery at Harvard, was among the first to advocate that pediatric surgery become a specialty.

In his first years at Children's, Koop found an immediate complication—very few patients. Sometimes he went for weeks without seeing one. Because the success rates for some kinds of pediatric surgery were so dismal, family physicians would not refer infants to the hospital unless a case grew desperate. And physicians often made no attempt whatsoever to intervene surgically when children were born with what are now considered correctable handicaps. The standard procedure for conditions such as inguinal hernia was to lace the children up in trusses and wait until age 5 or so, when theory dictated that they would be strong enough to endure surgery.

The only young children who were sent to a surgeon were acutely ill, making it even less likely that surgery would succeed, and perpetuating the cycle of gloom. Children younger than 3 years old who did have hernia operations, for example, were not operated on unless the intestine was incarcerated and irreducible. Then, Koop has written, "the operation was undertaken as though they were 55-year-olds and a recurrence was to be expected. The patient was laced up like a 59-cent football with an incision that went from the pubic tubercle to the anterior iliac spine." Two weeks of hospitalization followed, then another six weeks during which the child was given the highly practical advice not to strain, lift, sneeze, cough, or laugh.

Confronted with situations like these, Koop became outraged at how the adult world had been treating young patients. Children with correctable conditions such as simple duodenal atresia had died in the wards of Children's without so much as a surgical consult—no surgeon could be found who could be bothered to come over to the hospital and look at a "hopeless" case.

From his training with Gross and Ladd and from his own observations, Koop discerned several flaws in the way children were being operated upon. The most basic was the fundamental and far-reaching assumption that children should be treated like tiny adults. The drug quantity and administration sequence for anesthetizing a 10-pound infant, for example, were typically derived by taking the values for a 150-pound adult and dividing by 15. Yet tissue sensitivity, dose response, blood chemistry, disease resistance, cardiovascular behavior, and other aspects of human physiology are dramatically different in infants.

Modern pediatricians say the real equation is, adults are big kids. It is now known, for example, that the old practice of waiting until a child was 5 years old to do surgery made sense, though not because children become strong enough at that age. Rather, their physiology becomes similar enough to an adult's that they can bear the anesthesia and surgical techniques surgeons use for adults. (Even this was not fully understood until the 1960s.)

"Young doctors today find it difficult to believe there was once enormous resistance to the most basic notions about the need to view children as distinct biological and pathological entities," says Dr. Judah Folkman, former chief of surgery at Children's Hospital in Boston and now a researcher there.

The surgical errors that flowed from the faulty concept of children as miniature grown-ups were many. There was misunderstanding about issues as simple as the need for delicacy. The tissue of an otherwise healthy adult can withstand a little surgical insult, but surgeons who push or pull too roughly on newborn tissue may cause lasting trauma. Similarly, because adults are essentially static

SECURITY.

A BALANCE OF EFFICACY AND TOLERABILITY IN ARTHRITIS.
HELPING TO PROVIDE THE THERAPEUTIC SECURITY ELDERLY PATIENTS NEED.

NAPROSYN®
(NAPROXEN) 500 MG TABLETS.

THE MOST FREQUENT COMPLAINTS ARE GASTROINTESTINAL.
SEE "WARNINGS," "PRECAUTIONS," AND "ADVERSE REACTIONS" SECTIONS
OF PRESCRIBING INFORMATION.

IT IS PRUDENT TO USE THE LOWEST EFFECTIVE DOSE IN THE ELDERLY.

SYNTEX IS MAKING PROFOUND CONTRIBUTIONS TO MEDICINE.

YOU CAN LOCATE THE PRESCRIBING INFORMATION FOR **NAPROSYN** ON PAGES I-IV OF THE APPENDIX.
C

entities, surgeons plan procedures based on correcting conditions as observed. But pediatric surgeons must plan an attack based on what the patient's anatomy will become—a very different matter.

Ignorance of the differences between young and mature vascular systems further complicated matters. During his residency at Penn, Koop had worked in a unit investigating the new science of plasma substitution; the details of the physiology of the circulatory system were fresh in his mind. He soon realized that the response of a child's body to changes in blood volume and pressure, electrolyte loss, and especially hemorrhaging was fundamentally different from that of an adult.

"Infants have an elastic vascular bed," Koop says. "As they bleed out the bed contracts down around the site leaving no disproportion between the vascular tree and the circulating blood volume. So you're going along thinking everything is just fine and all of a sudden you fall off the edge. Boom, right off the edge, with none of the conventional warnings. So you try like mad to bring the patient back by the same techniques that would be quite effective with an adult, but which overload a child. Then he goes into cardiac failure and you've upset his physiology twice to an extreme, and it's too late to do anything about it. Surgeons were losing kids for years like this. Instead of stopping to question their own techniques and knowledge, they just shrugged and repeated the myth that children were too weak for operations. In fact, children have remarkable bounce relative to surgical invasion. They just have almost no reserve. The surgical establishment did not want to learn this kind of distinction because children were not considered worth worrying about."

Koop documented numerous differences between adults' and children's physiological responses to surgery, differences that would form the basis for many journal articles. But when it came to rapid improvements in survival rates, Koop's most important contribution had little to do with his own specialty. Rather, it concerned the field of anesthesiology.

At that time, pediatric anesthesia was generally administered by a nurse using open-drip ether; intubation of the young was rare. Reduced-dose versions of adult protocols were often death sentences for child patients. Emergency tracheostomies were distressingly common. Anesthesiologists who were M.D.'s took little interest in the very young. "Back then there were lots of people who could put kids to sleep, but not many could wake them up," Koop says.

Koop knew that to change this he would first need to find somebody who could figure out what was wrong with the way children were being put under. That was a straightforward medical inquiry. Then he'd have to woo the anesthesiologists over to his side, so they would care about pediatric surgery. In a sense this was a greater challenge since it involved medicine's internal politics. Because surgeons are infamous for viewing anesthesiologists as mere functionaries, Koop's overtures were sure to cause him embarrassment within the surgical old-boy network.

Koop found an ally in Dr. Margery Van Norden Deming, a young physician who had been an anesthesiology resident at Penn during Koop's surgical residency. With the help of a colleague, Koop persuaded Deming to become in effect, if not in title, one of the first subspecialists in pediatric anesthesiology. "Dr. Deming was an utterly selfless person and one of the great workaholics of all time," Koop says. "She took an entire category of medicine that was not then acceptable and transformed it into a field with intellectual respect."

"I've read some of the descriptions of Koop's and Deming's early work, and it was all pretty logical," says Dr. John Downes, now chief of anesthesiology at Children's of Philadelphia. "Ventilate the lungs, keep the baby warm, give fluids, maintain nutrition. It's hard to believe those things were big advances at the time, but they were."

Another basic expedient was the miniaturization of air-management equipment. Bits and pieces were cobbled together from various gizmos to form tiny intubation gear. Until the 1970s, when medical manufacturers caught up with the vast expansion in pediatric care, many devices found in children's hospitals were handmade and one of a kind.

Through their early years together, Koop and Deming achieved what was for the time a spectacular record: they performed their first 1,000 endotracheal anesthesias without an anesthesia death or an emergency tracheostomy. "People then did not believe it, and even now some refuse to believe it," Koop says. "We sat up with some kids all night, but we never did a trache."

Armed with the early techniques he and Deming had pioneered, Koop was able to make a rapid, dramatic leap in improving surgical survival rates for infants. He came to believe that improper anesthesia was the single greatest problem plaguing surgery on infants. Eventually it would be shown that children could tolerate nearly all the sleep drugs used on adults, including narcotics, and could benefit from continuous positive airway pressure, as long as everything was administered very carefully.

"I lost a few patients," Koop says, "but really, only a few. This built in me a great sense of outrage. Back then anytime you visited a hospital to do grand rounds or attend a mortality conference you'd find an anesthesia death from something as simple as a tonsillectomy, and the surgeons would act highly insulted if you called that an outrage. Which I frequently did."

Koop's professional reputation began to change one day in the late 1940s when he operated on a child with a herniated groin and discharged the patient the following day. When told that the child had been discharged, the referring physician, a prominent Philadelphia society doctor, was highly concerned. He had no idea, he said, how to care for a child who was convalescing from surgery. When told that the child was ambulatory, had no external sutures, and required no postoperative care, the physician was flabbergasted.

After examining the child, the referring physician called Koop. Was that operation a fluke, he inquired, or could you do it again? Soon a huge backlog of children aged 5 months to 5 years began appearing at Koop's doorstep, all enveloped in trusses. "The collection of trusses that accumulated during the next year made my office resemble a shrine like that at Lourdes," Koop wrote.

The success of the groin-hernia operation meant a big jump in Koop's income, plus enough patients to get his program rolling. To send the message that surgery on the very young would henceforth be a routine event, instead of something for the textbooks, he moved the surgical theater at Children's from a pit at the base of a 125-seat amphitheater to a smaller room. To drive the point home, Koop often scheduled 10 operations for the same day. The first time he did it, his entire nursing staff walked out.

This did not bother Koop. If anything, such reactions energized him. He had a vision of taking a significant portion of the country's population to a dramatic new plateau of care. Children were beginning to whiz through routine procedures. But why stop there? Why not assemble a team that could repair anything a scalpel could touch? Koop knew that it could be done, and that he was the person to do it.

The establishment view that he was crazy seemed to Koop an affirmation that his vision was genuine. He would experience that feeling again many times, in progressively more public circumstances. But for the moment, his attention was focused on the circle of intense white light that shone down from his operating lamps. Koop had demonstrated that little children could undergo conventional operations without incident. Now he set out to prove he could save babies that no one, absolutely no one, thought had a chance.

CHAPTER TWO

THE GIFT
OF A LIFETIME

ntil Koop's era, a baby born with a severe handicap posed a morbid choice for medical personnel: they could make a mad dash to find a general surgeon willing to perform an emergency operation that was all but certain to fail; or nurses could wrap the infant in a blanket, set it aside where others wouldn't see, and hope nature would swiftly take its course. The phrase *quality of life* did not come up; it was moot, because nobody had any idea what to do for such children.

After standing by helplessly as he watched a few handicapped babies expire, Koop may have looked into his soul and glimpsed a purpose to his life: he would become the person who would know exactly what to do. The ability to save seriously ill children held for him a satisfaction nothing else in medicine could match. The gift of life to a dying child could be enjoyed not just for months or years, as might be the case with adult patients, but for decades.

In the early 1950s, another incentive was added. Already some critics questioned the wisdom of performing expensive procedures to prolong the lives of the elderly; advanced surgery for infants, especially for those born prematurely, might be even more expensive. But in the long run, Koop thought, what could possibly be a more cost-effective intervention than one that saves the entire span of someone's life?

Koop concentrated his early surgical efforts on several birth conditions euphemistically labeled "incompatible with life"—esophageal atresia, intestinal obstructions of several kinds, omphalocele, imperforate anus, and diaphragmatic hernia.

Koop would later be most pleased by his accomplishments in treating esophageal atresia, once considered a hopeless defect be-

Koop did dexterity drills to keep his hands, above, supple enough to operate on neonates. Age and constant use would take their toll in the late '70s, when his fingers began to cramp during surgery.

cause the interior of a newborn's esophagus seemed too tiny for adult hands to reconstruct. Koop has likened the dexterity required for this operation to "sewing together two ends of a divided piece of wet spaghetti at the bottom of an ice-cream cone."

Dr. William Ladd at Children's in Boston had saved a few of these patients by performing a series of surgeries, each designed so that the invasion was brief enough for the famished newborn to survive. Koop's goal was to finish the entire repair in a single session. He did dexterity drills for hours on end in order to make himself ambidextrous and to hone his ability to manipulate extremely small objects. He grew one long fingernail and filed it so that he could use the nail for holding back blood vessels without having to make room for an additional instrument. His efforts paid off. Before Koop's appointment as chief of surgery at Children's of Philadelphia in 1948, no child in the city had ever survived surgery for esophageal atresia. From then until Koop retired in 1980, he performed the operation 425 times; after 1969 he never lost a full-term baby, and he lost only 12 percent of preemies.

Koop began to achieve similar results in correcting other birth defects. Speed was one of his allies, so much so that Koop eventually became known as a speed merchant. Carol Moyer, a nurse who worked with him for many years, says Koop often completed simple hernia operations in 10 minutes.

Because Koop wanted plenty of patients, he held his tongue when general surgeons sent him children whose operations they had botched, to ensure that the next botched patient would be referred, too. He developed good relations with many osteopaths (who are popular with Pennsylvania patients), going out of his way to share with them information about his work. As a result, nearly all the osteopaths of Philadelphia began to send their patients to Koop.

Perhaps it is no surprise that Koop got along well with osteopaths, for early in his career he too experienced hostility from the medical establishment. Organized surgery looked askance at those who claimed pediatric surgery ought to be a specialty or who impugned the ability of its members to treat children. "I would constantly hear from surgeons, 'If you're a real surgeon, how come you're not with us?'" Koop says. "It was impossible for the small band of progressive pediatric surgeons to get any professional recognition from the main medical establishment. Only the pediatricians, whose patients we were saving, would give us the time of day."

Surgical journals refused to accept articles on pediatric surgery, including Koop's, because the field was not recognized as a specialty. Finally, in 1963, Dr. Stephen L. Gans, now chairman of the Subdivision of Pediatric Surgery at Cedars-Sinai Medical Center in Los Angeles, founded the *Journal of Pediatric Surgery*. Koop became its first editor in chief, a post he held for 11 years.

In the 1960s, Koop was instrumental in convincing Japanese physicians and several royal colleges of physicians and surgeons in Britain to recognize pediatric surgery, but similar recognition in the U.S. evaded him and his "small band of progressives." By the time the American Board of Surgery finally certified pediatric surgeons in 1975, Koop was openly bitter toward the group. Even today Koop does not mince words about his distaste for the surgical establishment that rejected him for so many years.

"Now there are pediatric urologists, pediatric neurosurgeons, many subspecialties, with more coming," Koop says. "It makes me furious to think how many babies died needlessly because of the obstinacy of the general surgeons in recognizing the need for pediatric specialization. These people would operate on something like spina bifida and not give one hoot about the body that surrounds the lesion. Then they would charge some amazing fee, justifying the fee on how much they had put the patient through, I suppose."

Though the surgical establishment continued to disdain Koop's work throughout the 1950s and '60s, the academic world, particularly institutions like Harvard, had been open to the notion of children as separate medical entities since the '40s. In 1959, Koop became a professor of pediatric surgery at the University of Pennsylvania and began taking residents under his wing.

Children's Hospital in Boston, a Harvard affiliate, started ship-

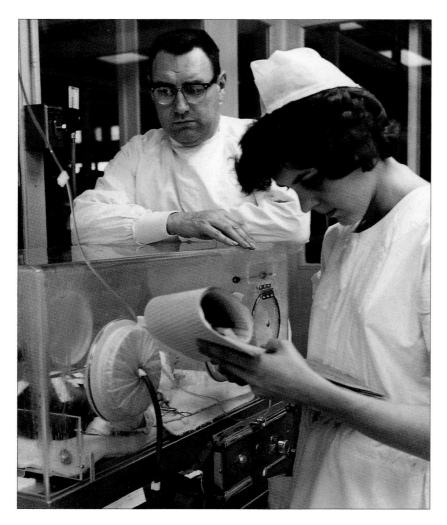

Koop observes a patient in an Isolette-Incubator, a device developed at Children's of Philadelphia in 1945 by Dr. Charles Chapple. The hospital opened the nation's first infant surgical ICU in 1962.

ping off young doctors to Children's of Philadelphia, a Penn affiliate, to study under Koop. This academic coup greatly endeared Koop to the Penn faculty. Older staff members there still cite this accomplishment with great pride, saying, "We sent our man to Harvard to be trained, and 10 years later, Harvard was sending its people to him." Today there are prominent Koop trainees in pediatric hospitals across the nation.

"Koop was rare in being both a great working surgeon and a great teacher," says Dr. John Templeton Jr., a pediatric surgeon at Children's of Philadelphia who did his residency under Koop. "Koop set high standards but was also willing to get involved in the lives of his students. And he had a gift for describing the most complicated operations in terms that practically anyone could understand. I think the fact that he was so oriented toward teaching made the transition to public life almost inevitable for him."

Meanwhile, Koop's surgical success continued apace. In 1957 he performed the first of many acts that would bring his name into the public eye, a separation of 1-week-old conjoined female twins. The operation was fairly straightforward by today's standards—the pair were of a type called pygopagus, joined back to back and sharing a single rectum and vagina—but in 1957 it caused a sensation. One of the twins died nine years later following open-heart surgery to correct a tetralogy of Fallot; the other grew into a happy and essentially normal adult. Koop has said his most prized possession is a picture of himself with the surviving twin on her wedding day.

By the time of that operation, Koop had achieved at least some success in correcting each entry on his target list of birth defects. He then began to devote more attention to his original interest from medical school days: cancer.

When Koop was a student, childhood cancers were thought to be extremely rare. But he was suspicious of this view. He had a hunch that many infant deaths ascribed to other causes or written up as "cause unknown" were in fact cancer cases. To support this view, Koop did studies of pediatric mortality data and of errors common in pediatric autopsy reports. His results helped convince the medical community that cancer in children was more common than previously thought. (Today, because many other causes of childhood mortality have been eliminated by vaccines or superior treatment, it is the number-two cause of death in children, after accidents.)

Koop was among the pioneers who demonstrated that it was possible to work with childhood cancers after they had metasta-

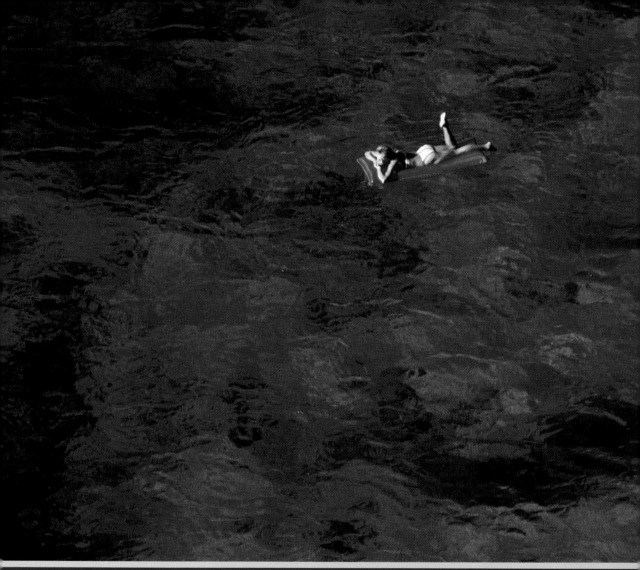

COMFORT.

PROVIDING EFFECTIVE MEDICATIONS
THAT ENABLE PHYSICIANS TO MANAGE PAIN, MAINTAIN COMFORT.
EMPOWERING PATIENTS TO TAKE AN ACTIVE ROLE
IN TREATMENT AND REHABILITATION.

 SYNTEX

SYNTEX IS MAKING PROFOUND CONTRIBUTIONS TO MEDICINE.

ACTIVITY.

CUTTING SHORT THE DISRUPTION CAUSED BY
ACUTE MUSCULOSKELETAL INJURY. PROMPT RELIEF OF PAIN.
QUICK RETURN TO ACTIVITY.

ANAPROX® DS
(NAPROXEN SODIUM) 550 MG TABLETS.

THE MOST FREQUENT COMPLAINTS ARE GASTROINTESTINAL.
SEE "WARNINGS," "PRECAUTIONS," AND "ADVERSE REACTIONS" SECTIONS
OF PRESCRIBING INFORMATION.

SYNTEX IS MAKING PROFOUND CONTRIBUTIONS TO MEDICINE.

YOU CAN LOCATE THE PRESCRIBING INFORMATION FOR **ANAPROX DS** ON PAGES IV-VII OF THE APPENDIX.
F

sized, something widely disbelieved when his generation went into practice. Eventually he came to focus on neuroblastomas and the Wilms tumor. Koop suspected that childhood tumors hold the secret to understanding one of medicine's ultimate questions: What causes cancer? "Whoever succeeds in the management of neuroblastomas will uncover the key to one of the great mysteries of cancer that could lead to its elimination," he has said.

Photographs of Children's of Philadelphia from the 1960s depict scenes that seem strangely remote in time. There are fluoroscopes, kids crudely secured to what look like cheap surfboards to keep them still during X-rays, doctors with Brylcreemed hair, nurses with beehive hairdos.

Yet many words in the captions that accompany those photos are just as strangely up to date: angioplasty, human growth hormone, outpatient surgery. It's easy to forget how often "new" developments in medicine are actually perfections of ideas that have been bouncing around for decades.

The key old-new phrase from Children's of Philadelphia of the 1960s is intensive-care unit. In 1962 the hospital became the first pediatric center in the United States to set up a neonatal surgical ICU. Koop and other staff members worked hard to secure federal funding for the concept, which at the time had science fiction status.

The new ICU was equipped with the latest in electronic devices and revival equipment. After its arrival the mortality rate at Children's declined further, as did the rate of surgical complications; increasing numbers of patients went on to lead normal or near-normal lives. About the same time, there was a boom in building pediatric hospitals nationwide. Because of the success of the new unit in Philadelphia, every major pediatric hospital soon had a neonatal surgical ICU or was planning one.

Thus, as the 1960s drew to a close, the life of C. Everett Koop seemed an unbroken string of successes. Pediatric care had improved markedly: between 1940 and 1970, the U.S. infant-mortality rate declined 58 percent. At Children's of Philadelphia, "hopeless" babies were being saved every day. And though the medical establishment groused about Koop's cocksure demeanor, his personal stature was nearing that of Great Surgeon. His name was as familiar to other doctors and to medical writers as those of, say, the heart surgeon Michael DeBakey or the transplant wizard Thomas E. Starzl. If surgeons' egos need feeding, Koop's had a balanced diet. Life seemed blissful.

But in April 1968, harsh reality intruded. Koop received the stiffly formal late-night telephone call that all parents instinctively dread. His third child, 20-year-old David Charles Everett, a Dartmouth student and an avid rock climber, had died in a fall. David, out of view of the other climbers, had slipped when a rock became dislodged. By the time a rescuer reached him the young man had nearly bled to death. His last words: "I'm sleepy."

Just two months before, Koop had published a *Reader's Digest* article entitled "What I Tell a Dying Child's Parents" (for some time afterward it was the magazine's most reprinted article). Suddenly he faced at a personal level the very worst aspect of the pediatric profession, the erasure of a beloved child's life.

Koop and his wife, Elizabeth, who have been together since 1938, tried to accept the news coolly. After all, they had three other healthy children, Allan, Norman, and Elizabeth. But soon the surgeon, who in the course of his work so often had to bear the distress of death at an early age, could not even mention David's name without sobbing. Friends said that if Koop encountered a young man who resembled David walking on the street, he would begin to shake, and would have to lock himself away for some time to regain his composure. Often Koop would sit grieving, repeating in despair, "I'm never going to see him again."

Dr. Patrick Pasquariello, a pediatrician at Children's and a long-time friend, says David's death was a turning point in Koop's life. One of the joys of his life was gone forever, and to assuage his grief, Koop looked to the teachings of his Christian faith. After his son's death, religion may have become even more important in the life of this already religious man.

Koop's family had long been churchgoers, active in the Evangelical Presbyterian denomination; the Bible in David's dorm room was open on his desk the day he died. Generally, Koop paused to pray before beginning an operation, though he says he did this not in the sense of asking for some dusting of magic but to help concentrate his thoughts on the task ahead and what really matters in life.

But in events like the death of a child, the world of faith takes on additional meaning. In Protestant doctrine, one who has tried to live a moral life and has accepted Christ not only goes to heaven, but is in every way better off than when on earth. So there is no cause to mourn his fate. Several Christian interpretations say that the real victim in the untimely death of a righteous person is not the deceased, but the surviving family and friends, who must go forward with a ray of light removed from their lives. Even if the loss is difficult, however, this view teaches that Christians must accept it as a manifestation of God's divine plan.

After David's death, Koop spent much time reflecting on this teaching, and on the related belief that the decision on when to end a human life should be God's and God's alone. These beliefs, Koop felt, must be applied not only to his personal life but to his professional life as well. Thus he began to ponder the morality of cases in which babies died because of the medical establishment's ignorance (in Koop's view, no longer tolerable), or (even worse) because of a conscious decision to stop life-sustaining treatment, or (just as bad) because of someone's active choice to cut short a fetus's journey to life. Koop concluded that as a Christian he had to do what he could to keep these things from happening.

And just as Everett Koop was becoming more focused on religion and the right to live, public opinion was tilting toward an acceptance of abortion and the right to die. Koop and the world around him were bound to collide.

CHAPTER THREE

THE FETUS EX UTERO

I n our unit, there [is] a growing tendency to seek early death as a management option," wrote Dr. Raymond Duff and Dr. A.G.M. Campbell in a celebrated 1973 article for the *New England Journal of Medicine*. They were referring to Yale-New Haven Hospital's special-care nursery where, they reported, 43 infant deaths over a two-year period were related to withheld treatment. The deaths were, in Duff and Campbell's words, of "very defective individuals": babies with trisomy, meningomyelocele, and other physical and mental abnormalities.

The article described the case of a child born with Down syndrome and intestinal atresia. The atresia, a condition readily correctable by 1973, was not operated on at the request of the parents; the child died of starvation a week later. In another case, after a long effort to save the life of a 5-month-old baby with chronic pulmonary disease, physicians withdrew oxygen supplementation and the child died within three hours. "The family settled down and 18 months later had another baby, who was healthy," the authors reported. They discussed the social costs of heroic intervention for severe birth defects and the strain severely defective babies can place on parents, suggesting that death can sometimes be a kindness.

Both the article and the wave of favorable media reaction it received threw Everett Koop into a frenzy. Babies allowed to starve do not just slip away peacefully; they probably wail in pain throughout their brief acquaintance with life. The baby from whom oxygen had been withdrawn died gasping for breath. At 5 months, many infants are old enough to look at those nearby in rage and bewilderment, wondering why they will not help. *This,* Koop thought, *is progress? This is death with dignity?*

It never occurred to him at the beginning of his medical career,

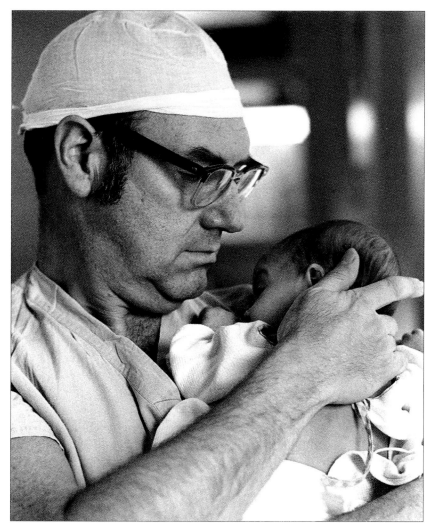

Koop carries a baby into an operating room in 1970. As he became increasingly able to repair conditions that had been considered hopeless, his opposition to abortion grew more intense.

Koop says, that he and so many others would end up debating terms like *quality of life* or questioning whether infants with advanced problems ought to receive advanced care. "If you had told me in 1946 that there would come a time when it was perfectly respectable in public debate to suggest it could be a bad thing to save a child's life, I would have thought you had taken leave of your senses," Koop notes. By 1973 such a time was coming. So was *Roe* v. *Wade*.

At Children's of Philadelphia, as everywhere else, the ICU had begun to play a role no one had anticipated. ICUs were intended to be places where patients with acute illnesses would be cared for briefly until their own bodies could resume functioning normally. High-tech devices like ventilators were never meant to replace organ function on a permanent basis. But as physicians acquired the ability to stave off death in increasing numbers of incurable cases, ICUs became the end of the line—places where some chronically ill patients would be maintained not for just a little while, but for the remainder of their lives.

"If you drew a cartoon diagram of a pediatric hospital in the early 1960s," Koop says, "there would be a neonatal ICU with patients coming in one end and going out the other either dead or on their way to fairly productive lives. As we began to understand things like respiratory reserve and as ventilators were developed, then you had to build a little annex for the patients who couldn't go home right away. Well, the annex got bigger than the entire ward."

To some, the use of extraordinary means to prolong the lives of the incurable, including children, was a misappropriation of social resources. Hundreds of thousands of dollars might be spent on a child who had no hope of ever leaving the hospital, while, because of quirks in the system, low-cost treatments like immunizations for poor children that could make a great difference in the life of an otherwise healthy child might be denied.

To others, the efforts of Koop and those like him to save permanently impaired babies—especially infants with serious mental defects—were in and of themselves scandalous. What was the point of saving a baby who could barely comprehend the existence of the world? Why struggle to maintain the life of a child with Down syndrome when caring for that child would handicap an entire normal family?

The generally favorable reaction to Duff's description of "early death as a management option" was a barometer of the times. Believing that it was a kindness to let handicapped babies die reflected a sentiment held by many in the "era of limits" of the 1970s that in a world as crummy as ours it was irresponsible to bring children into existence anyway. Others were made uncomfortable by the intrusive character of modern medical technology: by its ability to facilitate extensive surgical reconstructions, by the tethering of patients to life-support machines, and by physicians who played God, however unconvincingly.

This train of thought ran like an express into the abortion issue. Anyone who rereads accounts of the public debate on abortion during the late 1960s and early 1970s will be struck by the almost total emphasis on a woman's right to control her own body (a right with which this author agrees) to the exclusion of questions regarding the life of the fetus. By the 1970s, some commentators seemed to be saying that each new baby is just another generating mechanism for selfishness, corruption, and ecological abuse, a new curse upon the earth.

For Koop, the religious implications of this debate were great: the intentional taking of an innocent life, or the intentional failure to save that life, are sins of commission and omission, respectively. According to Koop's belief, withdrawal of care is, with few exceptions, as intolerable as abortion. (Koop nevertheless cites as justification for the death penalty the biblical verse Genesis 9:6, in which God instructs Noah and his sons, "Who sheds man's blood shall have his blood shed by man.")

But Koop kept his spiritual convictions out of hospital policymaking. "The staff here is really not all that religious, you know," says Dr. Louise Schnaufer, the surgeon who assisted Koop at the 1957 twins separation and who continues to practice at Children's of Philadelphia. "Chick always understood that only rational or ethical arguments would be entertained regarding patient care, and those were the only kind he ever offered." (Chick is Koop's nickname.)

One of Koop's secular arguments for heroic intervention was that such actions promote medical science by increasing surgeons' knowledge and skills. For instance, he says, "Constantly, pediatric surgeons hear, why are you spending so much effort and money to save 1,500-gram babies, or 1,000-gram babies, or whatever it was at each point down to today, when it's 600 grams. I would always explain that what we learned helping the 1,500-gram baby just barely make it would enable the 2,500-gram infant to breeze through without a problem. Today what we learn from the very intensive actions that save the 600-gram baby cuts the trauma and the costs for the 1,200-gram child, and so on."

Koop believes the same dynamic is exhibited in nearly every surgical setting in which the high expense of intensive intervention is criticized without regard for possible spillover effects on less expensive procedures and therapies.

Koop also used the "slippery slope" argument against abortion and the withholding of care: abortion today, euthanasia of your cranky grandparents tomorrow. Some of Koop's statements on this subject come across as hyperbolic—it has been his custom to use the term *infanticide* for nearly all instances of denial of care to the young.

But in what might be called the anti-life intellectual *Zeitgeist* of the 1970s, modestly phrased cautionary notes stood little chance of being noticed.

"Society's attitude toward the sanctity of human life may well affect the manner and immediate cause of your death," Koop told a group of physicians at a 1977 prayer breakfast in Atlantic City. "If Duff and Campbell can convince the medical profession and the public that the potential for such things as chronic shortness of breath, oxygen dependence, incontinence, paralysis of some portion of your body, a contracture, or a sexual handicap is a reason to kill a newborn baby, how long will it be before they shift their emphasis from the potential in a newborn baby to that existing defect in you, an adult?"

But perhaps Koop's most persuasive argument against the death-as-kindness concept is that he believes it is factually incorrect. Except in the rarest of cases, people with severe physical problems do not wish to die. "I have never had a parent come to me and ask, 'Dr. Koop, why did you fight so hard to save the life of my child?'" Koop says. "More important, I've never had a person who I saved as a child come to me as an adult and say, 'Dr. Koop, I wish you hadn't saved me.' This is true even though some of my patients have had to face their lives with very serious handicaps."

More compelling evidence for Koop's view began to emerge as the first generation of severely handicapped babies who had been saved by the new pediatric surgical techniques grew to adulthood. Not one would reject life, even life with severe problems, in favor of a cost-effective death.

Koop also asserted, though with less success, that a vegetative state is not always irreversible. He is fond of noting that at the time of the first Quinlan decision in 1975 (it prevented the withdrawal of life support, but was reversed in 1976), he was managing four patients who might have met the legal criteria for being unplugged. All later recovered and left the hospital.

After *Roe* v. *Wade* made most abortions legal in 1973, Children's of Philadelphia decided not to offer the procedure on its premises for the essentially humanistic reason that pediatric physicians are advocates first for the interests of the young, and allowing abortions could not serve the interest of the fetus.

The hospital further evolved an unofficial policy of almost always extending the maximum degree of care to children with severe defects, including profound retardation. As Schnaufer put it, "I believe that a doctor cannot ever allow a patient to die when there is

VISION.

OFFERING AN EFFECTIVE WEAPON AGAINST CMV RETINITIS.
A BEACON FOR PATIENTS THREATENED WITH LOSS OF VISION.

CYTOVENE®
(GANCICLOVIR SODIUM)
STERILE POWDER EQUIVALENT TO 500 MG GANCICLOVIR.

DUE TO THE RISK OF SERIOUS SIDE EFFECTS, SUCH AS
GRANULOCYTOPENIA (40%) AND THROMBOCYTOPENIA (20%),
CYTOVENE SHOULD ONLY BE USED IN THOSE PATIENTS
FOR WHOM THE BENEFITS OF THERAPY CLEARLY OUTWEIGH THE RISKS.

 SYNTEX

SYNTEX IS MAKING PROFOUND CONTRIBUTIONS TO MEDICINE.

YOU CAN LOCATE THE PRESCRIBING INFORMATION FOR **CYTOVENE** ON PAGES XXV-XXXI OF THE APPENDIX.

FREEDOM.

CHRONIC STABLE ANGINA AND HYPERTENSION
DEPENDABLY CONTROLLED. MORE FREEDOM AND CONFIDENCE
TO ENJOY LIFE'S PLEASURES.

CARDENE®
(NICARDIPINE HYDROCHLORIDE) 20, 30 MG CAPSULES.

THE MOST FREQUENT ADVERSE EVENTS ARE
FLUSHING, HEADACHE, PEDAL EDEMA, AND DIZZINESS.

SYNTEX IS MAKING PROFOUND CONTRIBUTIONS TO MEDICINE.

YOU CAN LOCATE THE PRESCRIBING INFORMATION FOR **CARDENE** ON PAGES XX-XXV OF THE APPENDIX.
H

any hope, even dim hope, of recovery." In cases in which parents were not inclined to operate on a handicapped newborn, hospital officials urged the parents to allow the procedure and put the baby up for adoption. When hope was absent altogether, however, Koop never insisted on the prolongation of life. Dr. Robert Kettrick, an anesthesiologist at Children's, has said that Koop knew when to quit, and that his hopeless patients did not die lingering deaths.

But it was abortion that transformed Everett Koop into a political doctor. Here were no vexing uncertainties about social costs or quality of life. Most aborted life is wholly normal, on its way to being exactly what parents are supposed to wish for and doctors are supposed to dedicate their lives to making possible. There was, however, the question of the point at which legal and spiritual rights to life begin.

Koop, of course, believes that life begins at conception. He was beside himself in 1971 when the medical school of the University of Pittsburgh amended the Declaration of Geneva to delete the last five words from the vow "I will maintain the utmost respect for human life *from the time of conception.*" In the absence of a scientific consensus on when life begins, Koop thought the amendment was professionally as well as spiritually corrupt.

Others argued with equal conviction that life begins with the first breath. In *Roe* v. *Wade*, the Supreme Court essentially posited that life begins (and the right to abortion stops) when that breath becomes possible, regardless of when it is actually taken. What really distressed Koop was that many medical professionals seemed uninterested in this pivotal aspect of the dispute, as if all that mattered was securing women's rights and being granted a federal sanction for what was sure to be a high-volume procedure. What Koop considered a new and frighteningly cold-hearted view by the medical establishment was summed up when he overheard a physician refer to a premature infant as a "fetus ex utero," a term chilling to him and one with potential legal power under *Roe*.

The fetus ex utero. In the early 1970s, James Watson, co-discoverer of the structure of the DNA molecule, had proposed that birth certificates for newborns not be issued until 72 hours after delivery so no legal consequences would ensue if parents or physicians wanted to let a "very defective individual" expire. A fetus ex utero would have no more legal status than a tumor or kidney or any other tissue cluster a physician might remove from a patient.

Koop's religious spirit recoiled at such developments, and his medical mind rebelled. The worst elements of the 1940s—doctors who seemed indifferent to little babies, who behaved as though you did not count as a full person until you were old enough to write your surgeon a check—were making a comeback in a new guise.

Koop felt that his numerous and elaborate surgical saves paled in comparison with the numbers of new lives that were being terminated by abortion every year in the United States. (Today that figure is 1.6 million a year, roughly equal to two and a half times the number that have died on battlefields in all U.S. wars combined.) Koop was staggered that physicians, people sworn to nurture life, considered this progress. Koop and the medical establishment were about to clash again.

CHAPTER FOUR

SODOM ENCROACHING

By the time C. Everett Koop entered the national spotlight in 1980, some saw him as a menace. Imperious in bearing, vain in professional demeanor, scathing in verbiage, Koop could come across as the worst kind of religious zealot. Once, for example, he implied that all members of denominations that support abortion rights would go to hell as "a reward for their depravity." As overblown as he sometimes was in public, Koop could be gentle in private—but this side of his personality was destined to become lost in the Washington battle of snippets and visuals. Koop often followed up on patients for months or years, particularly if the children had incurable diseases or disfigurements likely to cause psychological strain. Almost every Thursday night of his professional life, he drove around eastern Pennsylvania visiting young patients, not only to buck them up but also to eyeball their family circumstances and make sure the children were receiving adequate care.

Jane Kelso was one such patient. Karen Kelso of Philadelphia took her 8-year-old daughter, who had been experiencing leg pain for six months, to Koop in 1971. A succession of doctors had diagnosed Jane's problems as everything from spinal meningitis to arthritis. As soon as he saw her walk across the room, however, Koop suspected that Jane had something much more serious, like a malignant neoplasm. Her tumor, which turned out to be a neuroblastoma, was visible on X-ray, and Koop and a neurosurgeon decided to operate right away. The neurosurgeon removed as much of the growth as he could from the spinal column; a week later, Koop operated again to remove the remaining tissue. The tumor recurred after two months. Concluding that further surgical treat-

Koop and Karen Kelso, whose daughter, Jane, was Koop's patient from 1971 until she died in 1973. Koop took a deep interest in his patients' lives, and he and Kelso, shown here in 1980, remained friends.

ment was futile, Koop called in oncologists and started Jane on chemotherapy. He continued to coordinate her care.

Jane Kelso was regularly checked into Children's for chemotherapy after her surgery, and Koop was her constant visitor. They often read the Bible together or played board games. "I know she talked to Dr. Koop about some things she never even talked to me about," says Karen Kelso, "but I didn't mind. It meant so much to her that she had a friendship and private secrets with a famous man."

As Jane's malignancy progressed, the child lost control of her bowels. Once she soiled the hospital bed just as Koop was walking in. Thinking her daughter would be mortified, Karen Kelso tried to shoo the physician out of the room. Instead, Koop shooed her out. Listening at the door a moment later, the mother heard her daughter giggling happily. Looking in, she saw Koop cleaning up the mess, all the while making jokes to distract Jane's attention.

In the last year of Jane's life, Koop was a frequent visitor in her home. Koop gave Karen Kelso his private telephone number and urged her to call whenever she needed advice on Jane's treatment.

The physician advised against experimental therapies that might prolong her life but make Jane more conscious of her pain. As death neared, Koop gave the child's mother his weekly schedule so that she would always know where to call him.

Koop visited Jane at home shortly before her death in 1973. Coming down from the little girl's room, he sat on the sofa and wept, repeating, "Why is it taking her so long to die?" Karen Kelso called Koop's home two nights later to report that Jane was gone.

"One of the nice things about Chick was that he could talk about how really lousy life could be," says Kelso, who remained his friend. Koop's daughter-in-law suffered a miscarriage the same year Jane died. On Christmas Eve, he called Karen Kelso, saying, "It's going to be a really crummy Christmas for you this year, and for me too, but I just wanted you to know I'm thinking of you."

"Koop had buried his own child, so he knew some parts of life are unbearably awful," Kelso says. "I think it made him work that much harder with parents, so they wouldn't have to face the awfulness alone."

It's said that the pediatrician has an entire family for a patient, and medical wisdom holds that saintly patience and a self-effacing manner are required to excel in the specialty. Koop had neither. But in his own way, he labored to honor the injunction. Early in the Kelso case, for example, he took Karen Kelso aside and told her that Jane's ailment would either tear the family apart or bind the remaining members together forever. "I realized he was interested in the entire family right from the start," she says.

Though the standard clinical concern for family health turns on establishing a good psychology of recovery, it is not much of a leap to include spiritual well-being. As an evangelical Christian—one who accepts a duty to share with strangers what believers call the good news—Koop did not mind if troubled patients raised the subject of religion. Many physicians handle this situation by suggesting that the topic is more appropriate for a clergyman. But Koop would jump right in, eagerly pursuing the cause of drawing not just one patient, but a whole family closer to the Lord.

Karen Kelso was pleased that her child's surgeon was religious. She describes herself as a born-again Christian, though like many who use this term, she acknowledges that she rarely attends church. "Doctors can be very arrogant at times, and Chick was no exception," she says. "I felt better knowing there was something larger than his own ego directing him."

In his thoughts and writings, Koop embraces the orthodox view that God is omnipotent, a belief that might seem incongruous to many who deal with infant illness and birth defects. "This is a hard doctrine to accept," Koop has written, "but I think one must agree that if God is God . . . He is not able to make a mistake." That means God must desire that some babies be born with terrible problems.

Koop tried to interpret this "hard doctrine" in the best light. If parents feared some lapse on their parts had caused a child's illness, or if they felt guilty for having genes that caused a congenital defect, Koop would tell them the situation was in God's hands and therefore they should cease reproaching themselves. Koop often told parents of handicapped children that God was testing them or giving them a special challenge so that they could set an inspirational example for others.

Koop thought parents could actually learn to be happy about having a handicapped child. "I believe the adversity connected with rearing [such] youngsters has provided meaning and purpose to the lives of their families," he explains.

That it's good for your character to have a child with birth defects may sound like a rationalization for not facing the unpleasant side of quality-of-life issues—including what happens when the badly defective child ends up with a family that does not rise to the challenge. But some parents who have overcome the odds with retarded or disabled children do in fact say that the appreciation of life they have acquired in the process has made their own lives more meaningful. This is hardly a trivial result.

While many secular philosophies provide reasons to celebrate life, the atheist must assume that death brings oblivion. Physicians who do not believe in a god may help a dead child's family carry on, but they cannot honestly tell parents that an irrevocable wrong has not occurred. Religion at least holds out the prospect that a child cut down at the beginning of life does not perish pointlessly. Physicians like Koop who believe in a greater glory may or may not be right, but they have an important tool for helping patients cope.

Koop carried his beliefs to other countries as well, participating in several medicine-and-missionary projects during his years of active practice. Evangelicals have long placed special emphasis on reaching the native populations of the Americas, Africa, Asia, and Australia. Some proselytizing faiths teach that if you hear of Jesus and reject Him you are to blame, but if you never hear about Him at all, evangelicals feel the responsibility. Koop helped establish clinics to serve the Tarascan Indians of central Mexico, a children's hospital in Hong Kong, a medical school in Ghana, and a program that sends medical students to third-world nations. He also helped fight an epidemic of dysentery in the Dominican Republic. Such actions represent the best religion has to offer. Of course, they may also be useful for self-promotion; Koop's detractors noted that he rarely missed a chance to mention his rustic days tromping through mud with the Tarascans.

But Koop had possessed an instinct for publicity from early in his career. He was always readily accessible to reporters. During his days running the surgical department at Children's of Philadelphia, he told hospital personnel they could give his home number to practically anyone from the press, with only one proviso: no interviews after 6 p.m. Koop likes to relax with a dry martini after work, and alcohol and interviews do not mix. As his name recognition grew, Koop began to cultivate his abilities as a public speaker and missed few opportunities for the modest adulation such appearances confer. A computer scan of Philadelphia newspapers from the 1960s and 1970s reveals regular society-column mentions of Koop accepting a minor award or Koop speaking to a men's club, a civic club, a garden club—seemingly anyone who would, in Ronald Reagan's phrase, "pay for a microphone." A typical entry: a 1966 award from the League of Children's Hospital presented at a luncheon that offered the ladies in attendance a Koop acceptance speech plus "a fashion feature with B. Altman outfits coming in from the Main Line to be paraded."

But local press is one thing, national press quite another. In 1974, Koop gained valuable personal experience in both the power and malleability of the national press when the most challenging of his conjoined twins separations became a headline event worldwide.

Born 13 months earlier in the Dominican Republic, Clara and Alta Rodriguez (see photographs on pages 34-36) were conjoined twins of a type known as ischiopagus tetrapus. Connected from sternum to perineum, they shared one liver, one colon, one terminal ileum, and crossed ureters, which would make their separation a very difficult proposition. Shirley Bonnem, now a vice-president of Children's of Philadelphia but then its director of public relations, wanted to let the world know the Rodriguez twins were receiving their care without fee. She told Koop she would set up a press center for the day of the separation if there was a decent chance the girls would live. Koop thought this over for about 10 minutes, she says, and then declared, "They won't die. I won't let them."

Bonnem says she was amazed by the response to the forthcoming surgery. After the operation, reporters and television crews began arriving from around the country and from Europe. Playing the situation for all it was worth, Bonnem issued a series of midnight bulletins, hoping the story would become a lead item in the morning news. She strung out news of the operation brilliantly. On the day of the surgery, the press was allowed to photograph and interview Koop; on the next day, the twins' mother. The payoff came the third day, when reporters were allowed a glimpse of the girls themselves. This little tease kept Children's of Philadelphia on the front pages of the world's newspapers for weeks, during which the name C. Everett Koop and the phrase *medical miracle* became synonymous.

The connection was deserved. The Rodriguez operation was a masterpiece of surgical technique and creativity. The twins were brought to the operating theater at 6 a.m. on September 18 to be prepared for the separation. Koop made the first incision at 10:10 a.m., as a team of four surgeons, three nurses, and seven physicians tended the lifelines and anesthesia. After dividing the xiphoid process, the team reached the liver—actually a mass the size of two livers—and divided it between the girls. Then the surgeons worked their way down the gastrointestinal tract to the point where the two small intestines formed a T-shaped juncture with the single terminal ileum. Koop divided one terminal small bowel before the juncture of the terminal ileum and allocated about one-third of the single colon to Clara, the stronger twin, and two-thirds to Alta. Clara received the single rectum because she had the best blood supply. Reaching the conjoined pubis, the team encountered two normal bladders with crossed ureters—each twin had one ureter feeding into her own bladder and one connected to her sister's. The crossed ureters were detached and temporarily allowed to drip while the pubis was divided. An S-shaped incision was made across the perineum, and the twins were separated. The teams then proceeded to work on each child separately, anastomosing the severed ureters, repairing the intestines, performing a temporary perineal colostomy on Alta, and closing the huge abdominal wounds. The closures were completed by 5:15 p.m.

"Even the other surgeons were just in awe of Koop that day," said one who was present at Koop's triumphant postoperative press briefing in the hospital's auditorium. "It was as if he had worked a miracle in the true sense, done something beyond physical law."

Koop was the center of attention and admiration, and it's not unfair to speculate that somewhere in his subconscious, a voice might have been asking, "What else could keep me in the spotlight like this?" Koop's publicity-winning ways, combined with his growing dismay over the acceptance of "anti-life" ideas, probably made his future as a leader in the anti-abortion movement inevitable.

"One day when I was operating on three newborn babies," Koop once told an interviewer, "I realized that less than 100 feet away, at the Hospital of the University of Pennsylvania, they were destroying babies. Knowing what we can do with abnormal children, to know that we're destroying a million normal children a year just drives me crazy," Koop said.

Just as he had once infuriated general surgeons by taking his complaints about them public, Koop now began to criticize members of the very specialty he had helped nurture. Pediatric surgeons, Koop opined, were doing nowhere near enough to exert pressure to encourage the operations that keep handicapped infants alive. And pediatricians who supported abortion, he said, were traitors to the medical oath. Koop began to say these things bluntly, loudly, and publicly. Groups that once had cherished Koop as their champion and favorite speaker suddenly were uncomfortable when he showed up for a meeting. As he had done before, Koop took his complaints to an outside forum: this time, it was the right-to-life movement.

Koop's initial forays on the anti-abortion circuit consisted of relatively low-profile efforts—he made speeches to church groups and conservative organizations, and he wrote a short book, *The Right to Live, the Right to Die*, which enjoyed a small run by a religious press in 1976.

One of his first appearances on the national scene as a commentator on matters other than the health of children came in 1978. In an article about the first "test tube" baby, *The New York Times* identified Koop not only as the surgeon in chief at Children's but also as a Presbyterian elder. He was quoted as saying that since life begins at conception, no embryo conceived in vitro should be destroyed. Koop also expressed his fear that in vitro conception could become a tool for genetic engineering, which, he said, represented an attempt to usurp God's role at the center of creation. Eventually Koop would be cited as an unlikely ally of Jeremy Rifkin, the science gadfly who opposes a wide range of technological research, in their shared opposition to gene-manipulation experiments.

Koop developed a standard stump speech. In it he condemned both in vitro fertilization and, more forcefully, amniocentesis. He called the latter a "search-and-destroy mission."

(Text continues on page 37)

Separating the Rodriguez Twins

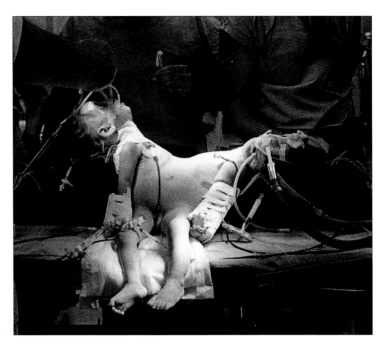

Preparation of the twins and administration of anesthesia began at 6 a.m. on September 18, 1974. Because their face-to-face position made intubation and other procedures awkward, the first incision was not made until four hours later.

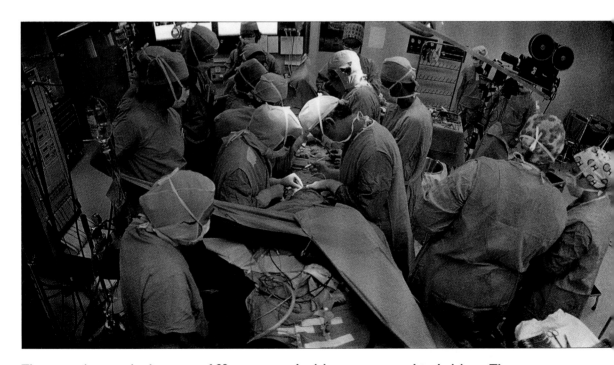

The operation required a team of 23 surgeons, physicians, nurses, and technicians. The twins were placed on two polyurethane triangles on operating tables joined footpiece-to-footpiece. At the moment of separation, the twins were drawn apart on the triangles.

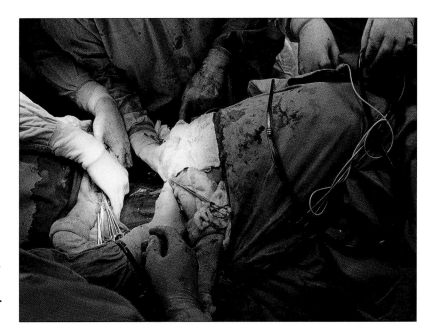

This picture shows the actual moment of separation. Afterward, each twin was surrounded by a separate surgical team.

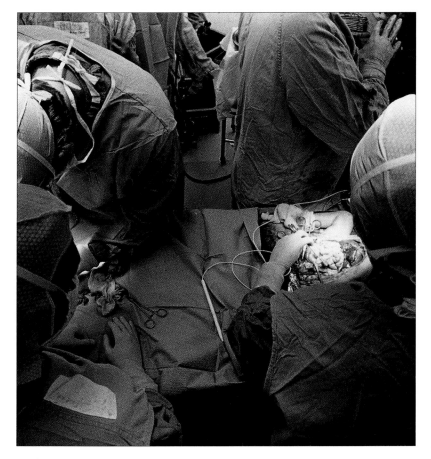

Separation entailed making a very large surgical wound. Here, Koop repairs one twin's bowels as Dr. John Duckett Jr. (not visible) anastomoses the other's ureter. Then the surgeons traded places.

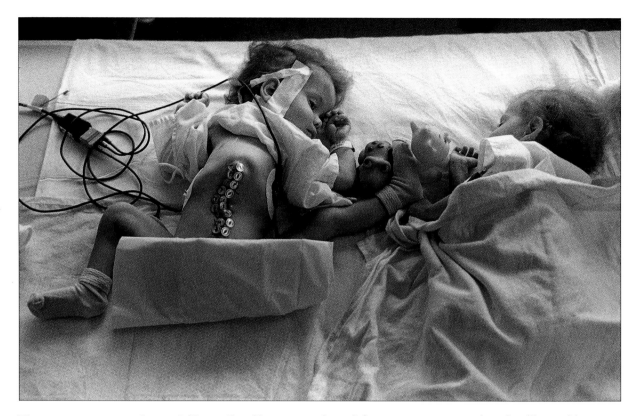

The surgery was complete at 5:15 p.m. Pearl buttons anchored the sutures to ensure that the silk would not pull through the tautly stretched skin. Recovery was surprisingly uneventful.

Alta died when she choked on a bean in 1976. Clara is now 18 years old. She is pictured with Koop at Children's of Philadelphia in 1985.

Amniocentesis often generates controversy among obstetricians. The procedure is thought to carry a low risk of aborting a fetus, and though it reliably detects gene defects related to retardation, it cannot predict whether the retardation will be profound. These limitations were a side issue to Koop. Even if there were a test that had no side effects and reliably identified only those fetuses that seemed hopeless in every way, he believed that using it would still be an abomination. Any procedure performed on a pregnant woman that might generate an argument in favor of abortion is an outrage, he felt.

Around the year 1979, the anti-abortion movement began to emerge as a potent political force, one that would help carry Ronald Reagan into office. That year Koop turned 63, and he began cutting back his surgical workload. Years of being on his feet, hunched over, straining to perform precise cuts and folds in tiny cavities, had taken their toll. Koop's fingers had begun to cramp during surgery, and he had to pause frequently to have nurses massage them. (In 1986, Koop awoke from a nap unable to move his hands at all. The paralysis, caused by bone spurs on a vertebra, was corrected surgically.)

Aging, his manual dexterity failing, Koop seemed unlikely to accomplish further breakthroughs as a working surgeon. Children's of Philadelphia, thanks in part to his work, was now an internationally renowned institution housed in a new building where the surgical center bore Koop's name. A career switch to public affairs seemed an inviting prospect, and the anti-abortion movement had what might be called job openings.

His big move came with the 1979 release of the anti-abortion film *Whatever Happened to the Human Race?*, with Koop as narrator and star. One scene shows the surgeon—looking more like a man who would frighten little children to death than a beloved doctor—standing on the salt wastes of the Dead Sea in Israel, at what is said to be the site of Sodom. Koop is surrounded by hundreds of smashed dolls that represent the souls of the unborn lost to abortion. Another scene shows Koop at Yad Vashem, the Israeli memorial to the Holocaust, making a comparison between Nazis and those who advocate pulling the plug on the elderly.

Whatever Happened to the Human Race? was a runaway box-office hit on the conservative circuit, bigger even than Ronald Reagan's favorite, *Silent Scream*. And unlike the latter, which was noted for its shock footage of aborted fetuses and its pseudoscientific claims, Koop's film offered no dubious medical assertions. *Whatever Hap-*

pened . . . ? was an opinionated but entirely straightforward film based on intellectual arguments. Koop's academic affiliation with the University of Pennsylvania medical school lent it a weight most of the anti-abortion movement's output sorely lacked.

The movie, which cost $1 million, was financed by supporters of Francis Schaeffer, a Christian evangelical minister and the author of numerous bestsellers (such as *The Christian Manifesto)* that combine old-fashioned insistence on biblical inerrancy with a modern approach to daily life. Schaeffer founded a religious retreat called L'Abri in the Swiss Alps, and Koop became close to him while attending retreats there. In a small shed on a snowswept peak above L'Abri, Koop built a memorial to his son David.

When news of *Whatever Happened . . . ?* became public, some of Koop's colleagues at Children's of Philadelphia thought he had gone off the deep end. "In the hospital environment Chick was always completely rational," said Dr. Anna Meadows, a pediatric oncologist and Koop's friend. "As he began to make public pronouncements, many of us felt he became less rational."

Then as now, most physicians supported the *Roe* decision, either because they endorsed women's right to choose or because they felt that government should keep out of decisions between doctor and patient. Those who agreed with the right to abortion but discouraged the practice deeply resented Koop's characterization of all pro-choice advocates as heartless fiends to whom life was cheap. Colleagues may also have been uncomfortable because as Koop began to be seen as a religious monomaniac, an unwelcome reflection could have been cast upon the hospital he had done so much to build.

Had Koop really gone over the edge? Or was he just saying things no one wanted to hear, as he so often had before?

Koop and Schaeffer had written a book, also called *Whatever Happened to the Human Race?*, that was released at the same time as their film. Although Koop's critics would frequently refer to this volume as crackpot literature during his 1981 confirmation hearings in Washington, it is well written, well argued, and well-grounded in the traditions of Western philosophy. In fact, although the film *Whatever Happened . . . ?* has its nutty moments, the book shows that Koop was not some daft revivalist but a man with a disciplined, independent mind—the kind of man who might have many surprises in store.

CHAPTER FIVE

A VERY FRIGHTENING INDIVIDUAL

When Ronald Reagan, a chortling, washed-up actor with a poor memory, defeated incumbent Jimmy Carter in 1980, the Washington establishment was stunned. The conservative voter sentiments Reagan represented—fear of military weakness, antipathy toward the expert set, bitterness toward any program that could be characterized as a handout, and the belief that Washington liberals hold traditional American values in contempt—were alien concepts to many of those safely barricaded inside the Beltway, the circular highway that bounds the nation's capital.

By early 1981, as Reagan's $750 billion supply-side tax cut (precursor to the deficits that have plagued the federal government since) sailed through Congress with hardly a word of opposition, there was palpable fear among liberals that the New Right revolution would succeed in rolling back 30 years of progress on civil rights, women's rights, Social Security, and environmental protection. Many political indicators suggested that once the supply-side fight was won, Reagan would focus on abortion, and liberals feared they would be steamrollered again. Then Reagan nominated C. Everett Koop as surgeon general—and Koop was just the sort who seemed as though he would drive a steamroller with glee.

Undoubtedly, Ronald Reagan chose Koop not because of his accomplishments in medicine but because of his high-profile crusade against abortion. This alone, in the Washington atmosphere of 1981, would have been sufficient to ensure an all-out flap. The Koop nomination sparked fear among the commentators, columnists, journalists, and others who form Washington's largely liberal opinion-making class that Reagan had assigned Koop the political task of leading the fight to make abortion illegal again. This was despite the fact that the surgeon general's office has no jurisdiction in this area. *Roe* v. *Wade* can be reversed only by another Supreme Court ruling or by a constitutional amendment.

During Reagan's presidency, many state legislatures nibbled around the edges of *Roe* by imposing conditions on how minors could obtain abortions, and Congress restricted public funding for abortions for the poor. But even these approaches are outside the surgeon general's mandate, which is to study public health and issue warnings regarding health hazards. Nevertheless, Koop resigned all his memberships in anti-abortion groups and declared that if confirmed he would decline from speaking further on the subject.

These gestures carried little weight with Koop's opponents. But they could not have known that Reagan would turn out to be all talk and no action on this most sensitive issue; although Reagan talked a great deal about abortion during his presidency, he never really did anything about it. He did not, for example, put the weight of the White House behind a constitutional amendment, and he did not send Congress a bill that defined abortion as an infringement of civil rights—an approach some conservative legal scholars thought might slip through a loophole in *Roe*.

Nevertheless, the intensity of the opposition to Koop was hard to explain on the merits of the case. Any decision to make a sustained push for something like an anti-abortion amendment would not be made by an official who reports to an assistant secretary of the Department of Health and Human Services (HHS), which is where the surgeon general sits on the federal depth chart. But the way power really flows in Washington is usually forgotten during confirmation fandangos. Koop's was no exception.

Throughout 1981, Koop found himself the target of the kind of political invective usually leveled at those who burglarize their opponents' political headquarters. Koop was, according to Representative Henry Waxman (D-Calif.), a top congressional player on health-care issues, "a very frightening individual." Koop was, according to Senator Ted Kennedy (D-Mass.), someone who endorsed "a cruel, outdated, patronizing, and discredited stereotype of women." He was, according to several columnists, "Dr. Kook."

Most major newspapers editorialized against the nomination. *The Louisville Times* dismissed Koop as "a religious extremist." *The Bul-*

SUPPORT.

PLACING A STRONG PRIORITY ON WOMEN'S HEALTHCARE ISSUES.
PROVIDING SUPPORT TO HELP MEET THE CHALLENGES OF THE FUTURE.

 SYNTEX

SYNTEX IS MAKING PROFOUND CONTRIBUTIONS TO MEDICINE.

I

REASSURANCE.

PROVIDING THE REASSURANCE OF EFFECTIVE, WELL-TOLERATED
RELIEF FOR THE MANAGEMENT OF ENDOMETRIOSIS. A BALANCED APPROACH
IN A UNIQUE INTRANASAL SPRAY.

SYNAREL®

(NAFARELIN ACETATE) NASAL SOLUTION 2 MG/ML (AS NAFARELIN BASE).

THE MOST COMMON ADVERSE EVENTS ARE HYPOESTROGENIC. PREGNANCY SHOULD
BE RULED OUT BEFORE THERAPY WITH **SYNAREL** IS INITIATED, AND PATIENTS
SHOULD BE ADVISED TO USE A NONHORMONAL METHOD OF CONTRACEPTION WHEN
TAKING **SYNAREL**. RETREATMENT CANNOT BE RECOMMENDED SINCE SAFETY DATA
FOR RETREATMENT ARE NOT CURRENTLY AVAILABLE.

SYNTEX IS MAKING PROFOUND CONTRIBUTIONS TO MEDICINE.

YOU CAN LOCATE THE PRESCRIBING INFORMATION FOR **SYNAREL** ON PAGES VIII-XI OF THE APPENDIX.

J

letin, in his hometown of Philadelphia, ran a vicious editorial cartoon depicting Koop as monstrous Siamese twins. Organizations that formally opposed his nomination included the American Public Health Association, Planned Parenthood, the National Organization for Women, the United Steelworkers, the United Mine Workers, the American Federation of State, County, and Municipal Employees, B'nai B'rith Women, and even the United Presbyterian Church in the U.S.A., the liberal wing of Koop's denomination. (The American Medical Association dodged this controversy by taking no stand at all.) Television networks edited snippets from the movie version of *Whatever Happened . . . ?* to leave the impression that Koop was deranged. *The New York Times* summed it up with a biting editorial headlined DR. UNQUALIFIED.

Though Koop's views and his off-putting personality were big factors in his confirmation struggle, what really unnerved opponents and some in the press was Koop's religiosity. It is common in Washington for public figures to make God-fearing noises at tactically advantageous moments. Actual religious fervor is another thing altogether. Thus, the Washington establishment was uncomfortable with Jimmy Carter, who seemed genuinely worried about the ultimate disposition of his soul; Ronald Reagan did not generate a similar level of discomfort. Though Reagan, like Carter, described himself as an old-time Christian, he rarely attended church, and his lifestyle gave scant indication that Christian teachings weighed heavily in his thinking.

Within the ranks of the Washington press corps, churchgoing is about as common as square-dancing. Religion tends to be viewed philosophically as a smattering of worn superstitions and sociologically as a complex of quaint, small-town customs. The press's distrust of religion is based partly on a commitment to the separation of church and state (which is sensible), but the attitude prevents many reporters from understanding a force that is, for better or worse, among the most powerful influences in the life of the typical American. In Koop's case, this antireligious sentiment was guaranteed to create hostilities.

In assessing Koop, for example, most journalists failed to grasp the difference between an evangelical Christian (Koop) and a fundamentalist. Evangelicals seek to win others to the faith, and one can be a liberal evangelical, though the species is rare. The term *fundamentalist* arose in the late 19th century as a response by conservative theologians to the Darwinian theory of evolution and other encroachments by natural science on religious beliefs. Originally, the fundamentalists were associated with institutions of higher learning—Princeton, for example—but because in recent decades their approach has acquired a connotation of closed-mindedness and anti-intellectualism, thoughtful conservatives like Koop want nothing to do with the fundamentalist label. The press corps missed this distinction entirely.

Meanwhile, at Children's of Philadelphia, the same colleagues who had been privately uneasy about Koop during his emergence as an anti-abortion activist in the late 1970s were dismayed that their friend was being slandered in the Washington reputation mill. Several Children's staff physicians, among them Koop's friend Dr. Anna Meadows, a *Roe* supporter, began calling reporters to speak in Koop's defense. But little of what they said filtered into the press's coverage of the confirmation fight.

Shirley Bonnem, who had manipulated the national press corps so masterfully during the 1974 twins operation, was frustrated in her attempts to exercise spin control. "*The Washington Post* absolutely refused to listen to me because I was saying things they didn't want to hear," Bonnem says. "I begged the *Post* to send a reporter here and ask anyone they wanted what Dr. Koop was like. No one came. This was for a story they were putting on the front page day after day. I begged them to call our doctors, nurses, or even patients who disagreed with Chick's views, and ask whether he was a man of principle. They would not."

There was little doubt where Koop stood on the issues. Adversaries in the Senate (which would judge his nomination) had plenty of material around which to rally an opposition. That was fair enough, since senatorial advice and consent traditionally takes into account political beliefs. But it was not long before fair disagreement with Koop's views gave way to vigorous attempts to take his statements out of context and overload the debate.

Koop was derided on Capitol Hill, for example, for a 1979 commencement speech to the graduating class of the Philadelphia College of Osteopathic Medicine. In remarks that opponents pulled out of context from the address, Koop appeared to declare his belief that by the year 1999 the worship of God would be outlawed in the United States and that genetically engineered homosexual test-tube babies would be mass-manufactured in clinics in order to increase gay political clout. Crackpot stuff to be sure, but Koop had prefaced these words by explaining that he was offering a satirical vision of where current political trends might lead. Koop's satire hardly rose to the level of Swift, but the sentences that the press began to quote

The controversy surrounding Koop's nomination was heated. This cartoon, which plays off the surgeon's success at separating conjoined twins, appeared in *The Bulletin*, a Philadelphia newspaper, in 1981.

to suggest that Koop was a nut had been clearly presented as fanciful in a speech that was otherwise sober and sharply reasoned.

As often happens when the ridiculous is used to attack a figure in public debate, the ridiculous began to be offered in Koop's defense. Against the charge that Koop was such a zealot on the prolongation of life that he would, in one critic's words, "ventilate an amoeba," Koop's defenders offered the sad tale of a 1977 separation of conjoined twins in which Koop deliberately killed an infant. In the Washington snippet wars, the fact that Koop had once been willing to terminate a handicapped infant became, with some factions, a point in his favor.

The twins, children of Orthodox Jewish parents, shared a single, normal heart that would have to go to one or the other at separation. For some 11 days a small army of rabbis and Talmudic scholars pitched camp in a wing of Children's of Philadelphia, trying to determine a course of action—whether to do nothing, in which case both babies would die, or operate, killing one to save the other— that would be consistent with an ancient body of law and tradition.

The rabbis interviewed Koop's entire surgical team, including the nurses, looking for opinions and information on subjects as arcane as exactly how the children would be touched in the moments when death was caused. Koop, who has said the day of the operation was the hardest of his life, has also said it took him only 10 minutes to decide that intervention was the moral course. Koop himself determined which baby would be let go, based on an assessment of their relative chances for survival. And he did the dirty work himself, clamping off Baby A's carotid artery as the table with Baby B, granted the heart, was pulled away. (It happened that Baby B died 47 days later of infections.)

Once it was apparent that the nomination controversy would not be resolved quickly, Koop moved from Philadelphia to Washington and took an acting position as deputy assistant secretary of health at HHS, filling a slot that did not require Senate confirmation. This move showed opponents that he would not be easily frightened off. It also betrayed how badly he wanted to become a top-level participant in American public affairs. "Chick wanted the surgeon general [position] like it was the last job in the world," said Koop's friend Dr. Patrick Pasquariello.

Koop knew the imprimatur of a high government job would give his views increased credibility and immediacy. And he thought the surgeon general's office, a low-profile operation during the 1970s, could be revived and used to press for reforms in a number of public-health categories. His surgeon's ego had, by now, become a commentator's ego. Koop had felt the sensation of the world hanging on his words, and he thirsted for more. Much as the opinion-making establishment was infuriating Koop by barraging him with snap judgments, the truth was that he longed to join their number.

Opponents trying to undermine Koop's credentials because they disagreed with his views also used arguments that were technically legitimate. The American Public Health Association, for example, complained that he had no degree in public health. No matter that decades of helping run a big inner-city hospital and setting up third-world health projects had given Koop plenty of de facto experience in this field. No matter that people with real-world experience often do better in government than people with impressive degrees. Most past surgeon generals had possessed public-health degrees. By declaring Koop academically unqualified to speak on matters of public health, adversaries could oppose his nomination without broaching the politically sensitive issue of abortion.

Koop's supporters were soon reduced to dredging up any incidents from Koop's past that seemed like the kinds of things holders of degrees in public health would have been involved in. In the late 1940s, for example, Koop conducted a public-relations campaign

Koop at his 1981 confirmation hearing before the Senate Labor and Human Resources Committee. Despite opposition that was sometimes fierce, he was confirmed by a vote of 68 to 24 on November 16.

against the use of X-ray machines in shoe stores to determine whether children's shoes had a "scientific fit." Promotional gimmicks popular in a period when anything with gee-whiz scientific touches projected an almost mystical aura, the machines were high-dose models that surely harmed salespeople even more than children. Koop's offensive helped get the machines removed. Another of his campaigns in the late '50s helped to end the now-forgotten practice of dosing household cleansing products with sickly sweet fragrances. Young children sometimes drank such products because they were attracted by the smell.

Though the confirmation hearings produced some negative publicity for Koop, they revealed nothing even faintly resembling the smoking guns of personal improprieties that are usually required to block a presidential choice. In fact the hearing records show that Koop's life had been squeaky-clean. Although he had said many controversial things, he had made few outright political gaffes. Representative Waxman's inability to lay a glove on Koop convinced many to vote in favor of the nomination. If Waxman, who wanted so dearly to see Koop's name withdrawn, could not produce any really damning evidence, perhaps the doctor was not as bad as he seemed. Koop's nomination was confirmed by the Senate, 68 to 24, on November 16, 1981. Given that the confirmation of nearly all presidential appointees except Supreme Court justices is essentially automatic, the 24 nays represented an unusually pronounced expression of negative sentiment.

As it happened, once confirmed in his post, Koop was true to his word. He did nothing that could be construed as violating the church-state boundary and, until the very end of his term, uttered nary a peep about abortion.

What Koop didn't say was surprising. What he did say was even more so.

VOICE OF MODERATION

I n his first big moment in the public spotlight, Surgeon General C. Everett Koop seemed to confirm his critics' very worst expectations.

In 1982, a baby with Down syndrome and esophageal atresia was born in a Bloomington, Indiana, hospital. After consulting with their obstetrician, the child's parents decided not to allow the atresia to be corrected, a course that would cause certain death. For several days, local prosecutors attempted to compel the hospital and the doctor to perform the surgery. While the fine points of the law were being argued, Baby Doe (as she was dubbed by the press) died.

Though Koop was not involved in the legal attempt to compel the operation, he spoke out on the issue. That the child had died of esophageal atresia, the very condition that Koop prided himself on having rendered correctable, was especially galling. Koop had often said that in pediatrics, the parents are patients as much as the child, but he never meant that the interests of parents were superior to those of children. To him, the essence of the Bloomington case was that the patient's interests were not served by the decision of the parents.

Not long afterward, in 1983, a second Baby Doe situation occurred. A child with spina bifida and the potential for an unknown degree of retardation was born in a hospital on New York's Long Island. When the child's parents refused to authorize surgery to correct the spina bifida, Justice Department attorneys demanded access to the child's medical files, contending that the baby was a victim of discrimination because it was being denied medical services that would have been granted to a person who was not handicapped. Again, the effort bogged down in court, but this time the baby survived. Her spine later closed naturally, and a 1990 article in *Newsday*, the Long Island newspaper, reported that the second Baby Doe has grown into a happy and active youngster.

Koop defended the government's actions. Appearing on the network television program *Face the Nation*, he argued that medieval misconceptions about the handicapped were at play. "I have never seen a child [with correctable spina bifida] live a life of pain," said Koop, responding to questions about whether the victim might somehow rather die. "And I don't think [the local physicians'] estimate of severe retardation or [a life of being] bedridden are necessarily facts. You cannot make those decisions at this early stage."

Koop then asked the television audience, "If we do not intrude into the life of a child such as this, whose civil rights may be abrogated? The next person may be you." The careful listener would have noted an important shift on Koop's part. A lifelong conservative, he was now arguing in favor of expanded government authority to preserve rights. This was not a slip of the tongue. Public pronouncements meant a great deal to Koop, and he thought them through carefully. His philosophy was changing.

Ronald Reagan took a personal interest in Baby Doe issues. His administration's attempts to deal with them led to a succession of measures, some wise, some comical. Frustrated by the inability of federal prosecutors to intervene in the cases directly, the White House counterattacked with several HHS regulations affecting hospitals that accept Medicare and Medicaid payments, which is to say, all hospitals. The first attempt at regulations, in March 1983, essentially required surgeons to operate on anything wrong with a newborn. Those rules also contained a universally despised clause that compelled hospitals to post a 25- by 30-inch sign in their waiting rooms, cautioning DISCRIMINATORY FAILURE TO FEED AND CARE FOR HANDICAPPED INFANTS IN THIS FACILITY IS PROHIBITED BY FEDERAL LAW. The sign listed a toll-free number at the Justice Department that people could call if they suspected the law was being violated.

Because Koop testified as the government's expert witness in legal hearings on the regulations, they were widely viewed as his idea. In fact he was anything but pleased with the language used, much less with the belief that he was responsible for it. "The idea was put together [by the White House and HHS] with tremendous consultation from the pro-life groups and no input from pediatricians," he says.

SIMPLICITY.

SIMPLIFYING TREATMENT FOR THE PATIENT WITH
VULVOVAGINAL CANDIDIASIS. THE EFFECTIVENESS AND SATISFACTION
OF A THREE-DAY THERAPY WITH THE EASE OF PREFILL CONVENIENCE.

FEMSTAT®
(BUTOCONAZOLE NITRATE) VAGINAL CREAM 2%.

IN PREGNANT PATIENTS (SECOND AND THIRD TRIMESTERS ONLY),
THERAPY SHOULD BE EXTENDED TO SIX DAYS.

 SYNTEX

SYNTEX IS MAKING PROFOUND CONTRIBUTIONS TO MEDICINE.

YOU CAN LOCATE THE PRESCRIBING INFORMATION FOR **FEMSTAT** ON PAGES XXXI-XXXIII OF THE APPENDIX.

K

The courts struck down the first set of Baby Doe regulations in April 1983, and HHS issued a second version in January 1984. This time the size of the warning sign was reduced, and it could be posted in doctors' and nurses' locker rooms instead of waiting areas. The courts voided these regulations in May 1984.

During the dispute over the Baby Doe regulations, Koop had gone to Margaret Heckler, the secretary of Health and Human Services, and told her that if he was going to take the blame for the regulations, he should be given a hand in composing them. With Heckler's assent, Koop convened a task force that included representatives of medical societies, anti-abortion groups, and public-interest organizations, among others. After overcoming their mutual hostilities, the group produced in 1984 a "bill of rights" for handicapped infants that was, Koop says, "a beautiful document." The compromise requires hospitals and physicians to perform all medically indicated treatments on all infants. The only exceptions to this rule involve heroic measures on the irreversibly comatose and procedures that would serve only to prolong suffering. A law based partly on Koop's document was passed by Congress in 1984, and that seemed to resolve the issue. But in 1986, the Supreme Court struck down a series of federal regulations written under the law's authority. Though the law still stands, confusion on the exact status of Baby Doe cases persists: the federal statute defines most forms of denial of care to the young as child abuse, but detecting and punishing such abuse is actually a matter of state jurisdiction.

Some were surprised that Koop acted as a moderating force rather than an extremist in these debates. Perhaps they shouldn't have been. Even as the Baby Doe cases were going forward, certain rather activist decisions were slipping out of the office of the surgeon general. In early 1982, for instance, Koop issued the strongest federal condemnation of cigarette smoking since the first surgeon general's report, which was released in 1964.

The surgeon general's office has been synonymous with crusades against smoking since Dr. Luther Terry, in Lyndon Johnson's administration, made a ban on television advertising of smoking products his personal cause. But in the years following Terry, the congressionally required publication of an annual surgeon general's antismoking report had become a ho-hum event. Koop changed that with a dramatic antismoking push that received great attention.

By 1985, Koop's office had raised the estimate of yearly U.S. smoking-related deaths to 350,000. He classified nicotine as an addictive drug and declared smoking an addiction, noting, "I use the term carefully and thoughtfully. Seventy-eight percent of smokers wish they could quit and cannot. There is no question that nicotine is addictive." Koop also concurred with assertions that passive smoke can have significant health effects. This proposition is especially vexing to the tobacco lobby, which tries to assert that smoking is a personal matter of no importance to anyone but the smoker. Though Koop did not favor outlawing cigarettes altogether, reasoning that Prohibition had proved people would always get bootleg products somehow, he did come up with the idea of declaring that since nicotine is a drug, cigarette sellers should be licensed to prevent sales to minors. The idea went nowhere, but it terrified the tobacco lobby for a time.

In 1984, Koop called for a ban on all forms of cigarette advertising, including that in newspapers and magazines. Strangely, the proposition seemed to receive much less play in the nation's newspapers and magazines than did other Koop pronouncements. Koop considered it significant that the American Medical Association did not endorse the proposal until a year later. Despite the delay, he believes that simple demographics are causing the AMA to take an increasingly strong position against tobacco. The older generation of doctors who smoke is gradually being replaced by a generation that hates smoke.

Luther Terry, Lyndon Johnson's surgeon general, sounded the first official warning on cigarettes in 1964.

Koop's aggressive antismoking campaign had political implications. During his 1980 campaign, Reagan had sought the support of tobacco companies, promising that his administration would not agitate against smoking. The White House was far from happy with Koop's decision to make smoking a high-profile issue.

Koop also spoke out against marijuana, but his language was not nearly as harsh as that he had used regarding cigarettes. The standard New Right practice at that time was to wax hysterical about "killer weed" while noting testily that tobacco is a legal product. Koop felt that the numbers for lung cancer proved conclusively which leafy product did society more harm, and he said so.

Koop's campaign against the dangers of cigarettes proved that he would not let the biases of others cloud his comprehension of the facts. It is a discipline every physician is supposed to practice, but institutional Washington had assumed Koop would be unable to do so. His early actions against tobacco were telling.

It now appeared that Koop would not shy from a fight—perhaps not even from a fight with the president.

CHAPTER SEVEN

NOTED ULTRALIBERAL

The Office of the Surgeon General is a small operation; the nation's chief physician has only five staff aides. Most of their work is routine: they produce studies, compilations of studies, and abstracts of studies that result in general precautionary statements about health. The standard public-health issues—the need for inoculations and hygiene, the importance of prevention over intervention, the sad state of health of the poor and uninsured—tend to stay roughly the same from generation to generation. The office comes to the attention of the average citizen only rarely, usually when a sudden health crisis threatens the nation.

Everett Koop made the post high-profile. To begin with, there was his physical appearance. Koop had grown his trademark Captain Ahab beard in the early '70s to cover a double chin, and photos from his clean-shaven period prove as good a case as any man has ever had to wear whiskers. Yet the publicity-conscious Koop could not have failed to notice that the beard gave him a more striking appearance and to suspect that it made his photo more likely to appear in the newspaper. Once in office, he made himself even more noticeable by reviving the practice of wearing the ceremonial uniform of the Public Health Service. He did this, he said, to emphasize that members of the service are officers who can be assigned away from their homes, like military personnel and diplomats. That a bearded government doctor in an *opéra-bouffe* uniform was irresistible to the media is not supposed to have entered his mind.

Even these touches, however, would have lost their novelty value had Koop himself remained the focus of attention. But in the early 1980s an unexpected development of historic proportions came

Koop in the full regalia of the U.S. Public Health Service, in a portrait taken near the end of his term in 1989. Robert Mapplethorpe, the photographer who shot this picture, died of AIDS later that year.

calling. Acquired immunodeficiency syndrome (AIDS) would change the politics of health—and change Koop's image as well.

It happened only a short time ago, but today it is difficult to recall the curious nature of the early public debate about AIDS. Much of it centered on the question of whether one ought to talk about the disease at all. It is hard to imagine that it ever could have been controversial to discuss tuberculosis or smallpox. Yet in the early 1980s, many conservatives were demanding what amounted to public silence about AIDS, because it was impossible to discuss the disease without mentioning its main modes of transmission—homosexual intercourse and intravenous drug use.

Some actually called the disease a blessing from God—a scourge sent to wipe out sodomites and drug users. As journalist Randy Shilts reports in his book *And the Band Played On* (St. Martin's Press, 1987), even factions within the gay community urged that news about AIDS be hushed up because it would be bad for homosexual businesses such as bathhouses, and because it might encourage homophobia. As late as 1985, President Reagan was following a strategy that ironically appealed to fringe groups on both the far right and gay left. The game plan called for Reagan to play down the possibility of an epidemic, call for no particular action, and make no funds available for crash research projects.

Abortion may not have fallen under Koop's jurisdiction as surgeon general, but as an emerging public-health issue, AIDS did. The nation's number-one health officer and best-known physician potentially had a great deal of impact on how the disease would be understood, how the victims would be treated by society, and whether Americans would take the steps necessary to impede the spread of the virus. There was an overpowering rationale for Koop to speak out. The question of whether or not he would do so became, itself, an issue.

During Reagan's first term (1981-85) the White House ordered Koop to say nothing on AIDS. This was not because Reagan feared Koop's views on the subject—the president's staff assumed that, as a conservative evangelical, Koop would hurl fire and brimstone upon the heads of the sufferers. It was because the president did not want anybody in his administration talking about the subject. So Koop watched from the sidelines, doubtless wondering what the consequences would be if he defied a direct order from the president on this issue.

By late 1985, public concern about AIDS had increased and Reagan's inaction was costing him political points with Middle America. Suddenly, the president reversed himself and announced there would be a major federal report on the new disease, to be written by Surgeon General Koop. Koop was not consulted in advance of the announcement; he said that he found out about it from Reagan's speech, just the way everybody else did. His charge was a brief letter from the president delivered to his office the next day. Reagan had no interest in sitting down and discussing this issue.

Koop's report on AIDS was released in October 1986. By that

time, the combination of concern about the disease and the growing notion that perhaps Koop was not a New Right windup doll had elevated speculation about the report's content to a high pitch. This was what Koop, in his private heart, liked best—the whole world was hanging on his words. He went for broke.

Koop laid it on the line about AIDS. He did not condemn homosexuals. He did not advocate sexual abstinence as a panacea. He stood up on national television, declared that condoms were the only short-term practical barrier to the spread of AIDS, and proceeded to give official U.S. government instructions for their use.

In a press conference, with the network cameras rolling, Koop urged teenage boys to think twice before having anal intercourse with one another. He explained that the worst thing about patronizing a prostitute, aside from the moral question, was the risk that he or she might use intravenous drugs.

"It was weird using words like *penis* and *vagina* on national TV," Koop noted later, "but how else was I supposed to say it?"

And then there was the matter of a 92-word paragraph buried in Koop's report. It advocated that children hear "frank, open discussions" about sex in "the lowest grade possible." The lowest grade possible—that is, in school. Koop had taken advantage of his presidential mandate to endorse one of organized conservatism's biggest bugaboos: mandatory sex education. Soon he would be saying in his standard stump speech that sex-education programs should be initiated as early as the third grade; high school was way too late.

The White House was stunned; the New Right was enraged. Secretary of Education William Bennett, a leading right-wing voice, began attacking Koop at every turn, saying his ideas were not only immoral, but an infringement of local control of schools. Phyllis Schlafly, leader of the Eagle Forum and an opponent of the women's movement, accused Koop of promoting promiscuity. The United Families Foundation, a conservative think tank, blasted him. *Conservative Digest*, once one of Koop's greatest fans, declared that he was "proposing instruction in buggery for schoolchildren." Schlafly and Paul Weyrich, a fellow New Right activist, urged conservatives to dissociate themselves from Koop because "his statements about AIDS are a cover for the homosexual community." Representative Jack Kemp, Senator Robert Dole, and former governor Pierre du Pont of Delaware, all candidates for the 1988 Republican presidential nomination, responded by dropping their sponsorship of a dinner in Koop's honor. The anti-abortion organi-

The surgeon general unveils the plain-language AIDS-information pamphlet that his office sent to every American household in 1988.

zation March for Life rescinded an award it had given Koop.

Koop's failure to pronounce a ritual invocation of the beauty of abstinence left many on the right especially peeved, since this see-no-evil position was its preferred way of weaseling out of the AIDS issue. Eventually Koop would advocate the airing of condom advertising on television, in order to reach those who "will not practice abstinence or monogamy."

"Many of my fellow conservatives did not seem to understand that there is a difference between what you recommend for a pluralistic society and what you might impose if you were king," Koop later reflected. "I strongly believe in sexual abstinence for the young, not only because it avoids pregnancy and disease but because it makes for better character and better marriages. I also believe in mutually faithful monogamy. Now if everybody in the world believed in those things we wouldn't have problems with abortion and AIDS. But we do have these problems and we have to face them in a practical way. If you tell the typical teenager today that the only thing you're going to discuss with him is abstinence, he will laugh at you."

In January 1988, Reagan was further dismayed when Assistant

Secretary for Health Robert E. Windom announced plans for Koop's office to send American households a plain-language brochure on AIDS and sexuality. But after the idea was widely praised in the media, Reagan grudgingly gave assent. The president then announced the formation of an AIDS study commission to be headed by Admiral James Watkins, the recently retired Chief of Naval Operations. Watkins was a firebrand conservative. More to the point, he was a devout Roman Catholic. Perhaps where a Presbyterian had failed to carry the ball on issuing condemnations of premarital sex and homosexuality, a Catholic would. The White House was foiled again when the Watkins report, released in June 1988, not only did not wag fingers but advocated that discrimination against people who were HIV-positive be made a violation of federal law.

Koop loyalists had a hard time understanding what had come over their man. In a speech in Washington, D.C., in 1987, Koop explained it this way: "I am surgeon general of the heterosexuals and the homosexuals, the moral and the immoral." The Bible, he noted, taught that one should hate the sin but love the sinner. So there was no time for self-righteous I-told-you-sos about the kinds of behavior linked to AIDS. All that mattered was trying to stop the disease and cure those already afflicted.

By 1988 Koop had gone so far as to endorse test programs on the distribution of sterile needles to IV-drug users. And he now thought that pregnant women with AIDS should receive counseling about all the options available, including abortion.

It left a bad taste in Koop's mouth that so many of his New Right allies abandoned him the instant he said things they found discomfiting. Speaking at Liberty University, the school founded by the Reverend Jerry Falwell, Koop noted, "One of the things that disturbed me most . . . is that my own constituency, namely political conservatives, and my own religious brethren, namely evangelicals, were most critical of what I said [about AIDS]. I cannot indulge the luxury of what I feel as an individual. I have to speak as a health officer."

Koop promptly shifted from hero of the right to hero of the left. Representative Henry Waxman, the congressman who had described Koop as "a frightening individual," now called him "a man of tremendous integrity." Senator Ted Kennedy sang Koop's praises from the Senate floor. Editorialists who had once delighted in the Dr. Kook tag now were practically the surgeon general's press agents. Planned Parenthood cited him as an authority on safe sex.

CONFIDENCE.

PRESCRIBED WITH CONFIDENCE FOR A WIDE VARIETY
OF CORTICOSTEROID-RESPONSIVE DERMATOSES.
REBUILDING CONFIDENCE ERODED BY THE EFFECTS
OF SKIN CONDITIONS ON APPEARANCE.

LIDEX®
(FLUOCINONIDE) CREAM 0.05%.

MINOR ADVERSE EFFECTS ARE REPORTED INFREQUENTLY.

SYNTEX IS MAKING PROFOUND CONTRIBUTIONS TO MEDICINE.

YOU CAN LOCATE THE PRESCRIBING INFORMATION FOR **LIDEX** ON PAGES XIII-XIV OF THE APPENDIX.

M

CONTROL.

HELPING PATIENTS WHO ARE VICTIMS OF THEIR ENVIRONMENT
TO START TAKING CONTROL OVER THEIR ALLERGIES.

NASALIDE®
(FLUNISOLIDE) NASAL SOLUTION 0.025%.

THE MOST FREQUENT COMPLAINT WITH **NASALIDE** IS MILD,
TRANSIENT NASAL STINGING AND BURNING.

SYNTEX IS MAKING PROFOUND CONTRIBUTIONS TO MEDICINE.

YOU CAN LOCATE THE PRESCRIBING INFORMATION FOR **NASALIDE** ON PAGES XIV-XVII OF THE APPENDIX.

N

The National Gay and Lesbian Task Force deemed Koop "someone whom we deeply admire."

One reason for Koop's instant liberal sainthood was that he seemed to have undergone a conversion. All political movements treasure converts. Just as the reformed alcoholic who once stole from the collection plate makes a better witness at revival meetings than the local tower of integrity, a former member of the opposition who switches sides is worth a hundred unyielding loyalists in politics. The Reagan wave had gathered up several highly publicized converts from liberalism; Democrats found it disconcerting that there was scant traffic in the other direction. Suddenly Everett Koop seemed to stand up as a man who had seen from the inside what Reagan speechwriter Peggy Noonan called "the revolution," become disenchanted, and defected.

But had the surgeon really changed his stripes? Koop would argue that he had simply followed his principles at each turn, and that if principle had led to unconventional conclusions, it was hardly the first time his life had worked out that way.

Koop possessed a keen sense of justice, but he had an equally keen sense of the value of bucking trends. In the 1970s, when liberal ideas were prevalent, Koop drew attention to himself by cutting directly to the kinds of issues conventional liberalism could not handle: what happens, for example, to those babies women now have the freedom to abort? In the 1980s, with Reaganism ascendant, Koop performed the same trick by homing in on the issues that struck New Right nerves: if we do save those babies, doesn't society have an obligation to help them grow up? Telling conservative truths in a liberal decade and liberal truths in a conservative decade turned out to be a formula for honoring an inner light of justice—and for making the evening news. To what degree Koop returned the liberals' embrace has never been clear. Ted Kennedy was hardly Koop's cup of tea, but few human beings can resist the sound of their names being praised, and Koop never went out of his way to renounce his liberal hero status.

Having broken with the New Right, Koop spent his final two years in office sharpening his views still further. His attacks on smoking became more focused. In 1989, his staff raised the estimate of smoke-related deaths once again, to 395,000 annually, or more than 1,000 Americans per day. Koop, who had criticized baseball players for endorsing chewing tobacco, urged the Department of Defense to eliminate PX discounts on cigarette purchases (it didn't). Noting that federal excise taxes on cigarettes raise billions of dollars per year, Koop proposed that the tax be increased tenfold, so that lung-cancer treatment would be self-financing. Cigarette companies recoiled; the cost of a pack would more than double.

When RJR Nabisco prepared to market a smokeless cigarette, Koop labeled the product a "drug delivery system" that should require certification by the Food and Drug Administration, an eventuality that the tobacco industry has long dreaded. Consumer and scientific reaction to the smokeless cigarette was negative, but RJR had even stronger reasons for withdrawing the product: among other things, it feared that Koop might succeed in convincing Congress that a new type of cigarette marketed with implied health claims justified the enactment of formal health-and-safety certification for every tobacco "delivery system." That could have set in motion a chain of events highly damaging to cigarette makers, since clinical trials were bound to reflect poorly on their product.

At many junctures during his dispute with cigarette makers, Koop slammed the assertions of the Tobacco Institute that, very strictly speaking, there is no proof that cigarettes cause lung cancer. Such claims show a "total lack of integrity," Koop said. Medical assertions of the cigarette lobby were "lies, open lies," he added. "If I ever lied in public like that I'd never get away with it. So how come they can?"

Another of Koop's targets was alcohol advertising. First he called for voluntary restrictions on television promotion of beer and wine, including the elimination of athletic sponsorships and celebrity endorsements. This relatively moderate idea went nowhere fast, and after leaving office, Koop would switch to a more drastic approach, saying that Congress should ban television advertising for beer and wine. He estimated that by age 18 the typical child will have seen 100,000 beer commercials, most of them associating the product with sex, fun, and robust good health. Beer and wine producers tried to protest that their ads did not lead to alcohol abuse. Koop's simple reply was that "advertising works."

Koop also called for a substantial increase in alcohol excise taxes, citing the estimate that there were 25,000 deaths per year in the United States in drinking-related auto accidents, which at the time made alcohol a greater cause of death than AIDS. Additional excise taxes would, Koop maintained, raise revenues to help finance the social costs of drinking (alcoholism treatment, for example) and reduce drunken-driving deaths by making prices high enough to discourage consumption. But Koop's alcohol-related proposals flopped on Capitol Hill.

Koop greets former critic and new friend Senator Edward Kennedy at a 1987 meeting on AIDS. Kennedy had once accused Koop of endorsing a "cruel, . . . patronizing, and discredited stereotype of women."

In other significant actions, Koop endorsed the value of breast milk and called for corporate policies that would make it practical for working women to nurse on the job. He issued a report on diet that was welcomed by nutritionists. It called for more lowfat, low-calorie food products and urged Americans to consume more fruits and vegetables. (Koop fails to follow some of his own dietary advice. Besides his fondness for dry martinis, he favors marbled steak and fatty macadamia nuts, for example.)

As an administrator, Koop was credited with reviving public awareness of the Public Health Service, a little-understood organization that, among other things, details physicians to the Centers for Disease Control and the National Institutes of Health. But he was not generally popular with the physician members of the service.

Members became peeved, for example, when Koop insisted that all purchase at their own expense and wear on certain occasions the PHS uniform Koop delighted in. They grew more peeved when Koop shook up the PHS hierarchy with a variety of rulings aimed at causing more frequent reassignments and making promotions competitive. He justified these actions by saying the service had been too slow to respond to AIDS. (For good measure, Koop took a swipe at the medical establishment by saying that too many doctors shunned AIDS patients, and those who did were guilty of "unprofessional conduct." This was easy for Koop to say, since he no longer worked around blood.)

Koop's final Washington controversy came just as Reagan was leaving office. For years, anti-abortion critics had contended that abortions harm women as well as fetuses. Although there was no documentation of the long-term psychological consequences to women who had legal abortions, it was said they were so ridden with guilt and sorrow that their mental health was damaged. Anti-abortion advocates assumed Surgeon General Koop might produce a study lending credence to this claim, and they pressed the White House to order Koop to do so.

The study was indeed begun, but as the final days of the Reagan presidency wound down, no results had been released. Reagan sent word to Koop that he was personally concerned that the study be made public before he left office. Koop sent Reagan a terse, coolly worded response—a payback, perhaps, for the tactless way in which Reagan had triggered the AIDS study—stating that his examination of the literature had convinced him that the data on the psychological aftermath of abortion were too vague to justify a scientifically defensible conclusion. Therefore the surgeon general's office would reach none.

Reagan is said to have blown his stack. Press reports played the event as another example of the converted right-winger revealing the shameful truth about a core assertion of conservative orthodoxy and taking a parting shot at the president. Because of this, Koop departed from the councils of government on sour terms with the Reagan administration—something that can be said of nearly everyone who had held a high-level post during Reagan's presidency. To Koop's great disappointment, he was not invited to serve under Bush.

Koop had hoped to land the only federal health position with greater visibility than surgeon general, that of secretary of the Department of Health and Human Services. A number of factors worked against him. One was his age (he was 72 years old when Bush took office in 1989). The second was that Bush staffers were intent on appointing a black to a high-ranking job. Qualified black Republicans are a rarity; of the few among them who were willing to

HOPE.

TAKING AN AGGRESSIVE APPROACH IN RESEARCH
ON ALZHEIMER'S DISEASE. NEW AVENUES OF THERAPY,
INNOVATIVE APPROACHES TO LONG-TERM CARE, KEEPING HOPE ALIVE.

 SYNTEX

SYNTEX IS MAKING PROFOUND CONTRIBUTIONS TO MEDICINE.

COMMUNICATION.

PURSUING PROMISING RESEARCH IN THE AREA OF STROKE.
DEFEATING THE FEAR OF ISOLATION, MAINTAINING THE ABILITY
TO COMMUNICATE WITH FAMILY AND FRIENDS.

SYNTEX IS MAKING PROFOUND CONTRIBUTIONS TO MEDICINE.

P

take an administration post, Dr. Louis Sullivan was custom-made for HHS, and got the position.

Finally, according to knowledgeable sources, Bush just didn't like Koop's style—he was too splashy and too egotistical. Bush tolerated the self-important verbiage of "drug czar" William Bennett because Bennett devoted time and energy to political attacks on Bush's Democratic Party foes. Koop would do none of this. And, although Bush shares many of Koop's views, the last thing he wanted was a cabinet official with enough public stature to divert attention from the president.

Perhaps it was just as well that Koop did not become secretary of HHS. In a cabinet-level job, where an official is to be a faithful exponent of administration policy, Koop would have been expected to do as he was told. And that would have spoiled all the fun.

CHAPTER EIGHT

UNMELLOWED

W hen Everett Koop left office in 1989, the media verdict was that he had mellowed. But that's not the right word. Koop may no longer see the world in the exaggerated us-versus-them terms of his late-1970s anti-abortion rhetoric. He may now count as friends many who once seemed enemies. But mellowed he has not. Moreover, Koop's work pace has increased since he retired from government. He is now among the most popular speakers on the lecture circuit, able to earn more from a month's worth of speeches than he did in a year as a public official (he earned $88,552 per year as surgeon general). Although they have not yet aired, he has hosted a series of five television specials on public-health issues (lots of Koop; no fields of twisted dolls or allusions to Sodom). Called *C. Everett Koop, M.D.*, the series was produced in conjunction with NBC. He is running a public-awareness organization called the National Safe Kids Campaign, which educates parents about accident prevention. He is also busy penning his memoirs (with no help from a ghost writer) to be published in September 1991 and trying to raise money to endow a Koop Institute for Health and Science. He is invited to appear on television as an interview subject so frequently that he now declines most requests, fearing the public will become sick of him.

Koop's transformation from practicing physician to public affairs commentator would seem complete: after he left the surgeon general's post he did not return to Philadelphia but elected to stay in Washington. For good or ill, Koop has cast his final lot with the inside-the-Beltway crowd.

Koop and his wife, whose health has begun to falter, recently bought a townhouse in a comfortable but not especially luxurious retirement community located a few hundred yards inside that Beltway in Bethesda, Maryland. The location leaves much to be desired, but it is possible to arrange for home care there, and the

Koop and his wife, Elizabeth, have moved to a townhouse in a modest retirement community just inside the Washington, D.C., Beltway.

Koops, older now, must consider such things. Above the fireplace of the townhouse hangs a spectacular photograph of their son David in his climber's gear, standing triumphant atop the pinnacle of a jagged rock face that pokes through the clouds.

Though the Koop of today is less likely to use the superheated rhetoric of the 1970s, his speech is still peppered with intensifiers. "Outrage," "amazement," "shock," "anger," and similar words come up frequently. And his surgeon's ego is intact. Even in casual conversation, Koop refers to his future television shows as "my five prime-time network specials." One physician who recently heard Koop speak at a medical conference notes, "I agreed with most of his points. But he overstates so much, makes everything a 10 when you know that most things in life are really a 6 or a 7. He talks like a television anchorman now."

Koop has taken on several new causes since leaving office. In 1990, he helped defeat California's "Big Green," an environmental ballot initiative, by appearing in TV commercials. Big Green would have banned any agricultural chemical judged by the state to cause cancer or reproductive damage. In his commercial Koop declared, "I know of absolutely no evidence whatever that the health of Americans is compromised in any way by tiny trace amounts of pesticides." The commercial was widely credited with being central to Big Green's defeat. Koop's high credibility among a heterodox group of religious conservatives, urban liberals, and homosexuals, three important California voting blocs, surely swayed the vote.

Supporters of California assemblyman Tom Hayden, the force behind Big Green, spun out an elaborate conspiracy theory concerning Koop's interest in the issue. Here it is: Johnson & Johnson helps fund Koop's Safe Kids campaign; Johnson & Johnson has a joint venture with Merck, the pharmaceutical firm; Merck has a joint venture with Du Pont; Du Pont is a major manufacturer of pesticides; therefore Koop fought Big Green hoping these three companies would repay him by endowing his Institute for Health and Science. The institute Koop hopes to create has not yet been capitalized by any corporation or foundation, and Koop calls the theory "one of the most farfetched of all time."

Another recent Koop target is Canada's health-care-financing system. Koop has a longstanding affection for Canadian physicians because they endorsed his call for the establishment of a specialty in pediatric surgery at a time when the message was being scoffed at in the United States. But he is unimpressed with Canada's health-care reimbursement system. "When National Health started in the United Kingdom it looked like a panacea," Koop says. "Soon it was a shambles. Canada is headed in the same direction. Four years ago 80 percent of Canadians were satisfied with their system. Now it's below 50 percent."

Remarking that Canadians are routinely placed on waiting lists for procedures Americans can have performed right away, Koop maintains that national health systems lead countries that adopt them to restrict all health services (including the basic ones). "Sav-

WELL-BEING.

WORKING TO CREATE REVOLUTIONARY MEDICINES
THAT ENABLE AGING PATIENTS TO MAINTAIN OPTIMUM COMFORT,
INDEPENDENCE, AND WELL-BEING.

SYNTEX IS MAKING PROFOUND CONTRIBUTIONS TO MEDICINE.

THE MEN AND WOMEN OF SYNTEX BRING THEIR PERSONAL VISION
OF A HEALTHIER FUTURE TO EVERY TASK, AND WE BELIEVE THIS SHOWS IN THE
QUALITY OF THE MEDICAL PRODUCTS THAT RESULT.

IN CLOSING, WE WISH TO ACKNOWLEDGE ONE OF OUR MOST IMPORTANT
RESOURCES — THE PRACTICING PHYSICIAN. WITH THE INVALUABLE INPUT OF
PHYSICIANS, WE AT SYNTEX ARE ABLE TO STAY CLOSELY LINKED WITH THE PEOPLE
WHO RELY UPON US FOR UNDERSTANDING AS WELL AS PRACTICAL SOLUTIONS.

SYNTEX IS MAKING PROFOUND CONTRIBUTIONS TO MEDICINE.

R

ing money is great, but it's very hard to sit around and see someone in your family suffer while waiting for care," Koop says.

Koop fears that the logic behind the goal of cost-effectiveness will eventually lead to the legalization of euthanasia. He was criticized for this view during his 1981 confirmation hearings, when opponents cited statements he had made loosely equating right-to-die advocacy with Nazism. The growing social acceptance of euthanasia in Germany during the 1930s, Koop has stated, created a psychology that led to acceptance of the Holocaust. That left many Washington liberals steaming. Nonetheless, Koop has not changed his opinion on this point.

"During my years in government the one phrase I heard most about medicine was *cost-effectiveness*," Koop says. "Today no one would say that euthanasia for the old is a good idea because it would save money. But I believe that day may be coming. When people talk about cutting back on expensive care for the terminally ill, they do not mean putting the money into health-care categories that are more efficient, like immunizing kids. I can sympathize with that. They mean putting the money into things like roads, bridges, and state parks, which I have a little trouble swallowing. Drive through the state of West Virginia, for example. Excellent roads. Gorgeous state parks. Abysmal health care for children. What is cost-effective about that arrangement?"

The passage of time and Koop's increased distance from anti-abortion politics have brought some of his views on technical medical issues back into line with the general thinking of the profession. "Once you get him away from public affairs, " says a colleague, "he's thinking like a Penn professor of surgery again." In return, the medical and scientific establishments have finally warmed to Koop. He was awarded the National Academy of Sciences' Public Welfare Medal in 1990 for his work on AIDS education and against cigarettes. The Dr. Kook of the movie *Whatever Happened to the Human Race?* could not have won this award.

Koop is no longer doctrinaire in his aversion to the prospects of genetic engineering. "If we can find a way to fix a Down's kid with gene therapy or perhaps even prevent the condition before the child is born, why would you ever be opposed to that?" he now asks. But he still worries that the sort of genetic knowledge that could eventually produce great boons for humankind will in the short run generate more reasons to have abortions.

For example, the fetal cystic fibrosis screening test now in development will be available years or decades before any kind of cure

Koop with a portrait of his third child, David, who died at age 20 in a 1968 rock-climbing accident. The portrait hangs above the fireplace in Koop's Bethesda, Maryland, home.

comes along. Parents who discover that their baby carries the cystic fibrosis marker face a difficult decision. Though the disease is incurable at present, it does not impair brain function. Should the parents abort the fetus, denying it the experience of life in order to spare it the tragedy of dying young? Technology that yields information that might be used to justify abortions or the withdrawal of care should not be released by genetic researchers, Koop believes.

On right-to-die questions, Koop now sounds much more like the American Medical Association of 1990 than the Everett Koop of the late 1970s. He explains, for instance, his opinion on the 1990 Supreme Court decision in the case of Nancy Cruzan, the young woman who had been in an irreversible coma since 1983 and who was finally allowed to die in 1990. Before the accident in which she was injured, Cruzan had said she would not wish to be sustained on life support. "If I were the Cruzans' doctor," Koop says, "knowing what I know about their family and believing what they have said about their daughter's wishes, even though . . . I can't go back in time and prove it, I would, at their request, have withdrawn the tubes." Still, Koop agreed with the Supreme Court order that, for a while, kept the tubes in place. "If I had been on the Court I would not have voted to allow [withdrawal] either," Koop said. "The question before the Court was not what you think about the tragedy of Nancy Cruzan. The question was the law in Missouri, and that law is terrifying. There's a clause about denial of 'assisted feeding.' If you had been in a car accident and needed spoon-feeding even briefly, under that law an uncaring relative might have had the legal power to switch you off." (The Missouri Attorney General's office says the law in question never contained a clause mentioning denial of assisted feeding.)

Koop is much less alarmist on Baby Doe questions than he once was. He believes that physicians are becoming less likely to let handicapped babies die. "A lot of pediatricians did some soul-searching on questions like, Do I really think a Down's child is not a person?" Koop explains. "Also doctors know that whatever they do on these issues will now be open to intense public scrutiny. It's the public focus more than anything else that protects these babies today . . . in the early 1980s I would get calls, both at the office and at home, from nurses at hospitals around the country saying, 'I can't give you my name but they are killing this baby.' I don't get those calls anymore."

Koop no longer makes appearances before anti-abortion groups. His ties with that community are frayed at best, though he remains the movement's best-known and most credible voice. "My position on abortion is exactly the same as it's always been," Koop says. "What has changed in me is that I am disenchanted with the rhetoric on both sides of the argument. Both sides have now been at it so long they've forgotten why they went into it. Each is intent solely on winning, meaning humiliating the other side. I have no interest in being wrapped up in that anymore."

Better understanding of contraception, Koop believes, is the one sure path out of the abortion quagmire. But most anti-abortion groups dodge this issue, which is another reason Koop has lost patience with them. Koop told the public television program *Nova* in 1989 that anti-abortion activists had "shot their wad" by failing to become birth-control advocates when their political influence was at its apex.

Koop attributes this failure to the internal politics of the movement. Before *Roe*, opposition to abortion was strongest among members of the Roman Catholic Church, which rejects both abortion and most forms of birth control. In the years following the decision, the born-again Protestant community, most of whose members see nothing wrong with contraception per se, became the driving force. Koop believes anti-abortion groups are dependent on contributions from Roman Catholics. This renders such groups terrified of even the tamest mention of contraception, however important it might be in reducing the number of abortions.

"I was talking recently to John Willke [the physician who is head of the National Right to Life Committee] and asked him what his position on birth control was," Koop says. "He said he did not have a position. I couldn't believe it. Polls show that 70 percent of Catholics practice contraception, that 30 percent of priests actively recommend it. It's time to start talking about these things openly."

Koop himself has often been described as opposed to family planning, but he tirelessly explains that he is in favor of any contraception that works before the sacred spark of conception is struck. Condoms, diaphragms, spermicides, most oral contraceptives, the rhythm method, and coitus interruptus are perfectly acceptable. What he opposes are methods that function after the union of sperm and egg: some oral contraceptives, the IUD, and abortion itself.

Koop departs from most of the medical profession in opposing the French drug RU 486. "In the year 1978, I predicted that someday the abortion issue would come to a grinding halt not because either side convinces the other but because some technical development would make abortion an entirely private decision between a woman and her pharmacist," Koop says. Back then he thought this would happen by means of something like a prostaglandin-tipped tampon. Only the chemical has changed, Koop believes. "If we allow RU 486 here," he says, "within two years there will not be any surgical abortions in the United States anymore."

Abortion is the second most common U.S. surgical procedure (procedures to assist in delivery are first), and it has been suggested that factions of the medical establishment will fight RU 486 not for reasons of moral principle but because the drug would eliminate a profitable line of business. If that's true, physicians who perform abortions may find themselves in an odd alliance with Koop on the subject.

Koop is equally disturbed by the potential of RU 486 as a birth-control mechanism. The idea is yet unproven and the protocol for administering the drug would have to be drastically simplified, but researchers have suggested that someday women might be better off taking one dose of RU 486 every four weeks (or at the end of any month in which they had sex) than taking a dose of conventional oral contraceptives almost every day. If that were to come to pass, women could have "abortions" before they know they are pregnant.

As he has been so many times before, Koop is outraged, shocked, and angered by the religious and sociological consequences of this development. In the years to come, the American public will probably hear his views on the matter—loudly, and in great detail.

EPILOGUE

The setting dials of your time machine have been recalibrated. The device shimmers and vibrates, and you emerge to this scene:

All around you specialists, RNs, and other skilled personnel are tending to children recovering from complex diseases and defects. Ten operating rooms are heavily booked from the early-morning hours onward. In them, surgeons perform open-heart surgery, correct lordosis and cleft palates, and control hydrocephalus. The spacious operating theaters are filled with the latest high-tech machinery, counterpointed, in every crevice where supplies can be stored, by stacks of Huggies disposable diapers. In critical-care nurseries, infants born as early as the 23rd week and weighing as little as 500 grams are surviving. On a pad overhead helicopters arrive, bearing accident victims or neonates born elsewhere with life-threatening defects.

Some of these children do not live, and others cannot be cured. But it is nearly unheard of for any to die for the reason they once did: human failing, rather than fate. The idea of a child dying here because of indifference, insufficient resources, or lack of attention from adults—all once as threatening to the health of children as any malady—would be entirely and justifiably shocking. It would be headline news in the local papers.

Many of the children's rooms in this place look out onto a huge, bustling atrium that forms the hospital's core. In one corner of the atrium is an institution that many adults can do without but that young patients find entirely appealing: a McDonald's restaurant. "You know a kid has turned the corner when he starts watching the other children heading for McDonald's and wanting to know how soon he gets to go," one of the surgeons says.

The scene, of course, is the Children's Hospital of Philadelphia in the here and now. It could as easily be any of a dozen other first-

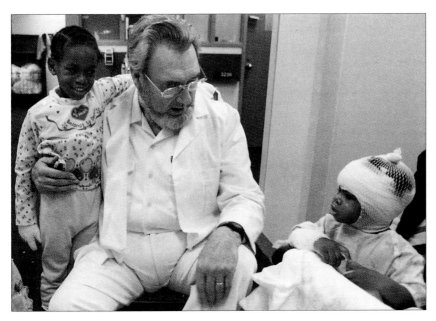

Koop in 1990 visiting young patients at Children's of Philadelphia, where the new surgical center was named for him in 1974.

rate pediatric hospitals scattered throughout the United States.

The true testament to Koop's life work is not the public personality he created for himself, or even the truths he told, but the revolution in pediatric care that he helped inspire.

Had Koop never been born, places such as the contemporary Children's of Philadelphia surely would have come into existence anyway. The discoveries and insights Koop championed, being fundamental, were inevitable. But without him the arrival of modern pediatric surgery might have come later. Many advances we now take for granted would have been slower in arriving, which might have made all the difference in your life, depending on what year you were born and whether anything about you was not quite right.

C. Everett Koop had a commitment to excellence, and he translated it into tangible aid to his fellow creatures. Would that all oversized egos accomplished as much.

Additional Copies

To order copies of *Surgeon Koop* for friends or colleagues, please write to The Grand Rounds Press, Whittle Books, 505 Market St., Knoxville, Tenn. 37902. Please include the recipient's name, mailing address, and, where applicable, primary specialty and ME number.

For a single copy, please enclose a check for $21.95 plus $1.50 for postage and handling, payable to The Grand Rounds Press. When ordering 10 or more books, enclose $20.95 for each plus $5 for postage and handling; for orders of 50 or more books, enclose $19.95 for each plus $20 for postage and handling. For more information about The Grand Rounds Press, please call 800-765-5889.

Also available, at the same prices, are copies of the previous books from The Grand Rounds Press:
The Doctor Watchers by Spencer Vibbert
The New Genetics by Leon Jaroff

Please allow four weeks for delivery.
Tennessee residents must add 7¾ percent sales tax.

NAPROSYN® (naproxen)

Tablets and Suspension

DESCRIPTION

NAPROSYN® (naproxen) tablets for oral administration each contain 250 mg, 375 mg or 500 mg of naproxen. NAPROSYN suspension for oral administration contains 125 mg/5 mL of naproxen. NAPROSYN is a member of the arylacetic acid group of nonsteroidal anti-inflammatory drugs.

The chemical name for naproxen is 2-naphthaleneacetic acid, 6-methoxy-α-methyl-,(+)-

It has the following structure:

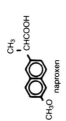

naproxen

Naproxen is an odorless, white to off-white crystalline substance. It is lipid soluble, practically insoluble in water at low pH and freely soluble in water at high pH.

Each tablet contains naproxen, the active ingredient, with the following inactive ingredients: croscarmellose sodium, iron oxides, magnesium stearate and povidone.

NAPROSYN suspension for oral administration contains 125 mg/5 mL of naproxen, the active ingredient, in a vehicle of FD&C Yellow #6, fumaric acid, imitation orange flavor, imitation pineapple flavor, magnesium aluminum silicate, methylparaben, purified water, sodium chloride, sorbitol solution and sucrose.

CLINICAL PHARMACOLOGY

NAPROSYN (naproxen) is a nonsteroidal anti-inflammatory drug with analgesic and antipyretic properties. Naproxen sodium, the sodium salt of naproxen, has been developed as an analgesic because it is more rapidly absorbed. The naproxen anion inhibits prostaglandin synthesis but beyond this its mode of action is unknown.

Naproxen is rapidly and completely absorbed from the gastrointestinal tract. After administration of naproxen, peak plasma levels of naproxen anion are attained in 2 to 4 hours, with steady-state conditions normally achieved after 4-5 doses. The mean biological half-life of the anion in humans is approximately 13 hours, and at therapeutic levels it is greater than 99% albumin bound. At doses of naproxen greater than 500 mg/day there is a lack of dose proportionality due to an increase in clearance caused by saturation of proteins at higher doses. Approximately 95% of the dose is excreted in the urine, primarily as naproxen, 6-0-desmethyl naproxen or their conjugates. The rate of excretion has been found to coincide closely with the rate of drug disappearance from the plasma. The drug does not induce metabolizing enzymes.

In children of 5 to 16 years of age with arthritis, plasma naproxen levels following a 5 mg/kg single dose of suspension were found to be similar to those found in normal adults following a 500 mg dose. The terminal half-life appears to be similar in children and adults. Pharmacokinetic studies of naproxen were not performed in children of less than 5 years of age.

The drug was studied in patients with rheumatoid arthritis, osteoarthritis, juvenile arthritis, ankylosing spondylitis, tendinitis and bursitis, and acute gout. It is not a corticosteroid. Improvement in patients treated for rheumatoid arthritis has been demonstrated by a reduction in joint swelling, a reduction in pain, a reduction in duration of morning stiffness, a reduction in disease activity as assessed by both the investigator and patient, and by increased mobility as demonstrated by a reduction in walking time.

analgesic drugs induce the syndrome of asthma, rhinitis, and nasal polyps. Both types of reactions have the potential of being fatal. Anaphylactoid reactions to NAPROSYN, ANAPROX or ANAPROX DS, whether of the true allergic type or the pharmacologic idiosyncratic (e.g., aspirin syndrome) type, usually but not always occur in patients with a known history of such reactions. Therefore, careful questioning of patients for such things as asthma, nasal polyps, urticaria, and hypotension associated with nonsteroidal anti-inflammatory drugs before starting therapy is important. In addition, if such symptoms occur during therapy, treatment should be discontinued.

WARNINGS

Risk of GI Ulceration, Bleeding and Perforation with NSAID Therapy:

Serious gastrointestinal toxicity such as bleeding, ulceration, and perforation, can occur at any time, with or without warning symptoms, in patients treated chronically with NSAID therapy. Although minor upper gastrointestinal problems, such as dyspepsia, are common, usually developing early in therapy, physicians should remain alert for ulceration and bleeding in patients treated chronically with NSAIDs even in the absence of previous GI tract symptoms. In patients observed in clinical trials of several months to two years duration, symptomatic upper GI ulcers, gross bleeding or perforation appear to occur in approximately 1% of patients treated for 3-6 months, and in about 2-4% of patients treated for one year. Physicians should inform patients about the signs and/or symptoms of serious GI toxicity and what steps to take if they occur.

Studies to date have not identified any subset of patients not at risk of developing peptic ulceration and bleeding. Except for a prior history of serious GI events and other risk factors known to be associated with peptic ulcer disease, such as alcoholism, smoking, etc., no risk factors (e.g., age, sex) have been associated with increased risk. Elderly or debilitated patients seem to tolerate ulceration or bleeding less well than other individuals and most spontaneous reports of fatal GI events are in this population. Studies to date are inconclusive concerning the relative risk of various NSAIDs in causing such reactions. High doses of any NSAID probably carry a greater risk of these reactions, although controlled clinical trials showing this do not exist in most cases. In considering the use of relatively large doses (within the recommended dosage range), sufficient benefit should be anticipated to offset the potential increased risk of GI toxicity.

PRECAUTIONS

General:

NAPROSYN (NAPROXEN) SHOULD NOT BE USED CONCOMITANTLY WITH THE RELATED DRUG ANAPROX OR ANAPROX DS (NAPROXEN SODIUM) SINCE THEY BOTH CIRCULATE IN PLASMA AS THE NAPROXEN ANION.

Renal Effects: As with other nonsteroidal anti-inflammatory drugs, long-term administration of naproxen to animals has resulted in renal papillary necrosis and other abnormal renal pathology. In humans, there have been reports of acute interstitial nephritis with hematuria, proteinuria, and occasionally nephrotic syndrome.

A second form of renal toxicity has been seen in patients with prerenal conditions leading to a reduction in renal blood flow or blood volume, where the renal prostaglandins have a supportive role in the maintenance of renal perfusion. In these patients, administration of a nonsteroidal anti-inflammatory drug may cause a dose-dependent reduction in prostaglandin formation and may precipitate overt renal decompensation. Patients at greatest risk of this reaction are those with impaired renal function, heart failure, liver dysfunction, those taking diuretics, and the elderly. Discontinuation of nonsteroidal anti-inflammatory therapy is typically followed by recovery to the pretreatment state.

NAPROSYN and its metabolites are eliminated primarily by the kidneys, therefore, the drug should be used with great caution in patients with significantly impaired renal function and the monitoring of serum creatinine and/or creatinine clearance is advised in these patients. Caution should be used if the drug is given to patients with creatinine clearance of less than 20 mL/minute because accumulation of naproxen metabolites has been seen in such patients.

Chronic alcoholic liver disease and probably other forms of cirrhosis reduce the total plasma concentration of naproxen, but the plasma concentration of unbound naproxen

In patients with osteoarthritis, the therapeutic action of the drug has been shown by a reduction in joint pain or tenderness, an increase in range of motion in knee joints, increased mobility as demonstrated by a reduction in walking time, and improvement in capacity to perform activities of daily living impaired by the disease.

In clinical studies in patients with rheumatoid arthritis, osteoarthritis, and juvenile arthritis, the drug has been shown to be comparable to aspirin and indomethacin in controlling the aforementioned measures of disease activity, but the frequency and severity of the milder gastrointestinal adverse effects (nausea, dyspepsia, heartburn) and nervous system adverse effects (tinnitus, dizziness, lightheadedness) were less than in both the aspirin- and indomethacin-treated patients. It is not known whether the drug causes less peptic ulceration than aspirin.

In patients with ankylosing spondylitis, the drug has been shown to decrease night pain, morning stiffness and pain at rest. In double-blind studies the drug was shown to be as effective as aspirin, but with fewer side effects.

In patients with acute gout, a favorable response to the drug was shown by significant clearing of inflammatory changes (e.g., decrease in swelling, heat) within 24-48 hours, as well as by relief of pain and tenderness.

The drug may be used safely in combination with gold salts and/or corticosteroids; however, in controlled clinical trials, when added to the regimen of patients receiving corticosteroids it did not appear to cause greater improvement over that seen with corticosteroids alone. Whether the drug could be used in conjunction with partially effective doses of corticosteroid for a "steroid-sparing" effect has not been adequately studied. When added to the regimen of patients receiving gold salts the drug did result in greater improvement. Its use in combination with salicylates is not recommended because data are inadequate to demonstrate that the drug produces greater improvement over that achieved with aspirin alone. Further, there is some evidence that aspirin increases the rate of excretion of the drug.

Generally, improvement due to the drug has not been found to be dependent on age, sex, severity or duration of disease.

In clinical trials in patients with osteoarthritis and rheumatoid arthritis comparing treatments of 750 mg per day with 1,500 mg per day, there were trends toward increased efficacy with the higher dose and a more clearcut increase in adverse reactions, particularly gastrointestinal reactions severe enough to cause the patient to leave the trial, which approximately doubled.

The drug was studied in patients with mild to moderate pain, and pain relief was obtained within 1 hour. It is not a narcotic and is not a CNS-acting drug. Controlled double-blind studies have demonstrated the analgesic properties of the drug in, for example, post-operative, post-partum, orthopedic and uterine contraction pain and dysmenorrhea. In dysmenorrheic patients, the drug reduces the level of prostaglandins in the uterus, which correlates with a reduction in the frequency and severity of uterine contractions. Analgesic action has been shown by such measures as a reduction of pain intensity scores, increase in pain relief scores, decrease in numbers of patients requiring additional analgesic medication, and delay in time for required remedication. The analgesic effect has been found to last for up to 7 hours.

In ^{51}Cr blood loss and gastroscopy studies with normal volunteers, daily administration of 1,000 mg of the drug has been demonstrated to cause statistically significantly less gastric bleeding and erosion than 3,250 mg of aspirin.

INDICATIONS AND USAGE

NAPROSYN (naproxen) is indicated for the treatment of rheumatoid arthritis, osteoarthritis, juvenile arthritis, ankylosing spondylitis, tendinitis and bursitis, and acute gout. It is also indicated in the relief of mild to moderate pain, and for the treatment of primary dysmenorrhea.

CONTRAINDICATIONS

The drug is contraindicated in patients who have had allergic reactions to NAPROSYN® (naproxen), ANAPROX® (naproxen sodium) or ANAPROX® DS (naproxen sodium). It is also contraindicated in patients in whom aspirin or other nonsteroidal anti-inflammatory/

is increased. Caution is advised when high doses are required and some adjustment of dosage may be required in these patients. It is prudent to use the lowest effective dose.

Studies indicate that, although total plasma concentration of naproxen is unchanged, the unbound plasma fraction of naproxen is increased in the elderly. Caution is advised when high doses are required and some adjustment of dosage may be required in elderly patients. As with other drugs used in the elderly, it is prudent to use the lowest effective dose.

As with other nonsteroidal anti-inflammatory drugs, borderline elevations of one or more liver tests may occur in up to 15% of patients. These abnormalities may progress, may remain essentially unchanged, or may be transient with continued therapy. The SGPT (ALT) test is probably the most sensitive indicator of liver dysfunction. Meaningful (3 times the upper limit of normal) elevations of SGOT or SGPT (AST) occurred in controlled clinical trials in less than 1% of patients. A patient with symptoms and/or signs suggesting liver dysfunction, or in whom an abnormal liver test has occurred, should be evaluated for evidence of the development of more severe hepatic reaction while on therapy with this drug. Severe hepatic reactions, including jaundice and cases of fatal hepatitis, have been reported with this drug as with other nonsteroidal anti-inflammatory drugs. Although such reactions are rare, if abnormal liver tests persist or worsen, if clinical signs and symptoms consistent with liver disease develop, or if systemic manifestations occur (e.g., eosinophilia, rash, etc.), this drug should be discontinued.

If steroid dosage is reduced or eliminated during therapy, the steroid dosage should be reduced slowly and the patients must be observed closely for any evidence of adverse effects, including adrenal insufficiency and exacerbation of symptoms of arthritis.

Patients with initial hemoglobin values of 10 grams or less who are to receive long-term therapy should have hemoglobin values determined periodically.

Peripheral edema has been observed in some patients. For this reason, the drug should be used with caution in patients with fluid retention, hypertension or heart failure.

NAPROSYN suspension contains 8 mg/mL of sodium. This should be considered in patients whose overall intake of sodium must be restricted.

The antipyretic and anti-inflammatory activities of the drug may reduce fever and inflammation, thus diminishing their utility as diagnostic signs in detecting complications of presumed non-infectious, non-inflammatory painful conditions.

Because of adverse eye findings in animal studies with drugs of this class, it is recommended that ophthalmic studies be carried out if any change or disturbance in vision occurs.

Information for Patients:

Naproxen, like other drugs of its class, is not free of side effects. The side effects of these drugs can cause discomfort and, rarely, there are more serious side effects, such as gastrointestinal bleeding, which may result in hospitalization and even fatal outcomes.

NSAIDs (Nonsteroidal Anti-Inflammatory Drugs) are often essential agents in the management of arthritis and have a major role in the treatment of pain, but they also may be commonly employed for conditions which are less serious.

Physicians may wish to discuss with their patients the potential risks (see Warnings, Precautions, and Adverse Reactions sections) and likely benefits of NSAID treatment, particularly when the drugs are used for less serious conditions where treatment without NSAIDs may represent an acceptable alternative to both the patient and physician.

Caution should be exercised by patients whose activities require alertness if they experience drowsiness, dizziness, vertigo or depression during therapy with the drug.

Laboratory Tests:

Because serious GI tract ulceration and bleeding can occur without warning symptoms, physicians should follow chronically treated patients for the signs and symptoms of ulceration and bleeding and should inform them of the importance of this follow-up (see Risk of GI Ulceration, Bleeding and Perforation with NSAID Therapy).

Drug Interactions:

In vitro studies have shown that naproxen anion, because of its affinity for protein, may displace from their binding sites other drugs which are also albumin-bound. Theoretically, the naproxen anion itself could likewise be displaced. Short-term controlled studies failed to show that taking the drug significantly affects prothrombin times when administered to individuals on coumarin-type anticoagulants. Caution is advised nonetheless, since interactions have been seen with other nonsteroidal agents of this class. Similarly, patients receiving the drug and a hydantoin, sulfonamide or sulfonylurea should be observed for signs of toxicity to these drugs.

The natriuretic effect of furosemide has been reported to be inhibited by some drugs of this class. Inhibition of renal lithium clearance leading to increases in plasma lithium concentrations has also been reported.

This and other nonsteroidal anti-inflammatory drugs can reduce the antihypertensive effect of propranolol and other beta-blockers.

Probenecid given concurrently increases naproxen anion plasma levels and extends its plasma half-life significantly.

Caution should be used if this drug is administered concomitantly with methotrexate. Naproxen and other nonsteroidal anti-inflammatory drugs have been reported to reduce the tubular secretion of methotrexate in an animal model, possibly enhancing the toxicity of that drug.

Drug/Laboratory Test Interactions:
The drug may decrease platelet aggregation and prolong bleeding time. This effect should be kept in mind when bleeding times are determined.

The administration of the drug may result in increased urinary values for 17-ketogenic steroids because of an interaction between the drug and/or its metabolites with m-dinitrobenzene used in this assay. Although 17-hydroxy-corticosteroid measurements (Porter-Silber test) do not appear to be artifactually altered, it is suggested that therapy with the drug be temporarily discontinued 72 hours before adrenal function tests are performed.

The drug may interfere with some urinary assays of 5-hydroxy indoleacetic acid (5HIAA).

Carcinogenesis:
A two-year study was performed in rats to evaluate the carcinogenic potential of the drug. No evidence of carcinogenicity was found.

Pregnancy:
Teratogenic Effects: Pregnancy Category B. Reproduction studies have been performed in rats, rabbits and mice at doses up to 6 times the human dose and have revealed no evidence of impaired fertility or harm to the fetus due to the drug. There are, however, no adequate and well-controlled studies in pregnant women. Because animal reproduction studies are not always predictive of human response, the drug should not be used during pregnancy unless clearly needed. Because of the known effect of drugs of this class on the human fetal cardiovascular system (closure of ductus arteriosus), use during late pregnancy should be avoided.

Non-teratogenic Effects: As with other drugs known to inhibit prostaglandin synthesis, an increased incidence of dystocia and delayed parturition occurred in rats.

Nursing Mothers:
The naproxen anion has been found in the milk of lactating women at a concentration of approximately 1% of that found in the plasma. Because of the possible adverse effects of prostaglandin-inhibiting drugs on neonates, use in nursing mothers should be avoided.

Pediatric Use:
Safety and effectiveness in children below the age of 2 years have not been established. Pediatric dosing recommendations for juvenile arthritis are based on well-controlled studies (see Dosage and Administration). There are no adequate effectiveness or dose-response data for other pediatric conditions, but the experience in juvenile arthritis and other use experience have established that single doses of 2.5-5 mg/kg, with total daily dose not exceeding 15 mg/kg/day, are safe in children over 2 years of age.

ADVERSE REACTIONS
The following adverse reactions are divided into 3 parts based on frequency and likelihood of causal relationship to naproxen.

Incidence greater than 1%

Probable Causal Relationship:
Adverse reactions reported in controlled clinical trials in 960 patients treated for rheu-

Central Nervous System: Depression, dream abnormalities, inability to concentrate, insomnia, malaise, myalgia and muscle weakness.

Dermatologic: Alopecia, photosensitive dermatitis, skin rashes.

Special Senses: Hearing impairment.

Cardiovascular: Congestive heart failure.

Respiratory: Eosinophilic pneumonitis.

General: Anaphylactoid reactions, menstrual disorders, pyrexia (chills and fever).

Causal Relationship Unknown:
Other reactions have been reported in circumstances in which a causal relationship could not be established. However, in these rarely reported events, the possibility cannot be excluded. Therefore, these observations are being listed to serve as alerting information to the physicians:

Hematologic: Aplastic anemia, hemolytic anemia.

Central Nervous System: Aseptic meningitis, cognitive dysfunction.

Dermatologic: Epidermal necrolysis, erythema multiforme, photosensitivity reactions resembling porphyria cutanea tarda and epidermolysis bullosa, Stevens-Johnson syndrome, urticaria.

Gastrointestinal: Non-peptic gastrointestinal ulceration, ulcerative stomatitis.

Cardiovascular: Vasculitis.

General: Angioneurotic edema, hyperglycemia, hypoglycemia.

OVERDOSAGE
Significant overdosage may be characterized by drowsiness, heartburn, indigestion, nausea or vomiting. A few patients have experienced seizures, but it is not clear whether or not these were drug related. It is not known what dose of the drug would be life threatening. The oral LD_{50} of the drug is 543 mg/kg in rats, 1,234 mg/kg in mice, 4,110 mg/kg in hamsters and greater than 1,000 mg/kg in dogs.

Should a patient ingest a large number of tablets or a large volume of suspension, accidentally or purposefully, the stomach may be emptied and usual supportive measures employed. In animals 0.5 g/kg of activated charcoal was effective in reducing plasma levels of naproxen. Hemodialysis does not decrease the plasma concentration of naproxen because of the high degree of its protein binding.

DOSAGE AND ADMINISTRATION
A measuring cup marked in 1/2 teaspoon and 2.5 milliliter increments is provided with the suspension. This cup or a teaspoon may be used to measure the appropriate dose.

For Rheumatoid Arthritis, Osteoarthritis, and Ankylosing Spondylitis:
The recommended dose of NAPROSYN® (naproxen) in adults is 250 mg (10 mL or 2 tsp of suspension), 375 mg (15 mL or 3 tsp), or 500 mg (20 mL or 4 tsp) twice daily (morning and evening). During long-term administration, the dose may be adjusted up or down depending on the clinical response of the patient. A lower daily dose may suffice for long-term administration. The morning and evening doses do not have to be equal in size and the administration of the drug more frequently than twice daily is not necessary. In patients who tolerate lower doses well, the dose may be increased to 1,500 mg per day for limited periods when a higher level of anti-inflammatory/analgesic activity is required. When treating such patients with the 1,500 mg/day dose, the physician should observe sufficient increased clinical benefits to offset the potential increased risk (see Clinical Pharmacology).

Symptomatic improvement in arthritis usually begins within 2 weeks. However, if improvement is not seen within this period, a trial for an additional 2 weeks should be considered.

For Juvenile Arthritis:
The recommended total daily dose of NAPROSYN is approximately 10 mg/kg given in 2 divided doses. One-half of the 250 mg tablet may be used to approximate this dose. The following table may be used as a guide for the suspension:

Child's Weight	Dose
13 kg (29 lb)	2.5 mL (1/2 tsp) b.i.d.
25 kg (55 lb)	5 mL (1 tsp) b.i.d.
38 kg (84 lb)	7.5 mL (1-1/2 tsp) b.i.d.

ANAPROX®/ANAPROX® DS
(naproxen sodium)

Tablets

DESCRIPTION

ANAPROX® (naproxen sodium) filmcoated tablets for oral administration each contain 275 mg of naproxen sodium, which is equivalent to 250 mg naproxen with 25 mg (about 1 mEq) sodium. ANAPROX® DS (naproxen sodium) filmcoated tablets for oral administration each contain 550 mg of naproxen sodium, which is equivalent to 500 mg naproxen with 50 mg (about 2 mEq) sodium. Naproxen sodium is a member of the arylacetic acid group of nonsteroidal anti-inflammatory drugs.

The chemical name of naproxen sodium is 2-naphthaleneacetic acid, 6-methoxy-α-methyl-, sodium salt,($-$). It has the following structure:

NAPROXEN SODIUM

Naproxen sodium is a white to creamy white, crystalline solid, freely soluble in water.

Each ANAPROX 275 mg tablet contains naproxen sodium, the active ingredient, with lactose, magnesium stearate, and microcrystalline cellulose. The coating suspension may contain hydroxypropyl methylcellulose 2910, Opaspray K-1-4210A, polyethylene glycol 8000 or Opadry YS-1-4215. Each ANAPROX DS 550 mg tablet contains naproxen sodium, the active ingredient, with magnesium stearate, microcrystalline cellulose, povi-

---

matoid arthritis or osteoarthritis are listed below. In general, these reactions were reported 2 to 10 times more frequently than they were in studies in the 962 patients treated for mild to moderate pain or for dysmenorrhea.

A clinical study found gastrointestinal reactions to be more frequent and more severe in rheumatoid arthritis patients taking 1,500 mg naproxen daily compared to those taking 750 mg daily (see Clinical Pharmacology).

In controlled clinical trials with about 80 children and in well-monitored open studies with about 400 children with juvenile arthritis, the incidences of rash and prolonged bleeding times were increased, the incidences of gastrointestinal and central nervous system reactions were about the same, and the incidences of other reactions were lower in children than in adults.

Gastrointestinal: The most frequent complaints reported related to the gastrointestinal tract. They were: constipation*, heartburn*, abdominal pain*, nausea*, dyspepsia, diarrhea, stomatitis.

Central Nervous System: Headache*, dizziness*, drowsiness*, lightheadedness, vertigo.

Dermatologic: Itching (pruritus)*, skin eruptions*, ecchymoses*, sweating, purpura.

Special Senses: Tinnitus*, hearing disturbances, visual disturbances.

Cardiovascular: Edema*, dyspnea*, palpitations.

General: Thirst.

*Incidence of reported reaction between 3% and 9%. Those reactions occurring in less than 3% of the patients are unmarked.

Incidence less than 1%

Probable Causal Relationship:

The following adverse reactions were reported less frequently than 1% during controlled clinical trials and through voluntary reports since marketing. The probability of a causal relationship exists between the drug and these adverse reactions:

Gastrointestinal: Abnormal liver function tests, colitis, gastrointestinal bleeding and/or perforation, hematemesis, jaundice, melena, peptic ulceration with bleeding and/or perforation, vomiting.

Renal: Glomerular nephritis, hematuria, hyperkalemia, interstitial nephritis, nephrotic syndrome, renal disease, renal failure, renal papillary necrosis.

Hematologic: Agranulocytosis, eosinophilia, granulocytopenia, leukopenia, thrombocytopenia.

For Acute Gout:

The recommended starting dose of NAPROSYN is 750 mg (30 mL or 6 tsp), followed by 250 mg (10 mL or 2 tsp) every 8 hours until the attack has subsided.

For Mild to Moderate Pain, Primary Dysmenorrhea and Acute Tendinitis and Bursitis:

The recommended starting dose of NAPROSYN is 500 mg (20 mL or 4 tsp), followed by 250 mg (10 mL or 2 tsp) every 6 to 8 hours as required. The total daily dose should not exceed 1,250 mg (50 mL or 10 tsp).

HOW SUPPLIED

NAPROSYN® (naproxen) is available as yellow 250 mg tablets in light-resistant bottles of 100 tablets (NDC 18393-272-42) (NSN 6505-01-026-9730) and 500 tablets (NDC 18393-272-62) (NSN 6505-01-046-0126) or in cartons of 100 individually blister-packed tablets (NDC 18393-272-53) (NSN 6505-01-097-9611). Peach 375 mg tablets are available in light-resistant bottles of 100 tablets (NDC 18393-273-42) (NSN 6505-01-135-8462) and 500 tablets (NDC 18393-273-62) (NSN 6505-01-204-5297) or in cartons of 100 individually blister-packed tablets (NDC 18393-273-53) (NSN 6505-01-204-5298). Yellow 500 mg tablets are available in light-resistant bottles of 100 tablets (NDC 18393-277-42) (NSN 6505-01-200-2474) and 500 tablets (NDC 18393-277-62) (NSN 6505-01-186-8758) or in cartons of 100 individually blister-packed tablets (NDC 18393-277-53). Store at room temperature in well-closed containers; dispense in light-resistant containers.

NAPROSYN® suspension is available in 1 pint (474 mL) light-resistant bottles (NDC 18393-278-20). Measuring cups are provided so that one can be dispensed with each prescription. Store at room temperature; avoid excessive heat, above 40°C (104° F). Dispense in light-resistant container.

CAUTION: Federal law prohibits dispensing without prescription.

U.S. Patent Nos. 3,904,682; 3,998,966 and others.

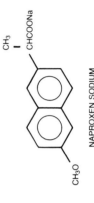

SYNTEX PUERTO RICO, INC.
HUMACAO, P.R. 00661

REVISED SEPTEMBER 1990
© 1990 SYNTEX PUERTO RICO, INC.
02-0273-53-02

done, and talc. The coating suspension may contain hydroxypropyl methylcellulose 2910, Opaspray K-1-4227, polyethylene glycol 8000 or Opadry YS-1-4216.

CLINICAL PHARMACOLOGY

The sodium salt of naproxen has been developed as an analgesic because it is more rapidly absorbed. Naproxen is a nonsteroidal anti-inflammatory drug with analgesic and antipyretic properties. Naproxen anion inhibits prostaglandin synthesis but beyond this its mode of action is unknown.

Naproxen sodium is rapidly and completely absorbed from the gastrointestinal tract. After administration of naproxen sodium, peak plasma levels of naproxen anion are attained at 1-2 hours with steady-state conditions normally achieved after 4-5 doses. The mean biological half-life of the anion in humans is approximately 13 hours, and at therapeutic levels it is greater than 99% albumin bound. Approximately 95% of the dose is excreted in the urine, primarily as naproxen, 6-0-desmethyl naproxen or their conjugates. The rate of excretion has been found to coincide closely with the rate of drug disappearance from the plasma. The drug does not induce metabolizing enzymes.

In children of 5 to 16 years of age with arthritis, plasma naproxen levels following a 5 mg/kg single dose of naproxen suspension (see Dosage and Administration) were found to be similar to those found in normal adults following a 500 mg dose. The terminal half-life appears to be similar in children and adults. Pharmacokinetic studies of naproxen were not performed in children of less than 5 years of age.

The drug was studied in patients with mild to moderate pain, and pain relief was obtained within 1 hour. It is not a narcotic and is not a CNS-acting drug. Controlled double-blind studies have demonstrated the analgesic properties of the drug in, for example, post-operative, post-partum, orthopedic and uterine contraction pain and dysmenorrhea. In dysmenorrheic patients, the drug reduces the level of prostaglandins in the uterus, which correlates with a reduction in the frequency and severity of uterine contractions. Analgesic action has been shown by such measures as reduction of pain intensity scores, increase in pain relief scores, decrease in numbers of patients requiring additional analgesic medication, and delay in time for required remedication. The analgesic effect has been found to last for up to 7 hours.

The drug was studied in patients with rheumatoid arthritis, osteoarthritis, juvenile arthritis, ankylosing spondylitis, tendinitis and bursitis, and acute gout. It is not a corticosteroid. Improvement in patients treated for rheumatoid arthritis has been demonstrated by a reduction in joint swelling, a reduction in pain, a reduction in duration of morning stiffness, a reduction in disease activity as assessed by both the investigator and patient, and by increased mobility as demonstrated by a reduction in walking time.

In patients with osteoarthritis, the therapeutic action of the drug has been shown by a reduction in joint pain or tenderness, an increase in range of motion in knee joints, increased mobility as demonstrated by a reduction in walking time, and improvement in capacity to perform activities of daily living impaired by the disease.

In clinical studies in patients with rheumatoid arthritis, osteoarthritis, and juvenile arthritis, the drug has been shown to be comparable to aspirin and indomethacin in controlling the aforementioned measures of disease activity, but the frequency and severity of the milder gastrointestinal adverse effects (nausea, dyspepsia, heartburn) and nervous system adverse effects (tinnitus, dizziness, lightheadedness) were less than in both the aspirin- and indomethacin-treated patients. It is not known whether the drug causes less peptic ulceration than aspirin.

In patients with ankylosing spondylitis, the drug has been shown to decrease night pain, morning stiffness and pain at rest. In double-blind studies the drug was shown to be as effective as aspirin, but with fewer side effects.

In patients with acute gout, a favorable response to the drug was shown by significant clearing of inflammatory changes (e.g., decrease in swelling, heat) within 24-48 hours, as well as by relief of pain and tenderness.

The drug may be used safely in combination with gold salts and/or corticosteroids; however, in controlled clinical trials, when added to the regimen of patients receiving corticosteroids it did not appear to cause greater improvement over that seen with corticosteroids alone. Whether the drug could be used in conjunction with partially effective doses of corticosteroid for a "steroid-sparing" effect has not been adequately studied. When added to the regimen of patients receiving gold salts, the drug did result in greater improvement. Its use in combination with salicylates is not recommended because data

Renal Effects: As with other nonsteroidal anti-inflammatory drugs, long-term administration of naproxen to animals has resulted in renal papillary necrosis and other abnormal renal pathology. In humans, there have been reports of acute interstitial nephritis with hematuria, proteinuria, and occasionally nephrotic syndrome.

Naproxen sodium and its metabolites are eliminated primarily by the kidneys, therefore the drug should be used with great caution in patients with significantly impaired renal function and the monitoring of serum creatinine and/or creatinine clearance is advised in these patients. Caution should be used if the drug is given to patients with creatinine clearance of less than 20 mL/minute because accumulation of naproxen metabolites has been seen in such patients.

Chronic alcoholic liver disease and probably other forms of cirrhosis reduce the total plasma concentration of naproxen, but the plasma concentration of unbound naproxen is increased. Caution is advised when high doses are required and some adjustment of dosage may be required in these patients. It is prudent to use the lowest effective dose.

Studies indicate that although total plasma concentration of naproxen is unchanged, the unbound plasma fraction of naproxen is increased in the elderly. Caution is advised when high doses are required and some adjustment of dosage may be required in elderly patients. As with other drugs used in the elderly, it is prudent to use the lowest effective dose.

As with other nonsteroidal anti-inflammatory drugs, borderline elevations of one or more liver tests may occur in up to 15% of patients. These abnormalities may progress, may remain essentially unchanged, or may be transient with continued therapy. The SGPT (ALT) test is probably the most sensitive indicator of liver dysfunction. Meaningful (3 times the upper limit of normal) elevations of SGPT or SGOT (AST) occurred in controlled clinical trials in less than 1% of patients. A patient with symptoms and/or signs suggesting liver dysfunction, or in whom an abnormal liver test has occurred, should be evaluated for evidence of the development of more severe hepatic reaction while on therapy with this drug. Severe hepatic reactions, including jaundice and cases of fatal hepatitis, have been reported with this drug as with other nonsteroidal anti-inflammatory drugs. Although such reactions are rare, if abnormal liver tests persist or worsen, if clinical signs and symptoms consistent with liver disease develop, or if systemic manifestations occur (e.g., eosinophilia, rash, etc.), this drug should be discontinued.

A second form of renal toxicity has been seen in patients with prerenal conditions leading to a reduction in renal blood flow or blood volume, where the renal prostaglandins have a supportive role in the maintenance of renal perfusion. In these patients, administration of a nonsteroidal anti-inflammatory drug may cause a dose-dependent reduction in prostaglandin formation and may precipitate overt renal decompensation. Patients at greatest risk of this reaction are those with impaired renal function, heart failure, liver dysfunction, those taking diuretics, and the elderly. Discontinuation of nonsteroidal anti-inflammatory therapy is typically followed by recovery to the pretreatment state.

If steroid dosage is reduced or eliminated during therapy, the steroid dosage should be reduced slowly and the patients must be observed closely for any evidence of adverse effects, including adrenal insufficiency and exacerbation of symptoms of arthritis.

Patients with initial hemoglobin values of 10 grams or less who are to receive long-term therapy should have hemoglobin values determined periodically.

Peripheral edema has been observed in some patients. Since each naproxen sodium tablet contains approximately 25 mg or 50 mg (about 1 or 2 mEq) of sodium, this should be considered in patients whose overall intake of sodium must be markedly restricted. For these reasons, the drug should be used with caution in patients with fluid retention, hypertension or heart failure.

The antipyretic and anti-inflammatory activities of the drug may reduce fever and inflammation, thus diminishing their utility as diagnostic signs in detecting complications of presumed non-infectious, non-inflammatory painful conditions.

Because of adverse eye findings in animal studies with drugs of this class it is recommended that ophthalmic studies be carried out if any change or disturbance in vision occurs.

Information for Patients:

Naproxen sodium, like other drugs of its class, is not free of side effects. The side effects of these drugs can cause discomfort and, rarely, there are more serious side effects, such as gastrointestinal bleeding, which may result in hospitalization and even fatal outcomes.

are inadequate to demonstrate that the drug produces greater improvement over that achieved with aspirin alone. Further, there is some evidence that aspirin increases the rate of excretion of the drug.

Generally, improvement due to the drug has not been found to be dependent on age, sex, severity or duration of disease.

In clinical trials in patients with osteoarthritis and rheumatoid arthritis comparing treatments of 825 mg per day with 1,650 mg per day, there were trends toward increased efficacy with the higher dose and a more clearcut increase in adverse reactions, particularly gastrointestinal reactions severe enough to cause the patient to leave the trial, which approximately doubled.

In ^{51}Cr blood loss and gastroscopy studies with normal volunteers, daily administration of 1,100 mg of naproxen sodium has been demonstrated to cause statistically significantly less gastric bleeding and erosion than 3,250 mg of aspirin.

INDICATIONS AND USAGE

Naproxen sodium is indicated in the relief of mild to moderate pain and for the treatment of primary dysmenorrhea.

It is also indicated for the treatment of rheumatoid arthritis, osteoarthritis, juvenile arthritis, ankylosing spondylitis, tendinitis and bursitis, and acute gout.

CONTRAINDICATIONS

The drug is contraindicated in patients who have had allergic reactions to ANAPROX® (naproxen sodium), ANAPROX® DS or to NAPROSYN® (naproxen). It is also contraindicated in patients in whom aspirin or other nonsteroidal anti-inflammatory/analgesic drugs induce the syndrome of asthma, rhinitis, and nasal polyps. Both types of reactions have the potential of being fatal. Anaphylactoid reactions to ANAPROX, ANAPROX DS or NAPROSYN, whether of the true allergic type or the pharmacologic idiosyncratic (e.g., aspirin syndrome) type, usually but not always occur in patients with a known history of such reactions. Therefore, careful questioning of patients for such things as asthma, nasal polyps, urticaria, and hypotension associated with nonsteroidal anti-inflammatory drugs before starting therapy is important. In addition, if such symptoms occur during therapy, treatment should be discontinued.

WARNINGS

Risk of GI Ulceration, Bleeding and Perforation with NSAID Therapy:

Serious gastrointestinal toxicity such as bleeding, ulceration, and perforation, can occur at any time, with or without warning symptoms, in patients treated chronically with NSAID therapy. Although minor upper gastrointestinal problems, such as dyspepsia, are common, usually developing early in therapy, physicians should remain alert for ulceration and bleeding in patients treated chronically with NSAIDs even in the absence of previous GI tract symptoms. In patients observed in clinical trials of several months to two years' duration, symptomatic upper GI ulcers, gross bleeding or perforation appear to occur in approximately 1% of patients treated for 3-6 months, and in about 2-4% of patients treated for one year. Physicians should inform patients about the signs and/or symptoms of serious GI toxicity and what steps to take if they occur.

Studies to date have not identified any subset of patients not at risk of developing peptic ulceration and bleeding. Except for a prior history of serious GI events and other risk factors known to be associated with peptic ulcer disease, such as alcoholism, smoking, etc., no risk factors (e.g., age, sex) have been associated with increased risk. Elderly or debilitated patients seem to tolerate ulceration or bleeding less well than other individuals and most spontaneous reports of fatal GI events are in this population. Studies to date are inconclusive concerning the relative risk of various NSAIDs in causing such reactions.

High doses of any NSAID probably carry a greater risk of these reactions, although controlled clinical trials showing this do not exist in most cases. In considering the use of relatively large doses (within the recommended dosage range), sufficient benefit should be anticipated to offset the potential increased risk of GI toxicity.

PRECAUTIONS

General:

ANAPROX (NAPROXEN SODIUM) OR ANAPROX DS (NAPROXEN SODIUM) SHOULD NOT BE USED CONCOMITANTLY WITH THE RELATED DRUG NAPROSYN (NAPROXEN) SINCE THEY BOTH CIRCULATE IN PLASMA AS THE NAPROXEN ANION.

NSAIDs (Nonsteroidal Anti-Inflammatory Drugs) are often essential agents in the management of arthritis and have a major role in the treatment of pain, but they also may be commonly employed for conditions which are less serious.

Physicians may wish to discuss with their patients the potential risks (see Warnings, Precautions, and Adverse Reactions sections) and likely benefits of NSAID treatment, particularly when the drugs are used for less serious conditions where treatment without NSAIDs may represent an acceptable alternative to both the patient and physician.

Caution should be exercised by patients whose activities require alertness if they experience drowsiness, dizziness, vertigo or depression during therapy with the drug.

Laboratory Tests:

Because serious GI tract ulceration and bleeding can occur without warning symptoms, physicians should follow chronically treated patients for the signs and symptoms of ulceration and bleeding and should inform them of the importance of this follow-up (see Risk of GI Ulcerations, Bleeding and Perforation with NSAID Therapy).

Drug Interactions:

In vitro studies have shown that naproxen anion, because of its affinity for protein, may displace from their binding sites other drugs which are also albumin-bound. Theoretically, the naproxen anion itself could likewise be displaced. Short-term controlled studies failed to show that taking the drug significantly affects prothrombin times when administered to individuals on coumarin-type anticoagulants. Caution is advised nonetheless, since interactions have been seen with other nonsteroidal agents of this class. Similarly, patients receiving the drug and a hydantoin, sulfonamide or sulfonylurea should be observed for signs of toxicity to these drugs.

The natriuretic effect of furosemide has been reported to be inhibited by some drugs of this class. Inhibition of renal lithium clearance leading to increases in plasma lithium concentrations has also been reported.

This and other nonsteroidal anti-inflammatory drugs can reduce the antihypertensive effect of propranolol and other beta-blockers.

Probenecid given concurrently increases naproxen anion plasma levels and extends its plasma half-life significantly.

Caution should be used if this drug is administered concomitantly with methotrexate. Naproxen and other nonsteroidal anti-inflammatory drugs have been reported to reduce the tubular secretion of methotrexate in an animal model, possibly enhancing the toxicity of that drug.

Drug/Laboratory Test Interactions:

The drug may decrease platelet aggregation and prolong bleeding time. This effect should be kept in mind when bleeding times are determined.

The administration of the drug may result in increased urinary values for 17-ketogenic steroids because of an interaction between the drug and/or its metabolites with m-dinitrobenzene used in this assay. Although 17-hydroxy-corticosteroid measurements (Porter-Silber test) do not appear to be artifactually altered, it is suggested that therapy with the drug be temporarily discontinued 72 hours before adrenal function tests are performed.

The drug may interfere with some urinary assays of 5-hydroxy indoleacetic acid (5HIAA).

Carcinogenesis:

A two-year study was performed in rats to evaluate the carcinogenic potential of the drug. No evidence of carcinogenicity was found.

Pregnancy:

Teratogenic Effects: Pregnancy Category B. Reproduction studies have been performed in rats, rabbits and mice at doses up to six times the human dose and have revealed no evidence of impaired fertility or harm to the fetus due to the drug. There are, however, no adequate and well-controlled studies in pregnant women. Because animal reproduction studies are not always predictive of human response, the drug should not be used during pregnancy unless clearly needed. Because of the known effect of drugs of this class on the human fetal cardiovascular system (closure of ductus arteriosus), use during late pregnancy should be avoided.

Non-teratogenic Effects: As with other drugs known to inhibit prostaglandin synthesis, an increased incidence of dystocia and delayed parturition occurred in rats.

Nursing Mothers:

The naproxen anion has been found in the milk of lactating women at a concentration of approximately 1% of that found in the plasma. Because of the possible adverse effects of prostaglandin-inhibiting drugs on neonates, use in nursing mothers should be avoided.

Pediatric Use:

Safety and effectiveness in children below the age of 2 years have not been established. Pediatric dosing recommendations for juvenile arthritis are based on well-controlled studies. There are no adequate effectiveness or dose-response data for other pediatric conditions, but the experience in juvenile arthritis and other use experience have established that single doses of 2.5-5 mg/kg (as naproxen suspension, see Dosage and Administration), with total daily dose not exceeding 15 mg/kg/day, are safe in children over 2 years of age.

ADVERSE REACTIONS

The following adverse reactions are divided into three parts based on frequency and likelihood of causal relationship to naproxen sodium.

Incidence greater than 1%

Probable Causal Relationship:

Adverse reactions reported in controlled clinical trials in 960 patients treated for rheumatoid arthritis or osteoarthritis are listed below. In general, these reactions were reported 2 to 10 times more frequently than they were in studies in the 962 patients treated for mild to moderate pain or for dysmenorrhea.

A clinical study found gastrointestinal reactions to be more frequent and more severe in rheumatoid arthritis patients taking 1,650 mg naproxen sodium daily compared to those taking 825 mg daily (see Clinical Pharmacology).

In controlled clinical trials with about 80 children and in well monitored open studies with about 400 children with juvenile arthritis, the incidences of rash and prolonged bleeding times were increased, the incidences of gastrointestinal and central nervous system reactions were about the same, and the incidences of other reactions were lower in children than in adults.

Gastrointestinal: The most frequent complaints reported related to the gastrointestinal tract. They were: constipation*, heartburn*, abdominal pain*, nausea*, dyspepsia, diarrhea, stomatitis.

Central Nervous System: Headache*, dizziness*, drowsiness*, lightheadedness, vertigo.

Dermatologic: Itching (pruritus)*, skin eruptions*, ecchymoses*, sweating*, purpura.

Special Senses: Tinnitus*, hearing disturbances, visual disturbances.

Cardiovascular: Edema*, dyspnea*, palpitations.

General: Thirst.

*Incidence of reported reaction between 3% and 9%. Those reactions occurring in less than 3% of the patients are unmarked.

Incidence less than 1%

Probable Causal Relationship:

The following adverse reactions were reported less frequently than 1% during controlled clinical trials and through voluntary reports since marketing. The probability of a causal relationship exists between the drug and these adverse reactions.

Gastrointestinal: Abnormal liver function tests, colitis, gastrointestinal bleeding and/or perforation, hematemesis, jaundice, melena, peptic ulceration with bleeding and/or perforation, vomiting.

Renal: Glomerular nephritis, hematuria, hyperkalemia, interstitial nephritis, nephrotic syndrome, renal disease, renal failure, renal papillary necrosis.

Hematologic: Agranulocytosis, eosinophilia, granulocytopenia, leukopenia, thrombocytopenia.

Central Nervous System: Depression, dream abnormalities, inability to concentrate, insomnia, malaise, myalgia and muscle weakness.

Dermatologic: Alopecia, photosensitive dermatitis, skin rashes.

Special Senses: Hearing impairment.

resembling porphyria cutanea tarda and epidermolysis bullosa, Stevens-Johnson syndrome, urticaria.

Gastrointestinal: Non-peptic gastrointestinal ulceration, ulcerative stomatitis.

Cardiovascular: Vasculitis.

General: Angioneurotic edema, hyperglycemia, hypoglycemia.

OVERDOSAGE

Significant overdosage may be characterized by drowsiness, heartburn, indigestion, nausea or vomiting. Because naproxen sodium may be rapidly absorbed, high and early blood levels should be anticipated. A few patients have experienced seizures, but it is not clear whether or not these were drug related. It is not known what dose of the drug would be life threatening. The oral LD_{50} of the drug is 543 mg/kg in rats, 1,234 mg/kg in mice, 4,110 mg/kg in hamsters and greater than 1,000 mg/kg in dogs.

Should a patient ingest a large number of tablets, accidentally or purposefully, the stomach may be emptied and usual supportive measures employed. In animals 0.5 g/kg of activated charcoal was effective in reducing plasma levels of naproxen. Hemodialysis does not decrease the plasma concentration of naproxen because of the high degree of its protein binding.

DOSAGE AND ADMINISTRATION

For Mild to Moderate Pain, Primary Dysmenorrhea and Acute Tendinitis and Bursitis:

The recommended starting dose is 550 mg, followed by 275 mg every 6 to 8 hours, as required. The total daily dose should not exceed 1,375 mg.

For Rheumatoid Arthritis, Osteoarthritis, and Ankylosing Spondylitis:

The recommended dose in adults is 275 mg or 550 mg twice daily (morning and evening). During long-term administration, the dose may be adjusted up or down depending on the clinical response of the patient. A lower daily dose may suffice for long-term administration. The morning and evening doses do not have to be equal in size and the administration of the drug more frequently than twice daily is not necessary.

In patients who tolerate lower doses well, the dose may be increased to 1,650 mg per day for limited periods when a higher level of anti-inflammatory/analgesic activity is required. When treating such patients with the 1,650 mg/day dose, the physician should observe sufficient increased clinical benefits to offset the potential increased risk (see Clinical Pharmacology).

Symptomatic improvement in arthritis usually begins within two weeks. However, if improvement is not seen within this period, a trial for an additional two weeks should be considered.

For Acute Gout:

The recommended starting dose is 825 mg, followed by 275 mg every eight hours until the attack has subsided.

For Juvenile Arthritis:

The recommended total daily dose is approximately 10 mg/kg given in two divided doses. The 275 mg ANAPROX tablet is not well suited to this dosage so use of the related drug NAPROSYN® (naproxen) as the 250 mg scored tablet or the 125 mg/5 mL suspension is recommended for this indication.

HOW SUPPLIED

ANAPROX® (naproxen sodium) is available in filmcoated tablets of 275 mg (light blue), in bottles of 100 tablets (NDC 18393-274-42) (NSN 6505-01-155-5157) and 500 tablets (NDC 18393-274-62) (NSN 6505-01-130-6832) or in cartons of 100 individually blister packed tablets (NDC 18393-274-53). ANAPROX® DS (naproxen sodium) is available in filmcoated tablets of 550 mg (dark blue), in bottles of 100 tablets (NDC 18393-276-42) (NSN 6505-01-305-8174) and 500 tablets (NDC 18393-276-62) or in cartons of 100 individually blister packed tablets (NDC 18393-276-53). Store at room temperature in well-closed containers.

CAUTION: Federal law prohibits dispensing without prescription.

U.S. Patent Nos. 4,009,197; 3,998,966 and others.

REVISED SEPTEMBER 1990
© 1990 SYNTEX PUERTO RICO, INC.
02-0276-42-04

SYNTEX PUERTO RICO, INC.
HUMACAO, P.R. 00661

SYNTEX

Cardiovascular: Congestive heart failure.

Respiratory: Eosinophilic pneumonitis.

General: Anaphylactoid reactions, menstrual disorders, pyrexia (chills and fever).

Causal Relationship Unknown:

Other reactions have been reported in circumstances in which a causal relationship could not be established. However, in these rarely reported events, the possibility cannot be excluded. Therefore these observations are being listed to serve as alerting information to the physicians.

Hematologic: Aplastic anemia, hemolytic anemia.

Central Nervous System: Aseptic meningitis, cognitive dysfunction.

Dermatologic: Epidermal necrolysis, erythema multiforme, photosensitivity reactions

SYNAREL® (nafarelin acetate)

Nasal Solution 2 mg/mL

(as nafarelin base)

DESCRIPTION

SYNAREL (nafarelin acetate) Nasal Solution is intended for administration as a spray to the nasal mucosa. Nafarelin acetate, the active component of SYNAREL Nasal Solution, is a decapeptide with the chemical name: 5-oxo-L-prolyl-L-histidyl-L-tryptophyl-L-seryl-L-tyrosyl-3-(2-naphthyl)-D-alanyl-L-leucyl-L-arginyl-L-prolyl-glycinamide acetate. Nafarelin acetate is a synthetic analog of the naturally occurring gonadotropin-releasing hormone (GnRH).

Nafarelin acetate has the following chemical structure:

SYNAREL Nasal Solution contains nafarelin acetate (2 mg/mL, content expressed as nafarelin base) in a solution of benzalkonium chloride, glacial acetic acid, sodium hydroxide or hydrochloric acid (to adjust pH), sorbitol, and purified water.

After priming the pump unit for SYNAREL, each actuation of the unit delivers approximately 100 μL of the spray containing approximately 200 μg nafarelin base. The contents of one spray bottle are intended to deliver at least 60 sprays.

CLINICAL PHARMACOLOGY

Nafarelin acetate is a potent agonistic analog of gonadotropin-releasing hormone (GnRH). At the onset of administration, nafarelin stimulates the release of the pituitary gonadotropins, LH and FSH, resulting in a temporary increase of ovarian steroidogenesis. Repeated dosing abolishes the stimulatory effect on the pituitary gland. Twice daily administration leads to decreased secretion of gonadal steroids by about 4 weeks; consequently, tissues and functions that depend on gonadal steroids for their maintenance become quiescent.

Nafarelin acetate is rapidly absorbed into the systemic circulation after intranasal administration. Maximum serum concentrations (measured by RIA) are achieved between 10 and 40 minutes. Following a single dose of 200 μg base, the observed average peak concentration is 0.6 ng/mL, whereas following a single dose of 400 μg base, the observed average peak concentration is 1.8 ng/mL. Bioavailability from a 400 μg dose averaged 2.8%. The average serum half-life of nafarelin following intranasal administration is approximately 3 hours. About 80% of nafarelin acetate is bound to plasma proteins at 4°C.

After subcutaneous administration of ^{14}C-nafarelin acetate, 44-55% of the dose was recovered in urine and 18.5-44.2% was recovered in feces. Approximately 3% of the administered dose appears as unchanged nafarelin in urine. The ^{14}C serum half-life of the metabolites is about 85.5 hours. Six metabolites of nafarelin have been identified of which the major metabolite is Tyr-D(2)-Nal-Leu-Arg-Pro-Gly-NH$_2$(5-10). The activity of the metabolites, the metabolism of nafarelin by nasal mucosa, and the pharmacokinetics of the drug in hepatic- and renal-impaired patients have not been determined.

The effect of rhinitis or a topical decongestant on SYNAREL has not been determined.

In controlled clinical studies, SYNAREL at doses of 400 and 800 μg/day for 6 months was shown to be comparable to danazol, 800 mg/day, in relieving the clinical symptoms of endometriosis (pelvic pain, dysmenorrhea, and dyspareunia) and in reducing the size of endometrial implants as determined by laparoscopy. The clinical significance of a decrease in endometriotic lesions is not known at this time and in addition, laparoscopic staging of endometriosis does not necessarily correlate with severity of symptoms.

SYNAREL 400 μg daily induced amenorrhea in approximately 65%, 80%, and 90% of the patients after 60, 90, and 120 days, respectively. In the first, second, and third post-treatment months, normal menstrual cycles resumed in 4%, 82%, and 100%, respectively, of those patients who did not become pregnant.

At the end of treatment, 60% of patients who received SYNAREL, 400 μg/day, were symptom free, 32% had mild symptoms, 7% had moderate symptoms and 1% had severe symptoms. Of the 60% of patients who had complete relief of symptoms at the end of treatment, 17% had moderate symptoms 6 months after treatment was discontinued, 33% had mild symptoms, 50% remained symptom free, and no patient had severe symptoms.

During the first two months use of SYNAREL, some women experience vaginal bleeding of variable duration and intensity. In all likelihood, this bleeding represents estrogen withdrawal bleeding, and is expected to stop spontaneously. If vaginal bleeding continues, the possibility of lack of compliance with the dosing regimen should be considered. If the patient is complying carefully with the regimen, an increase in dose to 400 μg twice a day should be considered.

There is no evidence that pregnancy rates are enhanced or adversely affected by the use of SYNAREL.

INDICATIONS AND USAGE

SYNAREL is indicated for management of endometriosis, including pain relief and reduction of endometriotic lesions. Experience with SYNAREL for the management of endometriosis has been limited to women 18 years of age and older treated for 6 months.

CONTRAINDICATIONS

1. Hypersensitivity to GnRH, GnRH agonist analogs or any of the excipients in SYNAREL;
2. Undiagnosed abnormal vaginal bleeding;
3. Use in pregnancy or in women who may become pregnant while receiving the drug. SYNAREL may cause fetal harm when administered to a pregnant woman. Major fetal abnormalities were observed in rats, but not in mice or rabbits after administration of SYNAREL throughout gestation. There was a dose-related increase in fetal mortality and a decrease in fetal weight in rats (see Pregnancy Section). The effects on rat fetal mortality are expected consequences of the alterations in hormonal levels brought about by the drug. If this drug is used during pregnancy or if the patient becomes pregnant while taking this drug, she should be apprised of the potential hazard to the fetus;
4. Use in women who are breast feeding (see Nursing Mothers Section).

WARNINGS

Safe use of nafarelin acetate in pregnancy has not been established clinically. Before starting treatment with SYNAREL, pregnancy must be excluded.

When used regularly at the recommended dose, SYNAREL usually inhibits ovulation and stops menstruation. Contraception is not insured, however, by taking SYNAREL, particularly if patients miss successive doses. Therefore, patients should use nonhormonal methods of contraception. Patients should be advised to see their physician if they believe they may be pregnant. If a patient becomes pregnant during treatment, the drug must be discontinued and the patient must be apprised of the potential risk to the fetus.

PRECAUTIONS

General

As with other drugs in this class, ovarian cysts have been reported to occur in the first two months of therapy with SYNAREL. Many, but not all, of these events occurred in patients with polycystic ovarian disease. These cystic enlargements may resolve spontaneously, generally by about four to six weeks of therapy, but in some cases may require discontinuation of drug and/or surgical intervention.

Information for Patients

An information pamphlet for patients is included with the product. Patients should be aware of the following information:

1. Since menstruation should stop with effective doses of SYNAREL, the patient should notify her physician if regular menstruation persists. The cause of vaginal spotting, bleeding or menstruation could be non-compliance with the treatment regimen, or it could be that a higher dose of the drug is required to achieve amenorrhea. The patient should be questioned regarding her compliance. If she is careful and compliant, and menstruation persists to the second month, consideration should be given to doubling the dose of SYNAREL. If the patient has missed several doses, she should be counseled on the importance of taking SYNAREL regularly as prescribed.

2. Patients should not use SYNAREL if they are pregnant, breast feeding, have undiagnosed abnormal vaginal bleeding, or are allergic to any of the ingredients in SYNAREL.

3. Safe use of the drug in pregnancy has not been established clinically. Therefore, a nonhormonal method of contraception should be used during treatment. Patients should be advised that if they miss successive doses of SYNAREL, breakthrough bleeding or ovulation may occur with the potential for conception. If a patient becomes pregnant during treatment, she should discontinue treatment and consult her physician.

4. Those adverse events occurring most frequently in clinical studies with SYNAREL are associated with hypoestrogenism; the most frequently reported are hot flashes, headaches, emotional lability, decreased libido, vaginal dryness, acne, myalgia, and reduction in breast size.

Nursing Mothers

It is not known whether SYNAREL is excreted in human milk. Because many drugs are excreted in human milk, and because the effects of SYNAREL on lactation and/or the breastfed child have not been determined, SYNAREL should not be used by nursing mothers.

Pediatric Use

Safety and effectiveness in children have not been established.

ADVERSE REACTIONS

As would be expected with a drug which lowers serum estradiol levels, the most frequently reported adverse reactions were those related to hypoestrogenism.

In controlled studies comparing SYNAREL (400 μg/day) and danazol (600 or 800 mg/day), adverse reactions most frequently reported and thought to be drug-related are shown in the figure below.

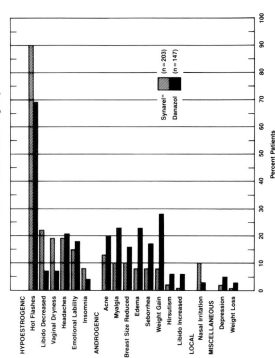

ADVERSE EVENTS DURING 6 MONTH TREATMENT WITH SYNAREL® 400 μg/day vs DANAZOL 600 OR 800 mg/day

In addition, less than 1% of patients experienced paresthesia, palpitations, chloasma, maculopapular rash, eye pain, urticaria, asthenia, lactation, breast engorgement, and arthralgia. In formal clinical trials, immediate hypersensitivity thought to be possibly or probably related to nafarelin occurred in 3 (0.2%) of 1509 healthy subjects or patients.

Changes in Bone Density

After six months of treatment with SYNAREL, vertebral trabecular bone density and total vertebral bone mass, measured by quantitative computed tomography (QCT), decreased by an average of 8.7% and 4.3%, respectively, compared to pretreatment levels. There was partial recovery of bone density in the post-treatment period; the average trabecular bone density and total bone mass were 4.9% and 3.3% less than the pretreatment levels, respectively. Total vertebral bone

Estrogen levels returned to normal after treatment was discontinued. Nasal irritation occurred in about 10% of all patients who used intranasal nafarelin.

5. The induced hypoestrogenic state results in a small loss in bone density over the course of treatment, some of which may not be reversible. During one six-month treatment period, this bone loss should not be important. In patients with major risk factors for decreased bone mineral content such as chronic alcohol and/or tobacco use, strong family history of osteoporosis, or chronic use of drugs that can reduce bone mass such as anticonvulsants or corticosteroids, SYNAREL therapy may pose an additional risk. In these patients the risks and benefits must be weighed carefully before therapy with SYNAREL is instituted. Repeated courses of treatment with gonadotropin-releasing hormone analogs are not advisable in patients with major risk factors for loss of bone mineral content.

6. Patients with intercurrent rhinitis should consult their physician for the use of a topical nasal decongestant. If the use of a topical nasal decongestant is required during treatment with SYNAREL, the decongestant must be used at least 30 minutes after SYNAREL dosing to decrease the possibility of reducing drug absorption.

7. Retreatment cannot be recommended since safety data beyond 6 months are not available.

Drug Interactions

No pharmacokinetic-based drug-drug interaction studies have been conducted with SYNAREL. However, because nafarelin acetate is a peptide that is primarily degraded by peptidase and not by cytochrome P-450 enzymes, and the drug is only about 80% bound to plasma proteins at 4°C, drug interactions would not be expected to occur.

Drug/Laboratory Test Interactions

Administration of SYNAREL in therapeutic doses results in suppression of the pituitary-gonadal system. Normal function is usually restored within 4 to 8 weeks after treatment is discontinued. Therefore, diagnostic tests of pituitary gonadotropic and gonadal functions conducted during treatment and up to 4 to 8 weeks after discontinuation of SYNAREL therapy may be misleading.

Carcinogenesis, Mutagenesis, Impairment of Fertility

Carcinogenicity studies of nafarelin were conducted in rats (24 months) at doses up to 100 µg/kg/day and mice (18 months) at doses up to 500 µg/kg/day using intramuscular doses (up to 110 times and 560 times the maximum recommended human intranasal dose, respectively). These multiples of the human dose are based on the relative bioavailability of the drug by the two routes of administration. As seen with other GnRH agonists, nafarelin acetate given to laboratory rodents at high doses for prolonged periods induced proliferative responses (hyperplasia and/or neoplasia) of endocrine organs. At 24 months, there was an increase in the related incidence of pituitary tumors (adenoma/carcinoma) in high-dose female rats and a dose-related increase in male rats. There was an increase in pancreatic islet cell adenomas in both sexes, and in benign testicular and ovarian tumors in the treated groups. There was a dose-related increase in benign adrenal medullary tumors in treated female rats. In mice, there was a dose-related increase in Harderian gland tumors in males and an increase in pituitary adenomas in high-dose females. No metastases of these tumors were observed. It is known that tumorigenicity in rodents is particularly sensitive to hormonal stimulation.

Mutagenicity studies have been performed with nafarelin acetate using bacterial, yeast, and mammalian systems. These studies provided no evidence of mutagenic potential.

Reproduction studies in male and female rats have shown full reversibility of fertility suppression when drug treatment was discontinued after continuous administration for up to 6 months.

Pregnancy, Teratogenic Effects

Pregnancy Category X. See 'Contraindications.' Intramuscular SYNAREL® was administered to rats throughout gestation at 0.4, 1.6, and 6.4 µg/kg/day (about 0.5, 2, and 7 times the maximum recommended human intranasal dose based on the relative bioavailability by the two routes of administration). An increase in major fetal abnormalities was observed in 4/80 fetuses at the highest dose. A similar, repeat study at the same doses in rats and studies in mice and rabbits at doses up to 600 µg/kg/day and 0.18 µg/kg/day, respectively, failed to demonstrate an increase in fetal abnormalities after administration throughout gestation. In rats and rabbits, there was a dose-related increase in fetal mortality and a decrease in fetal weight with the highest dose.

mass, measured by dual photon absorptiometry (DPA), decreased by a mean of 5.9% at the end of treatment. Mean total vertebral mass, re-examined by DPA six months after completion of treatment, was 1.4% below pretreatment levels. There was little, if any, decrease in the mineral content in compact bone of the distal radius and second metacarpal. Use of SYNAREL for longer than the recommended six months or in the presence of other known risk factors for decreased bone mineral content may cause additional bone loss.

Changes in Laboratory Values During Treatment

Plasma enzymes. During clinical trials with SYNAREL, regular laboratory monitoring revealed that SGOT and SGPT levels were more than twice the upper limit of normal in only one patient each. There was no other clinical or laboratory evidence of abnormal liver function and levels returned to normal in both patients after treatment was stopped.

Lipids. At enrollment, 9% of the patients in the SYNAREL 400 µg/day group and 2% of the patients in the danazol group had total cholesterol values above 250 mg/dL. These patients also had cholesterol values above 250 mg/dL at the end of treatment.

Of those patients whose pretreatment cholesterol values were below 250 mg/dL, 6% in the SYNAREL group and 18% in the danazol group, had post-treatment values above 250 mg/dL.

The mean ($\pm$SEM) pretreatment values for total cholesterol from all patients were 191.8 (4.3) mg/dL in the SYNAREL group and 193.1 (4.6) mg/dL in the danazol group. At the end of treatment, the mean values for total cholesterol from all patients were 204.5 (4.8) mg/dL in the SYNAREL group and 207.7 (5.1) mg/dL in the danazol group. These increases from the pretreatment values were statistically significant ($p < 0.05$) in both groups.

Triglycerides were increased above the upper limit of 150 mg/dL in 12% of the patients who received SYNAREL and in 7% of the patients who received danazol.

At the end of treatment, no patients receiving SYNAREL had abnormally low HDL cholesterol fractions (less than 30 mg/dL) compared with 43% of patients receiving danazol. None of the patients receiving SYNAREL had abnormally high LDL cholesterol fractions (greater than 190 mg/dL) compared with 15% of those receiving danazol. There was no increase in the LDL/HDL ratio in patients receiving SYNAREL, but there was approximately a 2-fold increase in the LDL/HDL ratio in patients receiving danazol.

Other changes. In comparative studies, the following changes were seen in approximately 10% to 15% of patients. Treatment with SYNAREL was associated with elevations of plasma phosphorous and eosinophil counts, and decreases in serum calcium and WBC counts. Danazol therapy was associated with an increase of hematocrit and WBC.

OVERDOSAGE

In experimental animals, a single subcutaneous administration of up to 60 times the recommended human dose (on a µg/kg basis, not adjusted for bioavailability) had no adverse effects. At present, there is no clinical evidence of adverse effects following overdosage of GnRH analogs.

Based on studies in monkeys, SYNAREL is not absorbed after oral administration.

DOSAGE AND ADMINISTRATION

For the management of endometriosis, the recommended daily dose of SYNAREL is 400 µg. This is achieved by one spray (200 µg) into one nostril in the morning and one spray into the other nostril in the evening. Treatment should be started between days 2 and 4 of the menstrual cycle.

In an occasional patient, the 400 µg daily dose may not produce amenorrhea. For these patients with persistent regular menstruation after 2 months of treatment, the dose of SYNAREL may be increased to 800 µg daily. The 800 µg dose is administered as one spray into each nostril in the morning (a total of two sprays) and again in the evening.

The recommended duration of administration is six months. Retreatment cannot be recommended since safety data for retreatment are not available. If the symptoms of endometriosis recur after a course of therapy, and further treatment with SYNAREL is contemplated, it is recommended that bone density be assessed before retreatment begins to ensure that values are within normal limits.

If the use of a topical nasal decongestant is necessary during treatment with SYNAREL, the decongestant should not be used until at least 30 minutes after SYNAREL dosing.

At 400 µg/day, a bottle of SYNAREL provides a 30-day (about 60 sprays) supply. If the daily dose is increased, increase the supply to the patient to ensure uninterrupted treatment for the recommended duration of therapy.

HOW SUPPLIED

Each 0.5 ounce bottle (NDC 0033-2260-40) contains 10 mL SYNAREL (nafarelin acetate) Nasal Solution 2 mg/mL (as nafarelin base), and is supplied with a metered spray pump that delivers 200 µg of nafarelin per spray. A dust cover and a leaflet of patient instructions are also included.

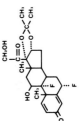

SYNTEX LABORATORIES, INC.
PALO ALTO, CA 94304

REVISED APRIL 1991
© 1991 SYNTEX LABORATORIES, INC.
02-2260-40-03

Store upright at room temperature. Avoid heat above 30°C (86°F). Protect from light. Protect from freezing.

CAUTION: Federal law prohibits dispensing without prescription.

U.S. Patent No. 4,234,571.

SYNALAR®
(fluocinolone acetonide)
Cream 0.025%
for initiation of therapy in inflammatory dermatoses.
Cream 0.01%
for occlusive or maintenance therapy.

description

SYNALAR creams are intended for topical administration. The active component is the corticosteroid fluocinolone acetonide, which has the chemical name pregna-1,4-diene-3,20-dione,6,9-difluoro-11,21-dihydroxy-16,17-[(1-methylethylidene)bis(oxy)]-,(6α,11β,16α)-. It has the following chemical structure:

The creams contain fluocinolone acetonide 0.25 mg/g or 0.1 mg/g in a water-washable aqueous base of stearyl alcohol, propylene glycol, cetyl alcohol, polyoxyl 20 cetostearyl ether, mineral oil, white wax, simethicone, butylated hydroxytoluene, edetate disodium, citric acid, and purified water, with methylparaben and propylparaben as preservatives.

3. The treated skin area should not be bandaged or otherwise covered or wrapped as to be occlusive unless directed by the physician.
4. Patients should report any signs of local adverse reactions especially under occlusive dressing.
5. Parents of pediatric patients should be advised not to use tight-fitting diapers or plastic pants on a child being treated in the diaper area, as these garments may constitute occlusive dressings.

Laboratory Tests
The following tests may be helpful in evaluating the HPA axis suppression:
Urinary free cortisol test
ACTH stimulation test

Carcinogenesis, Mutagenesis, and Impairment of Fertility
Long-term animal studies have not been performed to evaluate the carcinogenic potential or the effect on fertility of topical corticosteroids.
Studies to determine mutagenicity with prednisolone and hydrocortisone have revealed negative results.

Pregnancy Category C
Corticosteroids are generally teratogenic in laboratory animals when administered systemically at relatively low dosage levels. The more potent corticosteroids have been shown to be teratogenic after dermal application in laboratory animals. There are no adequate and well-controlled studies in pregnant women on teratogenic effects from topically applied corticosteroids. Therefore, topical corticosteroids should be used during pregnancy only if the potential benefit justifies the potential risk to the fetus. Drugs of this class should not be used extensively on pregnant patients, in large amounts, or for prolonged periods of time.

Nursing Mothers
It is not known whether topical administration of corticosteroids could result in sufficient systemic absorption to produce detectable quantities in breast milk. Systemically administered corticosteroids are secreted into breast milk in quantities *not* likely to have a deleterious effect on the infant. Nevertheless, caution should be exercised when topical corticosteroids are administered to a nursing woman.

Pediatric Use
Pediatric patients may demonstrate greater susceptibility to topical corticosteroid-induced HPA axis suppression and Cushing's syndrome than mature patients because of a larger skin surface area to body weight ratio.
Hypothalamic-pituitary-adrenal (HPA) axis suppression, Cushing's syndrome, and intracranial hypertension have been reported in children receiving topical corticosteroids. Manifestations of adrenal suppression in children include linear growth retardation, delayed weight gain, low plasma cortisol levels, and absence of response to ACTH stimulation.

clinical pharmacology

Topical corticosteroids share anti-inflammatory, anti-pruritic and vasoconstrictive actions.

The mechanism of anti-inflammatory activity of the topical corticosteroids is unclear. Various laboratory methods, including vasoconstrictor assays, are used to compare and predict potencies and/or clinical efficacies of the topical corticosteroids. There is some evidence to suggest that a recognizable correlation exists between vasoconstrictor potency and therapeutic efficacy in man.

Pharmacokinetics

The extent of percutaneous absorption of topical corticosteroids is determined by many factors including the vehicle, the integrity of the epidermal barrier, and the use of occlusive dressings.

Topical corticosteroids can be absorbed from normal intact skin. Inflammation and/or other disease processes in the skin increase percutaneous absorption. Occlusive dressings substantially increase the percutaneous absorption of topical corticosteroids. Thus, occlusive dressings may be a valuable therapeutic adjunct for treatment of resistant dermatoses. (See *DOSAGE AND ADMINISTRATION*.)

Once absorbed through the skin, topical corticosteroids are handled through pharmacokinetic pathways similar to systemically administered corticosteroids. Corticosteroids are bound to plasma proteins in varying degrees. Corticosteroids are metabolized primarily in the liver and are then excreted by the kidneys. Some of the topical corticosteroids and their metabolites are also excreted into the bile.

indications and usage

SYNALAR® (fluocinolone acetonide) creams are indicated for the relief of the inflammatory and pruritic manifestations of corticosteroid-responsive dermatoses.

contraindications

Topical corticosteroids are contraindicated in those patients with a history of hypersensitivity to any of the components of the preparation.

precautions

General

Systemic absorption of topical corticosteroids has produced reversible hypothalamic-pituitary-adrenal (HPA) axis suppression, manifestations of Cushing's syndrome, hyperglycemia, and glucosuria in some patients.

Conditions which augment systemic absorption include the application of the more potent steroids, use over large surface areas, prolonged use, and the addition of occlusive dressings.

Therefore, patients receiving a large dose of a potent topical steroid applied to a large surface area or under an occlusive dressing should be evaluated periodically for evidence of HPA axis suppression by using the urinary free cortisol and ACTH stimulation tests. If HPA axis suppression is noted, an attempt should be made to withdraw the drug, to reduce the frequency of application, or to substitute a less potent steroid.

Recovery of HPA axis function is generally prompt and complete upon discontinuation of the drug. Infrequently, signs and symptoms of steroid withdrawal may occur, requiring supplemental systemic corticosteroids.

Children may absorb proportionally larger amounts of topical corticosteroids and thus be more susceptible to systemic toxicity. (See *PRECAUTIONS—Pediatric Use.*)

If irritation develops, topical corticosteroids should be discontinued and appropriate therapy instituted.

As with any topical corticosteroid product, prolonged use may produce atrophy of the skin and subcutaneous tissues. When used on intertriginous or flexor area, or on the face, this may occur even with short term use.

In the presence of dermatological infections, the use of an appropriate antifungal or antibacterial agent should be instituted. If a favorable response does not occur promptly, the corticosteroid should be discontinued until the infection has been adequately controlled.

Information for the Patient

Patients using topical corticosteroids should receive the following information and instructions:

1. This medication is to be used as directed by the physician. It is for external use only. Avoid contact with the eyes.
2. Patients should be advised not to use this medication for any disorder other than for which it was prescribed.

Manifestations of intracranial hypertension include bulging fontanelles, headaches, and bilateral papilledema.

Administration of topical corticosteroids to children should be limited to the least amount compatible with an effective therapeutic regimen. Chronic corticosteroid therapy may interfere with the growth and development of children.

adverse reactions

The following local adverse reactions are reported infrequently with topical corticosteroids, but may occur more frequently with the use of occlusive dressings. These reactions are listed in an approximate decreasing order of occurrence:

Burning	Hypertrichosis
Itching	Acneiform eruptions
Irritation	Hypopigmentation
Dryness	Perioral dermatitis
Folliculitis	Allergic contact dermatitis
Maceration of the skin	
Secondary infection	
Skin atrophy	
Striae	
Miliaria	

overdosage

Topically applied corticosteroids can be absorbed in sufficient amounts to produce systemic effects. (See *PRECAUTIONS*.)

dosage and administration

SYNALAR® (fluocinolone acetonide) creams are generally applied to the affected area as a thin film from two to four times daily depending on the severity of the condition. In hairy sites, the hair should be parted to allow direct contact with the lesion.

Occlusive dressing may be used for the management of psoriasis or recalcitrant conditions. Some plastic films may be flammable and due care should be exercised in their use. Similarly, caution should be employed when such films are used on children or left in their proximity, to avoid the possibility of accidental suffocation.

If an infection develops, the use of occlusive dressings should be discontinued and appropriate antimicrobial therapy instituted.

how supplied

SYNALAR® (fluocinolone acetonide) cream 0.025%

15 g Tube	—**NDC**	0033-2501-13
30 g Tube	—**NDC**	0033-2501-14
60 g Tube	—**NDC**	0033-2501-17
425 g Jar	—**NDC**	0033-2501-23

SYNALAR® (fluocinolone acetonide) cream 0.01%

15 g Tube	—**NDC**	0033-2502-13
30 g Tube	—**NDC**	0033-2502-14
60 g Tube	—**NDC**	0033-2502-17
425 g Jar	—**NDC**	0033-2502-23

Store tubes at room temperature; avoid freezing and excessive heat, above 40°C (104°F).

Store jars at controlled room temperature, 15°–30°C (59°–86°F).

CAUTION: Federal law prohibits dispensing without prescription.

SYNTEX LABORATORIES, INC.
PALO ALTO, CA 94304

Revised OCTOBER 1989
© SYNTEX LABORATORIES, INC.

02-2502-14-00

LIDEX®
Products 0.05%
(fluocinonide)

Description LIDEX® (fluocinonide) products are intended for topical administration. Their active component is the corticosteroid fluocinonide, which is the 21-acetate ester of fluocinolone acetonide and has the chemical name pregna-1, 4-diene-3, 20-dione, 21-(acetyloxy)-6, 9-difluoro-11-hydroxy-16, 17-[(1-methyl-ethylidene) bis (oxy)]-, (6α-, 11β, 16α-)-.

LIDEX cream 0.05% contains fluocinonide 0.5 mg/g in FAPG® cream, a specially formulated cream base consisting of citric acid, 1,2,6-hexanetriol, polyethylene glycol 8000, propylene glycol and stearyl alcohol. This white cream vehicle is greaseless, non-staining, anhydrous and completely water miscible. The base provides emollient and hydrophilic properties. In this formulation, the active ingredient is totally in solution.

LIDEX ointment 0.05% contains fluocinonide 0.5 mg/g in a specially formulated ointment base consisting of glyceryl monostearate, white petrolatum, propylene carbonate, propylene glycol and white wax. It provides the occlusive and emollient effects desirable in an ointment. In this formulation, the active ingredient is totally in solution.

LIDEX-E cream 0.05% contains fluocinonide 0.5 mg/g in a water-washable aqueous emollient base of cetyl alcohol, citric acid, mineral oil, polysorbate 60, propylene glycol, sorbitan monostearate, stearyl alcohol and water (purified).

LIDEX topical solution 0.05% contains fluocinonide 0.5 mg/mL in a solution of alcohol (35%), citric acid, diisopropyl adipate and propylene glycol. In this formulation, the active ingredient is totally in solution.

LIDEX gel 0.05% contains fluocinonide 0.5 mg/g in a specially formulated gel base consisting of carbomer 940, edetate disodium, propyl gallate, propylene glycol, sodium hydroxide and/or hydrochloric acid (to adjust pH) and water (purified). This clear, colorless thixotropic vehicle is greaseless, non-staining and completely water miscible. In this formulation, the active ingredient is totally in solution.

Clinical Pharmacology Topical corticosteroids share anti-inflammatory, antipruritic and vasoconstrictive actions.

The mechanism of anti-inflammatory activity of the topical corticosteroids is unclear. Various laboratory methods, including vasoconstrictor assays, are used to compare and predict potencies and/or clinical efficacies of the topical corticosteroids. There is some evidence to suggest that a recognizable correlation exists between vasoconstrictor potency and therapeutic efficacy in man.

Pharmacokinetics The extent of percutaneous absorption of topical corticosteroids is determined by many factors including the vehicle, the integrity of the epidermal barrier and the use of occlusive dressings. A significantly greater amount of fluocinonide is absorbed from the solution than from the cream or gel formulations.

Topical corticosteroids can be absorbed from normal intact skin. Inflammation and/or other disease processes in the skin increase percutaneous absorption. Occlusive dressings substantially increase the percutaneous absorption of topical corticosteroids. Thus, occlusive dressings may be a valuable therapeutic adjunct for treatment of resistant dermatoses. (See DOSAGE AND ADMINISTRATION.)

Once absorbed through the skin, topical corticosteroids are handled through pharmacokinetic pathways similar to systemically administered corticosteroids. Corticosteroids are bound to plasma proteins in varying degrees. Corticosteroids are metabolized primarily in the liver and are then excreted by the kidneys. Some of the topical corticosteroids and their metabolites are also excreted into the bile.

Indications and Usage These products are indicated for the relief of the inflammatory and pruritic manifestations of corticosteroid-responsive dermatoses.

Contraindications Topical corticosteroids are contraindicated in those patients with a history of hypersensitivity to any of the components of the preparation.

Precautions General Systemic absorption of topical corticosteroids has produced reversible hypothalamic-pituitary-adrenal (HPA) axis suppression, manifestations of Cushing's syndrome, hyperglycemia, and glucosuria in some patients.

Conditions which augment systemic absorption include the application of the more potent steroids, use over large surface areas, prolonged use, the addition of occlusive dressings, and a large surface form.

Therefore, patients receiving a large dose of a potent topical steroid applied to a large surface area or under an occlusive dressing should be evaluated periodically for evidence of HPA axis suppression by using the urinary free cortisol and ACTH stimulation tests. If HPA axis suppression is noted, an attempt should be made to withdraw the drug, to reduce the frequency of application, or to substitute a less potent steroid.

Recovery of HPA axis function is generally prompt and complete upon discontinuation of the drug. Infrequently, signs and symptoms of steroid withdrawal may occur, requiring supplemental systemic corticosteroids.

1. This medication is to be used as directed by the physician. It is for external use only. Avoid contact with the eyes. If there is contact with the eyes and severe irritation occurs, immediately flush the eyes with a large volume of water.

2. Patients should be advised not to use this medication for any disorder other than for which it was prescribed.

3. The treated skin area should not be bandaged or otherwise covered or wrapped as to be occlusive unless directed by the physician.

4. Patients should report any signs of local adverse reactions especially under occlusive dressing.

5. Parents of pediatric patients should be advised not to use tight-fitting diapers or plastic pants on a child being treated in the diaper area, as these garments may constitute occlusive dressings.

Laboratory Tests The following tests may be helpful in evaluating the HPA axis suppression:
Urinary free cortisol test
ACTH stimulation test

Carcinogenesis, Mutagenesis, and Impairment of Fertility Long-term animal studies have not been performed to evaluate the carcinogenic potential or the effect on fertility of topical corticosteroids.

Studies to determine mutagenicity with prednisolone and hydrocortisone have revealed negative results.

Pregnancy Category C Corticosteroids are generally teratogenic in laboratory animals when animals are administered systemically at relatively low dosage levels. The more potent corticosteroids have been shown to be teratogenic after dermal application in laboratory animals. There are no adequate and well-controlled studies in pregnant women on teratogenic effects from topically applied corticosteroids. Therefore, topical corticosteroids should be used during pregnancy only if the potential benefit justifies the potential risk to the fetus. Drugs of this class should not be used extensively on pregnant patients, in large amounts, or for prolonged periods of time.

Nursing Mothers It is not known whether topical administration of corticosteroids could result in sufficient systemic absorption to produce detectable quantities in breast milk. Systemically administered corticosteroids are secreted into breast milk in quantities not likely to have a deleterious effect on the infant. Nevertheless, caution should be exercised when topical corticosteroids are administered to a nursing woman.

Pediatric Use Pediatric patients may demonstrate greater susceptibility to topical corticosteroid-induced HPA axis suppression and Cushing's syndrome than mature patients because of a larger skin surface area to body weight ratio.

Hypothalamic-pituitary-adrenal (HPA) axis suppression, Cushing's syndrome, and intracranial hypertension have been reported in children receiving topical corticosteroids. Manifestations of adrenal suppression in children include linear growth retardation, delayed weight gain, low plasma cortisol levels, and absence of response to ACTH stimulation. Manifestations of intracranial hypertension include bulging fontaneles, headaches, and bilateral papilledema.

Administration of topical corticosteroids in children should be limited to the least amount compatible with an effective therapeutic regimen. Chronic corticosteroid therapy may interfere with the growth and development of children.

Adverse Reactions The following local adverse reactions are reported infrequently with topical corticosteroids, but may occur more frequently with the use of occlusive dressings. These reactions are listed in an approximate decreasing order of occurrence: burning, itching, irritation, dryness, folliculitis, hypertrichosis, acneiform eruptions, hypopigmentation, perioral dermatitis, allergic contact dermatitis, maceration of the skin, secondary infection, skin atrophy, striae, miliaria.

Overdosage Topically applied corticosteroids can be absorbed in sufficient amounts to produce systemic effects. (See PRECAUTIONS.)

Dosage and Administration These products are generally applied to the affected area as a thin film from two to four times daily depending on the severity of the condition.

Occlusive dressings may be used for the management of psoriasis or recalcitrant conditions.

If an infection develops, the use of occlusive dressings should be discontinued and appropriate antimicrobial therapy instituted.

How Supplied LIDEX® (fluocinonide) cream 0.05%: 15 g Tube—NDC 0033-2511-13; 30 g Tube—NDC 0033-2511-14; 60 g Tube—NDC 0033-2511-17; 120 g Tube—NDC 0033-2511-22. Store at room temperature. Avoid excessive heat, above 40°C (104°F).

LIDEX® (fluocinonide) ointment 0.05%: 15 g Tube—NDC 0033-2514-13; 30 g Tube—NDC 0033-2514-14; 60 g Tube—NDC 0033-2514-17; 120 g Tube—NDC 0033-2514-22. Store at room temperature. Avoid temperature above 30°C (86°F).

LIDEX-E® (fluocinonide) cream 0.05%: 15 g Tube—NDC 0033-2513-13; 30 g Tube—NDC 0033-2513-14; 60 g Tube—NDC 0033-2513-17; 120 g Tube—NDC 0033-2513-22. Store at room temperature. Avoid excessive heat, above 40°C (104°F).

LIDEX® (fluocinonide) topical solution 0.05%: plastic squeeze bottles: 20 cc. NDC 0033-2517-44; 60 cc. NDC 0033-2517-46. Store at room temperature. Avoid excessive heat, above 40°C (104°F).

Children may absorb proportionally larger amounts of topical corticosteroids and thus be more susceptible to systemic toxicity. (See PRECAUTIONS-Pediatric Use.)

Not for ophthalmic use. Severe irritation is possible if fluocinonide contacts the eye. If that should occur, immediate flushing of the eye with a large volume of water is recommended.

If irritation develops, topical corticosteroids should be discontinued and appropriate therapy instituted.

As with any topical corticosteroid product, prolonged use may produce atrophy of the skin and subcutaneous tissues. When used on intertriginous or flexor area, or on the face, this may occur even with short-term use.

In the presence of dermatological infections, the use of an appropriate antifungal or antibacterial agent should be instituted. If a favorable response does not occur promptly, the corticosteroid should be discontinued until the infection has been adequately controlled.

Information for the Patient Patients using topical corticosteroids should receive the following information and instructions:

SYNTEX LABORATORIES, INC.
PALO ALTO, CA 94304

NASALIDE®
(flunisolide)
Nasal Solution 0.025%
For Nasal Use Only

DESCRIPTION

NASALIDE® (flunisolide) nasal solution is intended for administration as a spray to the nasal mucosa. Flunisolide, the active component of NASALIDE nasal solution, is an anti-inflammatory steroid with the chemical name: 6α-fluoro-11β,16α,17,21-tetrahydroxypregna-1,4-diene-3,20-dione cyclic 16,17-acetal with acetone (USAN). It has the following chemical structure:

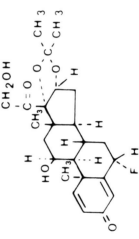

Flunisolide is a white to creamy white crystalline powder with a molecular weight of 434.49. It is soluble in acetone, sparingly soluble in chloroform, slightly soluble in methanol, and practically insoluble in water. It has a melting point of about 245°C.

Each 25 mL spray bottle contains flunisolide 6.25 mg (0.25 mg/mL) in a solution of propylene glycol, polyethylene glycol 3350, citric acid, sodium citrate, butylated hydroxyanisole, edetate disodium, benzalkonium chloride, and purified water, with NaOH and/or HCl added to adjust the pH to approximately 5.3. It contains no fluorocarbons.

After priming the delivery system for NASALIDE, each actuation of the unit delivers a metered droplet spray containing approximately 25 mcg of flunisolide. The size of the droplets produced by the unit is in excess of 8 microns to facilitate deposition on the nasal mucosa. The contents of one nasal spray bottle deliver at least 200 sprays.

CLINICAL PHARMACOLOGY

NASALIDE® (flunisolide) has demonstrated potent glucocorticoid and weak mineralocorticoid activity in classical animal test systems. As a glucocorticoid it is several hundred times more potent than the cortisol standard. Clinical studies with flunisolide have shown therapeutic activity on nasal mucous membranes with minimal evidence of systemic activity at the recommended doses.

A study in approximately 100 patients which compared the recommended dose of flunisolide nasal solution with an oral dose providing equivalent systemic amounts of flunisolide has shown that the clinical effectiveness of NASALIDE, when used topically as recommended, is due to its direct local effect and not to an indirect effect through systemic absorption.

Following administration of flunisolide to man, approximately half of the administered dose is recovered in the urine and half in the stool; 65-70% of the dose recovered in urine is the primary metabolite, which has undergone loss of the 6α fluorine and addition of a 6β hydroxy group. Flunisolide is well absorbed but is rapidly converted by the liver to the much less active primary metabolite and to glucuronate and/or sulfate conjugates. Because of first-pass liver metabolism, only 20% of the flunisolide reaches the systemic circulation when it is given orally whereas 50% of the flunisolide administered intranasally reaches the systemic circulation unmetabolized. The plasma half-life of flunisolide is 1-2 hours.

The effects of flunisolide on hypothalamic-pituitary-adrenal (HPA) axis function have been studied in adult volunteers. NASALIDE was administered intranasally as a spray in total doses over 7 times the recommended dose (2200 mcg, equivalent to 88 sprays/ day) in 2 subjects for 4 days, about 3 times the recommended dose (800 mcg, equivalent to 32 sprays/day) in 4 subjects for 4 days, and over twice the recommended dose (700 mcg, equivalent to 28 sprays/day) in 6 subjects for 10 days. Early morning plasma cortisol concentrations and 24-hour urinary 17-ketogenic steroids were measured daily. There was evidence of decreased endogenous cortisol production at all three doses.

In controlled studies, NASALIDE was found to be effective in reducing symptoms of stuffy nose, runny nose and sneezing in most patients. These controlled clinical studies have been conducted in 488 adult patients at doses ranging from 8 to 16 sprays (200-400 mcg) per day and 127 children at doses ranging from 6 to 8 sprays (150-200 mcg) per day for periods as long as 3 months. In 170 patients who had cortisol levels evaluated at baseline and after 3 months or more of flunisolide treatment, there was no unequivocal flunisolide-related depression of plasma cortisol levels.

The mechanisms responsible for the anti-inflammatory action of corticosteroids and for the activity of the aerosolized drug on the nasal mucosa are unknown.

INDICATIONS

NASALIDE® (flunisolide) is indicated for the topical treatment of the symptoms of seasonal or perennial rhinitis when effectiveness of or tolerance to conventional treatment is unsatisfactory.

Clinical studies have shown that improvement is based on a local effect rather than systemic absorption, and is usually apparent within a few days after starting NASALIDE. However, symptomatic relief may not occur in some patients for as long as two weeks. Although systemic effects are minimal at recommended doses, NASALIDE should not be continued beyond 3 weeks in the absence of significant symptomatic improvement.

NASALIDE should not be used in the presence of untreated localized infection involving nasal mucosa.

CONTRAINDICATIONS

Hypersensitivity to any of the ingredients.

WARNINGS

The replacement of a systemic corticosteroid with a topical corticoid can be accompanied by signs of adrenal insufficiency, and in addition some patients may experience symptoms of withdrawal, e.g., joint and/or muscular pain, lassitude and depression. Patients previously treated for prolonged periods with systemic corticosteroids and transferred to NASALIDE® (flunisolide) should be carefully monitored to avoid acute adrenal insufficiency in response to stress.

When transferred to NASALIDE, careful attention must be given to patients previously treated for prolonged periods with systemic corticosteroids. This is particularly important in those patients who have associated asthma or other clinical conditions, where too rapid a decrease in systemic corticosteroids may cause a severe exacerbation of their symptoms.

The use of NASALIDE with alternate-day prednisone systemic treatment could increase the likelihood of HPA suppression compared to a therapeutic dose of either one alone. Therefore, NASALIDE treatment should be used with caution in patients already on alternate-day prednisone regimens for any disease.

PRECAUTIONS

General: In clinical studies with flunisolide administered intranasally, the development of localized infections of the nose and pharynx with *Candida albicans* has occurred only rarely. When such an infection develops it may require treatment with appropriate local therapy or discontinuance of treatment with NASALIDE® (flunisolide).

Flunisolide is absorbed into the circulation. Use of excessive doses of NASALIDE may suppress hypothalamic-pituitary-adrenal function.

Flunisolide should be used with caution, if at all in patients with active or quiescent tuberculosis infections of the respiratory tract or in untreated fungal, bacterial or systemic viral infections or ocular herpes simplex.

Because of the inhibitory effect of corticosteroids on wound healing, in patients who have experienced recent nasal septal ulcers, recurrent epistaxis, nasal surgery or trauma, a nasal corticosteroid should be used with caution until healing has occurred.

Although systemic effects have been minimal with recommended doses, this potential increases with excessive dosages. Therefore, larger than recommended doses should be avoided.

Information for Patients: Patients should use NASALIDE at regular intervals since its effectiveness depends on its regular use. The patient should take the medication as directed. It is not acutely effective and the prescribed dosage should not be increased. Instead, nasal vasoconstrictors or oral antihistamines may be needed until the effects of NASALIDE are fully manifested. One to two weeks may pass before full relief is obtained. The patient should contact the physician if symptoms do not improve, or if the condition worsens, or if sneezing or nasal irritation occurs.

For the proper use of this unit and to attain maximum improvement, the patient should read and follow the accompanying Patient Instructions carefully.

Carcinogenesis: Long-term studies were conducted in mice and rats using oral administration to evaluate the carcinogenic potential of the drug. There was an increase in the incidence of pulmonary adenomas in mice, but not in rats.

Female rats receiving the highest oral dose had an increased incidence of mammary adenocarcinoma compared to control rats. An increased incidence of this tumor type has been reported for other corticosteroids.

Impairment of fertility: Female rats receiving high doses of flunisolide (200 mcg/kg/day) showed some evidence of impaired fertility. Reproductive performance in the low (8 mcg/kg/day) and mid-dose (40 mcg/kg/day) groups was comparable to controls.

Pregnancy: Teratogenic effects: Pregnancy Category C. As with other corticosteroids, flunisolide has been shown to be teratogenic in rabbits and rats at doses of 40 and 200 mcg/kg/day respectively. It was also fetotoxic in these animal reproductive studies. There are no adequate and well-controlled studies in pregnant women. Flunisolide should be used during pregnancy only if the potential benefit justifies the potential risk to the fetus.

Nursing Mothers: It is not known whether this drug is excreted in human milk. Because other corticosteroids are excreted in human milk, caution should be exercised when flunisolide is administered to nursing women.

ADVERSE REACTIONS

Adverse reactions reported in controlled clinical trials and long-term open studies in 595 patients treated with NASALIDE are described below. Of these patients, 409 were treated for 3 months or longer, 323 for 6 months or longer, 259 for 1 year or longer, and 91 for 2 years or longer.

In general, side effects elicited in the clinical studies have been primarily associated with the nasal mucous membranes. The most frequent complaints were those of mild transient nasal burning and stinging, which were reported in approximately 45% of the patients treated with NASALIDE in placebo-controlled and long-term studies. These complaints do not usually interfere with treatment; in only 3% of patients was it necessary to decrease dosage or stop treatment because of these symptoms. Approximately the same incidence of mild transient nasal burning and stinging was reported in patients on placebo as was reported in patients treated with NASALIDE in controlled studies, implying that these complaints may be related to the vehicle or the delivery system. The incidence of complaints of nasal burning and stinging decreased with increasing duration of treatment.

Other side effects reported at a frequency of 5% or less were: nasal congestion, sneezing, epistaxis and/or bloody mucus, nasal irritation, watery eyes, sore throat, nausea and/or vomiting, headaches and loss of sense of smell and taste. As is the case with other nasally inhaled corticosteroids, nasal septal perforations have been observed in rare instances.

Systemic corticosteroid side effects were not reported during the controlled clinical trials. If recommended doses are exceeded, or if individuals are particularly sensitive, symptoms of hypercorticism, i.e., Cushing's syndrome, could occur.

OVERDOSAGE

I.V. flunisolide in animals at doses up to 4 mg/kg showed no effect. One spray bottle contains 6.25 mg of NASALIDE; therefore acute overdosage is unlikely.

The therapeutic effects of corticosteroids, unlike those of decongestants, are not immediate. This should be explained to the patient in advance in order to ensure cooperation and continuation of treatment with the prescribed dosage regimen. Full therapeutic benefit requires regular use, and is usually evident within a few days. However, a longer period of therapy may be required for some patients to achieve maximum benefit (up to 3 weeks). If no improvement is evident by that time, NASALIDE® (flunisolide) should not be continued.

Patients with blocked nasal passages should be encouraged to use a decongestant just before NASALIDE administration to ensure adequate penetration of the spray. Patients should also be advised to clear their nasal passages of secretions prior to use.

Adults: The recommended starting dose of NASALIDE is 2 sprays (50 mcg) in each nostril 2 times a day (total dose 200 mcg/day). If needed, this dose may be increased to 2 sprays in each nostril 3 times a day (total dose 300 mcg/day).

Children 6 to 14 years: The recommended starting dose of NASALIDE is one spray (25 mcg) in each nostril 3 times a day or two sprays (50 mcg) in each nostril 2 times a day (total dose 150-200 mcg/day). NASALIDE is not recommended for use in children less than 6 years of age as safety and efficacy studies, including possible adverse effects on growth, have not been conducted.

Maximum total daily doses should not exceed 8 sprays in each nostril for adults (total dose 400 mcg/day) and 4 sprays in each nostril for children under 14 years of age (total dose 200 mcg/day). Since there is no evidence that exceeding the maximum recommended dosage is more effective and increased systemic absorption would occur, higher doses should be avoided.

After the desired clinical effect is obtained, the maintenance dose should be reduced to the smallest amount necessary to control the symptoms. Approximately 15% of patients with perennial rhinitis may be maintained on as little as 1 spray in each nostril per day.

HOW SUPPLIED

Each 25 mL NASALIDE® (flunisolide) nasal solution spray bottle (NDC 0033-2906-40) (NSN 6505-01-132-9979) contains 6.25 mg (0.25 mg/mL) of flunisolide and is supplied in a nasal pump dispenser with dust cover and with a patient leaflet of instructions.

Store at controlled room temperature, 15°-30°C (59°-86°F).

SYNTEX

SYNTEX LABORATORIES, INC.
PALO ALTO, CA 94304

02-2906-42-00

© Revised July 1988

TORADOL® IM
(ketorolac
tromethamine)

Plasma Levels After Recommended
Ketorolac Tromethamine I.M. Dosing Schedules

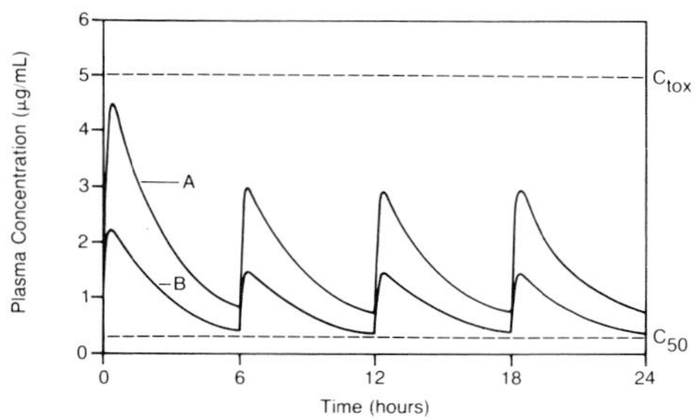

DESCRIPTION

TORADOL* (ketorolac tromethamine) is a member of the pyrrolo-pyrrole group of nonsteroidal anti-inflammatory drugs (NSAIDs).
The chemical name for ketorolac tromethamine is (±)-5-benzoyl-2,3-dihydro-1H-pyrrolizine-1-carboxylic acid,2-amino-2-(hydroxymethyl)-1,3-propanediol and it has the following structure:

Ketorolac tromethamine is soluble in water, has a pKa of 3.54 and an n-octanol/water partition coefficient of 0.26. The molecular weight of ketorolac tromethamine is 376.41.

TORADOL Injection is available for intramuscular (IM) administration as: 15 mg in 1 mL (1.5%), 30 mg in 1 mL (3%), or 60 mg in 2 mL (3%) of ketorolac tromethamine in sterile solution. The 15 mg/mL solution contains 10% (w/v) alcohol, USP, and 6.68 mg of sodium chloride in sterile water. The 30 mg/mL solution contains 10% (w/v) alcohol, USP, and 4.35 mg sodium chloride in sterile water. The pH is adjusted with sodium hydroxide or hydrochloric acid. The sterile solutions are clear and slightly yellow in color.

CLINICAL PHARMACOLOGY

Pharmacodynamics

TORADOL is a nonsteroidal anti-inflammatory drug (NSAID) that exhibits analgesic, anti-inflammatory, and antipyretic activity. TORADOL inhibits synthesis of prostaglandins and may be considered a peripherally acting analgesic. Pain relief, following extraction of third impacted molars, is clinically evident when steady state plasma levels exceed 0.3 μg/mL, while side effects are frequent above concentrations of 5 μg/mL. Pain relief is often perceptible in about 10 minutes after TORADOL administration, but peak analgesia lags peak plasma levels by 45 to 90 minutes. Ketorolac tromethamine does not have any known effects on opiate receptors.

Table of Estimated Pharmacodynamic Parameters Following Intramuscular Doses of TORADOL

$C_{50}est^1$	0.1 – 0.3 μg/mL
$C_{tox}est^2$	5 μg/mL

1 Estimated concentration required to obtain 50% decreases in pain intensity scores in dental surgery pain
2 Estimated concentration above which side effects are frequent

Pharmacokinetics (see Tables and Graph)

TORADOL is completely absorbed following intramuscular administration with mean peak plasma concentrations of 2.2 – 3.0 μg/mL occurring an average of 50 minutes after a single 30 mg dose. The terminal plasma half-life is 3.8 – 6.3 hours in young adults and 4.7 – 8.6 hours in elderly subjects (mean age 72). More than 99% of the ketorolac tromethamine in plasma is protein bound over a wide concentration range.

The pharmacokinetics of ketorolac tromethamine in man, following single or multiple intramuscular doses, are apparently linear, e.g., plasma levels are approximately proportional to dosage. Steady state plasma levels are achieved after dosing every 6 hours for one day. No changes in clearance occur with chronic dosing. Ketorolac, following intravenous and intramuscular administration, displays characteristics of a two-compartment model. In order to minimize the time delay in achieving adequate analgesic effect from the initial dose of a given regimen, a loading dose equal to twice the maintenance dose is recommended. This is based upon the pharmacokinetic principle that when the dosing interval is near the drug's half-life, the target steady-state plasma level is achieved faster if the first dose is twice the maintenance dose. Due to the two-compartment characteristics of TORADOL, the loading dose results in plasma levels during the first dosing interval that are higher than in subsequent intervals (see graph).

The primary route of excretion of ketorolac tromethamine and its metabolites (conjugates and a para-hydroxy metabolite) is in the urine (mean 91.4%) and the remainder (mean 6.1%) is excreted in the feces. In patients with serum creatinine values ranging from 1.9 to 5.0 mg/dL the rate of ketorolac clearance was reduced to approximately half of normal.

Table of Approximate† Average Pharmacokinetic Parameters Following Intramuscular Doses of TORADOL

	15 mg	30 mg	60 mg
Bioavailability (extent)	100%	100%	100%
T_{max}^1 (min)	30 – 60	30 – 60	30 – 60
C_{max}^2 (μg/mL) [single dose]	1.0 – 1.4	2.2 – 3.0	4.0 – 4.5
C_{max}^2 (μg/mL) [steady state qid]	1.1 – 1.7	2.3 – 3.5	N/A*
C_{min}^3 (μg/mL) [steady state qid]	0.2 – 0.3	0.3 – 0.7	N/A
C_{ave}^4 (μg/mL) [steady state qid]	0.6 – 0.8	1.3 – 1.5	N/A
$Vd(\beta)^5$	– – – – – – –	0.15 – 0.33 L/kg	– – – – – – – –
Dose metabolized ≈ ~50%			
% Dose excreted in urine = 91%			
% Dose excreted in feces = 6%			
% Plasma protein binding = 99%			

* Not applicable because 60 mg is only recommended as a loading dose
1 Time-to-peak plasma concentration
2 Peak Plasma concentration
3 Trough plasma concentration
4 Average plasma concentration
5 Volume of distribution (calculated from mean clearance and terminal half-life)

† Derived from pharmacokinetic studies in 32 normal volunteers.

A = Ketorolac tromethamine 60 mg followed by 30 mg doses (Q 6 hr)
B = Ketorolac tromethamine 30 mg followed by 15 mg doses (Q 6 hr)
C_{tox} = Estimated concentration above which side effects are frequent
C_{50} = Estimated concentration required to obtain 50% decreases in pain intensity scores in dental surgery pain

The Influence of Age, Liver and Kidney Function on the Clearance and Terminal Half-life of TORADOL[1]

Types of Subjects:	Total Clearance:[2] [in L/h/kg] mean (range)	Terminal Half-life: [in hours] mean (range)
Normal subjects (n = 8)	0.026 (0.017 – 0.046)	4.5 (3.8 – 5.0)
Patients with hepatic dysfunction (n = 7)	0.029 (0.013 – 0.066)	5.4 (2.2 – 6.9)
Patients with renal impairment (n = 10)	0.016 (0.007 – 0.043)	9.6 (3.2 – 15.7)
Healthy elderly subjects (n = 13)	0.019 (0.013 – 0.034)	7.0 (4.7 – 8.6)

1 Estimated from 30 mg single doses of ketorolac tromethamine
2 liters/hour/kilogram

Decreases in serum albumin, such as encountered in liver cirrhosis, would be expected to change ketorolac tromethamine clearance. However, in a study of 7 patients with liver cirrhosis, no correlation was found between serum albumin concentration and ketorolac tromethamine clearance.

Hemodynamics of anaesthetized patients were not altered by parenteral administration of TORADOL.

Ketorolac tromethamine poorly penetrates the blood-brain barrier (levels in the cerebrospinal fluid were found to be .002 times or less than those in plasma).

Clinical Studies

The analgesic efficacy of intramuscularly administered TORADOL was investigated in two post-operative pain models: general surgery (orthopedic, gynecologic and abdominal) and oral surgery (removal of impacted third molars). The studies were primarily double-blind, single-dose, parallel trial designs, in which TORADOL was compared to meperidine or morphine administered intramuscularly to patients with moderate to severe pain at baseline.

During the first hour, the onset of analgesic action was similar for TORADOL and the narcotics. TORADOL 30 or 90 mg intramuscularly, gave pain relief comparable to meperidine 100 mg or morphine 12 mg. TORADOL 10 mg was comparable to 50 mg of meperidine or 6 mg of morphine. The duration of analgesia was longer with all three doses of TORADOL. The percentage of patients who did not remedicate by 6 hours, i.e., by the end of the studies, was roughly 70%, 60%, and 50% for TORADOL 90, 30 and 10 mg respectively, as compared to 30% and 20% for the high and low doses of the two narcotics.

In a multi-dose (10 doses), post-operative (general surgery) double-blind trial of TORADOL 30 mg versus morphine 6 and 12 mg, each drug given on an "as needed" basis, the overall analgesic effect of TORADOL 30 mg was in between that of morphine 6 and 12 mg. TORADOL 30 mg caused less drowsiness, nausea and vomiting than morphine 12 mg.

INDICATIONS AND USAGE

Intramuscular injection of TORADOL is indicated for the short-term management of pain (see "Clinical Studies" in CLINICAL PHARMACOLOGY).

TORADOL is not recommended for use as an obstetrical preoperative medication or for obstetrical analgesia because it has not been adequately studied for use in these circumstances and because of the known effects of drugs that inhibit prostaglandin biosynthesis on uterine contraction and fetal circulation.

TORADOL is not recommended for routine use with other nonsteroidal anti-inflammatory drugs (NSAIDs) because of the potential for additive side effects. TORADOL protein-binding is affected by aspirin (see PRECAUTIONS) but not by acetaminophen, ibuprofen, naproxen or piroxicam. Studies with other nonsteroidals have not been performed. TORADOL has been used concomitantly with morphine and meperidine without apparent adverse interactions.

CONTRAINDICATIONS

TORADOL should not be used in patients with previously demonstrated hypersensitivity to ketorolac tromethamine or in individuals with the complete or partial syndrome of nasal polyps, angioedema, and bronchospastic reactivity to aspirin or other nonsteroidal anti-inflammatory drugs (NSAIDs).

WARNINGS

Though TORADOL Injection is recommended for short-term use only, long-term administration of ketorolac tromethamine oral formulation has shown that this drug shares the risks that other nonsteroidal anti-inflammatory drugs (NSAIDs) pose to patients when taken chronically.

Risk of GI Ulcerations, Bleeding and Perforation with NSAID Treatment: Serious gastrointestinal toxicity, such as bleeding, ulceration, and perforation, can occur at any time, with or without warning symptoms, in patients treated chronically with NSAIDs. Although minor upper gastrointestinal problems, such as dyspepsia, are common, usually developing early in therapy, physicians should remain alert for ulceration and bleeding in patients treated chronically with NSAIDs, even in the absence of previous GI tract symptoms. In patients observed in clinical trials of such agents for several months to two years, symptomatic upper GI ulcers, gross bleeding or perforation appear to occur in approximately 1% of patients treated for 3-6 months, and in about 2-4% of patients treated for one year. Physicians should inform patients about the signs and/or symptoms of serious GI toxicity and what steps to take if they occur.

Studies to date have not identified any subset of patients not at risk of developing peptic ulceration and bleeding. Except for a prior history of serious GI events, and other risk factors known to be associated with peptic ulcer disease, such as alcoholism, smoking, etc., no risk factors (e.g., age, sex) have been associated with increased risk. Elderly or debilitated patients seem to tolerate ulceration or bleeding less well than other individuals, and most spontaneous reports of fatal GI events are in this population.

Studies to date are inconclusive concerning the relative risk of various nonsteroidal anti-inflammatory drugs (NSAIDs) in causing such reactions. High doses of any such agent probably carry a greater risk of these reactions, although controlled clinical trials showing this do not exist in most instances. In considering the use of relatively large doses (within the recommended dosage range), sufficient benefit should be anticipated to offset the potential increased risk of GI toxicity.

Because serious GI tract ulceration and bleeding can occur without warning symptoms, physicians should follow chronically treated patients for the signs and symptoms of ulceration and bleeding, and should inform the patients of the importance of this follow-up.

PRECAUTIONS

General Precautions

Impaired Renal or Hepatic Function: As with other nonsteroidal anti-inflammatory drugs (NSAIDs), TORADOL* should be used with caution in patients with impaired renal or hepatic function, or a history of kidney or liver disease. Studies to assess the pharmacokinetics of TORADOL in patients with active hepatitis or cholestasis have not been done.

Renal Effects: As with other nonsteroidal anti-inflammatory drugs, long-term administration of ketorolac tromethamine to animals resulted in renal papillary necrosis and other abnormal renal pathology. In humans, hematuria and proteinuria have been observed in long-term trials with oral ketorolac tromethamine treatment with a frequency and degree similar to the aspirin control group.

A second form of renal toxicity has been seen in patients with conditions leading to a reduction in blood volume and/or renal blood flow, where renal prostaglandins have a supportive role in the maintenance of renal perfusion. In these patients, administration of a nonsteroidal anti-inflammatory drug may cause a dose-dependent reduction in renal prostaglandin formation and may precipitate overt renal failure. Patients at greatest risk of this reaction are those with impaired renal function, heart failure, liver dysfunction, those taking diuretics and the elderly. Discontinuation of NSAID therapy is typically followed by recovery to the pretreatment state.

TORADOL and its metabolites are eliminated primarily by the kidneys which, in patients with reduced creatinine clearance, will result in diminished clearance of the drug (see CLINICAL PHARMACOLOGY). Therefore, TORADOL should be used with caution in patients with impaired renal function (see DOSAGE and ADMINISTRATION section) and such patients should be followed closely. TORADOL has not been studied in patients with serum creatinine above 5.0 mg/dl, nor was it studied in patients on renal dialysis.

Fluid Retention and Edema: Fluid retention and edema have been reported with the use of NSAIDs; therefore, TORADOL should be used with caution in patients with cardiac decompensation, hypertension, or similar conditions.

Hepatic Effects: As with other nonsteroidal anti-inflammatory drugs (NSAIDs), borderline elevations of one or more liver tests may occur in up to 15% of patients. These abnormalities may progress, may remain essentially unchanged, or may disappear with continued therapy. The ALT (SGPT) test is probably the most sensitive indicator of liver injury. Meaningful (3 times the upper limit of normal) elevations of ALT or AST (SGOT) have been reported in controlled clinical trials (with the oral formulations of ketorolac tromethamine) in less than 1% of patients. A patient with symptoms and/or signs suggesting liver dysfunction, or in whom an abnormal liver test has occurred, should be evaluated for evidence of the development of a more severe hepatic reaction while on therapy with TORADOL. (See also Pharmacokinetics).

Hematologic Effects: TORADOL inhibits platelet aggregation and may prolong bleeding time. TORADOL does not affect platelet count, prothrombin time (PT) or partial thromboplastin time (PTT). Patients who have coagulation disorders or are receiving drug therapy that interferes with hemostasis should be carefully observed when TORADOL is administered. Unlike the prolonged effects from aspirin, the inhibition of platelet function by TORADOL disappears within 24 to 48 hours after the drug is discontinued. In controlled clinical studies, the incidence of clinically significant postoperative bleeding was 5/1170 (0.4%) compared to 1/570 (0.2%) in the control groups receiving opiates.

Drug Interactions

TORADOL is highly bound to human plasma protein (mean 99.2%) and binding is independent of concentration.

The in vitro binding of warfarin to plasma proteins is only slightly reduced by TORADOL (99.5% control vs 99.3% binding with TORADOL concentrations of 5 to 10 µg/mL). TORADOL does not alter digoxin protein binding.

In vitro studies indicated that at therapeutic concentrations of salicylate (300 µg/mL), the binding of TORADOL was reduced from approximately 99.2% to 97.5%, representing a potential two-fold increase in unbound TORADOL plasma levels; hence, TORADOL should be used with caution (or at a reduced dosage) in patients being treated with high dose salicylate regimens. Therapeutic concentrations of digoxin, warfarin, ibuprofen, naproxen, acetaminophen, phenytoin, tolbutamide and piroxicam did not alter TORADOL protein binding.

In a study of 12 healthy volunteers given TORADOL 10 mg orally for 6 days prior to co-administration of a single dose of warfarin 25 mg, no significant changes in pharmacokinetics or pharmacodynamics of warfarin were detected.

In another study of 12 healthy volunteers, co-administration of heparin 5000 U s.c. and TORADOL did not show any pharmacodynamic effects of the combination on template bleeding time or kaolin cephalin clotting time.

There is no evidence, in animal or human studies, that TORADOL induces or inhibits the hepatic enzymes capable of metabolizing itself or other drugs.

Lactation and Nursing

After a single oral administration of 10 mg of TORADOL to humans, the maximum milk concentration observed was 7.3 ng/mL and the maximum milk-to-plasma ratio was 0.037. After one day of dosing (qid), the maximum milk concentration was 7.9 ng/mL and the maximum milk-to-plasma ratio was 0.025. Caution should be exercised when TORADOL is administered to a nursing woman.

Pediatric Use

Safety and efficacy in children have not been established. Therefore, TORADOL is not recommended for use in children.

Use in the Elderly

Because ketorolac tromethamine is cleared somewhat more slowly by the elderly (see CLINICAL PHARMACOLOGY) who are also more sensitive to the renal effects of NSAIDs (see PRECAUTIONS Renal Effects), extra caution and reduced dosages (see DOSAGE AND ADMINISTRATION) should be used when treating the elderly with TORADOL.

ADVERSE REACTIONS

Adverse reactions rates from short-term use of NSAIDs are generally from 1/2 to 1/10 the rates associated with chronic usage. This is also true for TORADOL.

In studies of patients with chronic painful conditions treated for up to 1 year, the incidence of serious and nonserious ADRs, including GI tract ulceration and bleeding (yearly rate 1.2 to 5.4%), associated with 10 mg of ketorolac tromethamine orally, 1 to 4 times per day prn, was comparable to treatment with aspirin 650 mg on a similar prn schedule. Physicians using TORADOL Injection should be alert for the usual complications of NSAID-treatment.

The adverse reactions listed below were reported to be probably related to TORADOL in clinical trials in which patients received up to 20 doses, in five days, of intramuscularly administered TORADOL 30 mg. Reactions are listed under body systems which are arranged alphabetically.

Incidence greater than 1%

Body as a whole: edema

Gastrointestinal: nausea*, dyspepsia*, gastrointestinal pain*, diarrhea

Nervous system: drowsiness*, dizziness, headache, sweating

*Injection site pain was reported by 2% of patients in multidose studies (vs. 5% for morphine control group).

*Incidence of reported reaction between 3% and 9%. Those reactions occurring in less than 3% of the patients are unmarked.

Incidence 1% or less

Body as a whole: asthenia, myalgia

Cardiovascular: vasodilation, pallor

Dermatologic: pruritus, urticaria

Gastrointestinal: constipation, flatulence, gastrointestinal fullness, liver function abnormalities, melena, peptic ulcer, rectal bleeding, stomatitis, vomiting

Hemic and lymphatic: purpura

Nervous system: dry mouth, nervousness, paresthesia, abnormal thinking, depression, euphoria, excessive thirst, inability to concentrate, insomnia, stimulation, vertigo

Respiratory: dyspnea, asthma

Special senses: abnormal taste, abnormal vision

Urogenital: increased urinary frequency, oliguria

DRUG ABUSE AND PHYSICAL DEPENDENCE

TORADOL is not a narcotic agonist or antagonist. Subjects did not show any subjective symptoms or objective signs of drug withdrawal upon abrupt discontinuation of intravenous or intramuscular dosing. Patients receiving TORADOL orally for six months or longer have not developed tolerance to the drug and there is no pharmacologic basis to expect addiction. TORADOL did not exhibit activity in classical animal studies which are reasonable predictors of opiate analgesic action. In vitro, TORADOL does not bind to opiate receptors. These studies demonstrate that TORADOL does not have central opiate-like activity.

OVERDOSAGE

The absence of experience with acute overdosage precludes characterization of sequelae and assessment of antidotal efficacy at this time. At single oral doses greater than 100 mg/kg in rats, mice and monkeys, symptoms such as decreased activity, diarrhea, pallor, labored breathing, rales, and vomiting were observed.

DOSAGE AND ADMINISTRATION

TORADOL may be used on a regular schedule or prn ('as needed'), although current recommendations for pain management are to use analgesics on a regular schedule, rather than using them prn based on the return of pain. For the short-term management of pain (see CLINICAL PHARMACOLOGY for details of clinical trials), the recommended initial dose is 30 or 60 mg IM, as a loading dose, followed by half of the loading dose, e.g., 15 or 30 mg, every 6 hours as long as needed to control pain. The rationale for the recommended loading dose (LD) and the maintenance dosages (MD) is based upon pharmacokinetic and pharmacodynamic considerations (see CLINICAL PHARMACOLOGY). 60 mg LD/30 mg MD and 30 mg LD/15 mg MD achieve average plasma levels of 1.5 and 0.8 µg/mL respectively, which lie within the therapeutic range of 0.3 – 5 µg/mL. The recommended maximum total daily dose is 150 mg for the first day and 120 mg/day thereafter.

Inhibition of renal lithium clearance leading to an increase in plasma lithium concentration has been reported with some prostaglandin synthesis inhibiting drugs. The effect of TORADOL on plasma lithium levels has not been studied.

Concomitant administration of methotrexate and some NSAIDs has been reported to reduce the clearance of methotrexate, enhancing the toxicity of methotrexate. The effect of TORADOL on methotrexate clearance has not been studied.

Ketorolac tromethamine has been administered concurrently with morphine in several clinical trials of post-operative pain without evidence of adverse interactions.

Carcinogenesis, Mutagenesis, and Impairment of Fertility

An 18-month study in mice at oral doses of ketorolac tromethamine equal to the parenteral MRHD (Maximum Recommended Human Dose) and a 24-month study in rats at oral doses 2.5 times the parenteral MRHD, showed no evidence of tumorigenicity.

Ketorolac tromethamine was not mutagenic in tests performed with S. typhimurium, S. cerevisiae, or E. coli. Ketorolac did not cause chromosome breakage in the *in vivo* mouse micronucleus assay.

Impairment of fertility did not occur in male or female rats at oral doses of 9 mg/kg (4.5 times the parenteral MRHD) and 16 mg/kg (8 times the parenteral MRHD), respectively.

Pregnancy:

Pregnancy – Category B

Reproduction studies have been performed in rabbits, using daily oral doses equal to 3.6 mg/kg (1.8 times the parenteral Maximum Recommended Human Dose – MRHD) and, in rats, equal to 10 mg/kg (5 times the parenteral MRHD), respectively, and did not reveal evidence of harm to the fetus. Ketorolac tromethamine caused delayed parturition and dystocia in rats at oral doses higher than the parenteral MRHD, like other inhibitors of prostaglandin synthesis. Because animal reproduction studies are not always predictive of human response, this drug should be used during pregnancy only if clearly needed and no known safer alternatives are available.

Labor and Delivery

TORADOL is not recommended for use during labor and delivery (see INDICATIONS).

If prn managment is elected, however, since the half-life of TORADOL is approximately 6 hours, an assessment of the size of a repeat dose can be based on the duration of pain relief from the previous dose. For example, if pain returns within 3-5 hours the next dose could be increased by up to 50%. (Note: The recommended maximum total daily dose is 120 mg (150 mg on the first day). An alternative would be to use morphine or meperidine concomitantly (see INDICATIONS and DRUG INTERACTIONS). Alternatively, if pain does not return for 8 to 12 hours, the next dose could be decreased by as much as 50%, or the previous dose could be given every 8 to 12 hours.

The lower end of the recommended dosage range is recommended for patients under 50 kg (110 pounds), for patients over 65 years of age, and for patients with reduced renal function (see CLINICAL PHARMACOLOGY and PRECAUTIONS).

CARDENE®
(nicardipine hydrochloride)
Capsules

DESCRIPTION

CARDENE® capsules for oral administration each contain 20 mg or 30 mg of nicardipine hydrochloride. CARDENE is a calcium influx inhibitor (slow channel blocker or calcium channel blocker).

Nicardipine hydrochloride is a dihydropyridine structure with the IUPAC (International Union of Pure and Applied Chemistry) chemical name 2-(benzyl-methyl amino)ethyl methyl 1,4-dihydro-2,6-dimethyl-4-(m-nitrophenyl)-3,5-pyridinedicarboxylate monohydrochloride, and it has the following structure:

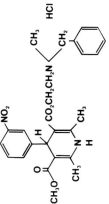

NICARDIPINE HYDROCHLORIDE

Nicardipine hydrochloride is a greenish-yellow, odorless, crystalline powder that melts at about 169°C. It is freely soluble in chloroform, methanol, and glacial acetic acid, sparingly soluble in anhydrous ethanol, slightly soluble in n-butanol, water, 0.01 M potassium dihydrogen phosphate, acetone, and dioxane, very slightly soluble in ethyl acetate, and practically insoluble in benzene, ether and hexane. It has a molecular weight of 515.99.

CARDENE is available in hard gelatin capsules containing 20 mg or 30 mg nicardipine hydrochloride with magnesium stearate and pregelatinized starch as the inactive ingredients. The 20 mg strength is provided in opaque white-white capsules made tamper evident by a brilliant blue gelatin band while the 30 mg capsules are opaque light blue-powder blue with a brilliant blue gelatin band. The colorants used in the 20 mg capsules are titanium dioxide, D&C Red #7 Calcium Lake and FD&C Blue #1 and the 30 mg capsules use titanium dioxide, FD&C Blue #1, D&C Yellow #10 Aluminum Lake, D&C Red #7 Calcium Lake, and FD&C Blue #2.

CLINICAL PHARMACOLOGY

Mechanism of Action

CARDENE is a calcium entry blocker (slow channel blocker or calcium ion antagonist) which inhibits the transmembrane influx of calcium ions into cardiac muscle and smooth muscle without changing serum calcium concentrations. The contractile processes of cardiac muscle and vascular smooth muscle are dependent upon the movement of extracellular calcium ions into these cells through specific ion channels. The effects of CARDENE are more selective to vascular smooth muscle than cardiac muscle. In animal models, CARDENE produces relaxation of coronary vascular smooth muscle at drug levels which cause little or no negative inotropic effect.

Pharmacokinetics and Metabolism

CARDENE is completely absorbed following oral doses administered as capsules. Plasma levels are detectable as early as 20 minutes following an oral dose and maximal plasma levels are observed within 30 minutes to two hours (mean T_{max} = 1 hour). While CARDENE is completely absorbed, it is subject to saturable first pass metabolism and the systemic bioavailability is about 35% following a 30 mg oral dose at steady state.

When CARDENE was administered one (1) or three (3) hours after a high fat meal, the mean Cmax and mean AUC were lower (20% to 30%) than when CARDENE was given to fasting subjects. These decreases in plasma levels observed following a meal may be significant but the clinical trials establishing the efficacy and safety of CARDENE were done in patients without regard to the timing of meals. Thus the results of these trials reflect the effects of meal-induced variability.

The pharmacokinetics of CARDENE are nonlinear due to saturable hepatic first pass metabolism. Following oral administration, increasing doses result in a disproportionate increase in plasma levels. Steady state Cmax values following 20, 30, and 40 mg doses every 8 hours averaged 36, 88, and 133 ng/mL, respectively. Hence, increasing the dose from 20 to 30 mg every 8 hours more than doubled Cmax and increasing the dose from 20 to 40 mg every 8 hours increased Cmax more than 3-fold. A similar disproportionate increase in AUC with dose was observed. Considerable inter-subject variability in plasma levels was also observed.

Post-absorption kinetics of CARDENE are also non-linear, due to non-linear, plasma clearance. A reproducible terminal plasma half-life that averaged 8.6 hours following 30 and 40 mg doses at steady state (TID). The terminal half-life represents the elimination of less than 5% of the absorbed drug (measured by plasma concentrations). Elimination over the first 8 hours after dosing is much faster with a half-life of 2-4 hours. Steady state plasma levels are achieved after 2 to 3 days of TID dosing (every 8 hours) and are 2-fold higher than after a single dose.

CARDENE is highly protein bound (>95%) in human plasma over a wide concentration range.

CARDENE is metabolized extensively by the liver; less than 1% of intact drug is detected in the urine. Following a radioactive oral dose in solution, 60% of the radioactivity was recovered in the urine and 35% in feces. Most of the dose (over 90%) was recovered within 48 hours of dosing. CARDENE does not induce its own metabolism and does not induce hepatic microsomal enzymes.

The steady-state pharmacokinetics of CARDENE in elderly hypertensive patients ($\geq$65 years) are similar to those obtained in young normal adults. After one week of CARDENE dosing at 20 mg three times a day, the Cmax, Tmax, AUC, terminal plasma half-life, and the extent of protein binding of CARDENE observed in healthy elderly hypertensive patients did not differ significantly from those observed in healthy young normal volunteers.

CARDENE plasma levels were higher in patients with mild renal impairment (baseline serum creatinine concentration ranged from 1.2 to 5.5 mg/dl) than in normal subjects. After 30 mg CARDENE TID at steady state, Cmax and AUC were approximately 2-fold higher in these patients.

Because CARDENE is extensively metabolized by the liver, the plasma levels of the drug are influenced by changes in hepatic function. CARDENE plasma levels were higher in patients with severe liver disease (hepatic cirrhosis confirmed by liver biopsy or presence of endoscopically-confirmed esophageal varices) than in normal subjects. After 20 mg CARDENE BID at steady state, Cmax and AUC were 1.8 and 4-fold higher, and the terminal half-life was prolonged to 19 hours in these patients.

Hemodynamics

In man, CARDENE produces a significant decrease in systemic vascular resistance. The degree of vasodilation and the resultant hypotensive effects are more prominent in hypertensive patients. In hypertensive patients, nicardipine reduces the blood pressure at rest and during isometric and dynamic exercise. In normotensive patients, a small decrease of about 8/8 mmHg in systolic and 7 mmHg in diastolic blood pressure may accompany this fall in peripheral resistance. An increase in heart rate may occur in response to the vasodilation and decrease in blood pressure, and in a few patients the heart rate may be pronounced. In clinical studies, an increase in heart rate at time of peak plasma levels was usually minimal compared to placebo, with the greater increases at higher doses, while there was no difference from placebo at end of the dosing interval. Hemodynamic studies following intravenous dosing in patients with coronary artery disease and normal or moderately abnormal left ventricular function have shown significant increases in ejection fraction and cardiac output with no significant change, or a small decrease, in left ventricular end-diastolic pressure (LVEDP). Although there is evidence that CARDENE increases coronary blood flow, there is no evidence that this property plays any role in its effectiveness in stable angina. In patients with coronary artery disease, intracoronary administration of nicardipine caused no direct myocardial depression. CARDENE does, however, have a negative inotropic effect in some patients with severe left ventricular dysfunction and could, in patients with very impaired function, lead to worsened failure.

"Coronary Steal", the detrimental redistribution of coronary blood flow in patients with coronary artery disease (diversion of blood from underperfused areas toward better perfused areas), has not been observed during nicardipine treatment. On the contrary, nicardipine has been shown to improve systolic shortening in normal and hypokinetic segments of myocardial muscle, and radio-nuclide angiography has confirmed that wall motion remained improved during an increase in oxygen demand. Nonetheless, occasional patients have developed increased angina upon receiving nicardipine. Whether this represents steal in those patients, or is the result of increased heart rate and decreased diastolic pressure, is not clear.

In patients with coronary artery disease nicardipine improves L.V. diastolic distensibility during the early filling phase, probably due to a faster rate of myocardial relaxation in previously underperfused areas. There is little or no effect on normal myocardium, suggesting the improvement is mainly by indirect mechanisms such as afterload reduction, and reduced ischemia. Nicardipine has no negative effect on myocardial relaxation at therapeutic doses. The clinical consequences of these properties are as yet undemonstrated.

Electrophysiologic Effects

In general, no detrimental effects on the cardiac conduction system were seen with the use of CARDENE.

CARDENE increased the heart rate when given intravenously during acute electrophysiologic studies, and prolonged the corrected QT interval to a minor degree. The sinus node recovery times and SA conduction times were not affected by the drug. The PA, AH, and HV intervals* and the functional and effective refractory periods of the atrium were not prolonged by CARDENE and the relative and effective refractory periods of the His-Purkinje system were slightly shortened after intravenous CARDENE.

*PA = conduction time from high to low right atrium, AH = conduction time from low right atrium to His bundle deflection, or AV nodal conduction time, HV = conduction time through the His bundle and the bundle branch-Purkinje system.

Renal Function

There is a transient increase in electrolyte excretion, including sodium. CARDENE does not cause generalized fluid retention, as measured by weight changes, although 7-8% of the patients experience pedal edema.

Effects in Angina Pectoris

In controlled clinical trials of up to 12 weeks duration in patients with chronic stable angina, CARDENE increased exercise tolerance and reduced nitroglycerin consumption and the frequency of anginal attacks. The antianginal efficacy of CARDENE (20-40 mg) has been demonstrated in four placebo-controlled studies involving 258 patients with chronic stable angina. In exercise tolerance testing, CARDENE significantly increased time to angina, total exercise duration and time to 1 mm ST segment depression. Included among these four studies was a dose-definition study in which dose-related improvements in exercise tolerance at one and four hours post-dosing and reduced frequency of anginal attacks were seen at doses of 10, 20 and 30 mg TID. Effectiveness at 10 mg TID was, however, marginal. In a fifth placebo-controlled study, the antianginal efficacy of CARDENE was demonstrated at 8 hours post-dose (trough). The sustained efficacy of CARDENE has been demonstrated over long-term dosing. Blood pressure fell in patients with angina by about 10/8 mmHg at peak blood levels and was little different from placebo at trough blood levels.

Effects in Hypertension

CARDENE produced dose-related decreases in both systolic and diastolic blood pressure in clinical trials. The antihypertensive efficacy of CARDENE administered

Three times daily has been demonstrated in three placebo-controlled studies involving 517 patients with mild to moderate hypertension. The blood pressure responses in the three studies were statistically significant from placebo at peak (1 hour post-dosing) and trough (8 hours post-dosing) although it is apparent that well over half of the antihypertensive effect is lost by the end of the dosing interval. The results from placebo controlled studies of CARDENE given three times daily are shown in the following table:

	SYSTOLIC BP (mmHg)					DIASTOLIC BP (mmHg)			
Dose	Number of Patients	Mean Peak Response	Mean Trough Response	Trough/ Peak	Dose	Number of Patients	Mean Peak Response	Mean Trough Response	Trough/ Peak
20 mg	50 52	−10.3 −17.6	−4.9 −7.9	48% 45%	20 mg	50 52	−10.6 −9.0	−4.6 −2.9	43% 32%
30 mg	45 44	−14.5 −14.6	−7.2 −7.5	50% 51%	30 mg	45 44	−12.8 −14.2	−4.9 −4.3	38% 30%
40 mg	50 38	−16.3 −15.9	−9.5 −6.0	58% 38%	40 mg	50 38	−15.4 −14.8	−5.9 −3.7	38% 25%

The responses are shown as differences from the concurrent placebo control group. The large changes between peak and trough effects were not accompanied by observed side effects at peak response times. In a study using 24 hour intra-arterial blood pressure monitoring, the circadian variation in blood pressure remained unaltered, but the systolic and diastolic blood pressures were reduced throughout the whole 24 hours.

When added to beta-blocker therapy, CARDENE further lowers both systolic and diastolic blood pressure.

INDICATIONS AND USAGE

I. Stable Angina

CARDENE is indicated for the management of patients with chronic stable angina (effort-associated angina). CARDENE may be used alone or in combination with beta-blockers.

II. Hypertension

CARDENE is indicated for the treatment of hypertension. CARDENE may be used alone or in combination with other antihypertensive drugs. In administering nicardipine it is important to be aware of the relatively large peak to trough differences in blood pressure effect. (See DOSAGE AND ADMINISTRATION.)

CONTRAINDICATIONS

CARDENE is contraindicated in patients with hypersensitivity to the drug.

Because part of the effect of CARDENE is secondary to reduced afterload, the drug is also contraindicated in patients with advanced aortic stenosis. Reduction of diastolic pressure in these patients may worsen rather than improve myocardial oxygen balance.

WARNINGS

Increased Angina

About 7% of patients in short term placebo-controlled angina trials have developed increased frequency, duration or severity of angina on starting CARDENE or at the time of dosage increases, compared with 4% of patients on placebo. Comparisons with beta-blockers also show a greater frequency of increased angina, 4% vs 1%. The mechanism of this effect has not been established. (See ADVERSE REACTIONS.)

Use in Patients with Congestive Heart Failure

Although preliminary hemodynamic studies in patients with congestive heart failure have shown that CARDENE reduced afterload without impairing myocardial contractility, it has a negative inotropic effect in vitro and in some patients. Caution should be exercised when using the drug in congestive heart failure patients, particularly in combination with a beta-blocker.

Beta-Blocker Withdrawal

CARDENE is not a beta-blocker and therefore gives no protection against the dangers of abrupt beta-blocker withdrawal; any such withdrawal should be by gradual reduction of the dose of beta-blocker, preferably over 8-10 days.

PRECAUTIONS

GENERAL

Blood Pressure: Because CARDENE decreases peripheral resistance, careful monitoring of blood pressure during the initial administration and titration of CARDENE is suggested. CARDENE, like other calcium channel blockers, may occasionally produce symptomatic hypotension. Caution is advised to avoid systemic hypotension when administering the drug to patients who have sustained an acute cerebral infarction or hemorrhage. Because of prominent effects at the time of peak blood levels, initial titration should be performed with measurements of blood pressure at peak effect (1-2 hours after dosing) and just before the next dose.

Use in patients with impaired hepatic function: Since the liver is the major site of biotransformation and since CARDENE is subject to first pass metabolism, the drug should be used with caution in patients having impaired liver function or reduced hepatic blood flow. Patients with severe liver disease developed elevated blood levels (4-fold increase in AUC) and prolonged half-life (19 hours) of CARDENE. (See DOSAGE AND ADMINISTRATION.)

Use in patients with impaired renal function: When CARDENE 20 mg or 30 mg TID was given to hypertensive patients with mild renal impairment, mean plasma concentrations, AUC, and Cmax were approximately 2-fold higher in renally impaired patients than in healthy controls. Doses in these patients must be adjusted. (See CLINICAL PHARMACOLOGY and DOSAGE AND ADMINISTRATION.)

DRUG INTERACTIONS

Beta-Blockers

In controlled clinical studies, adrenergic beta-receptor blockers have been frequently administered concomitantly with CARDENE. The combination is well tolerated.

Cimetidine

Cimetidine increases CARDENE plasma levels. Patients receiving the two drugs concomitantly should be carefully monitored.

Digoxin

Some calcium blockers may increase the concentration of digitalis preparations in the blood. CARDENE usually does not alter the plasma levels of digoxin, however, serum digoxin levels should be evaluated after concomitant therapy with CARDENE is initiated.

Maalox

Co-administration of Maalox TC had no effect on CARDENE absorption.

Fentanyl Anesthesia

Severe hypotension has been reported during fentanyl anesthesia with concomitant use of a beta-blocker and a calcium channel blocker. Even though such interactions were not seen during clinical studies with CARDENE, an increased volume of circulating fluids might be required if such an interaction were to occur.

Cyclosporine

Concomitant administration of nicardipine and cyclosporine results in elevated plasma cyclosporine levels. Plasma concentrations of cyclosporine should therefore be closely monitored, and its dosage reduced accordingly, in patients treated with nicardipine.

When therapeutic concentrations of *furosemide, propranolol, dipyridamole, warfarin, quinidine, or naproxen* were added to human plasma *(in vitro)*, the plasma protein binding of CARDENE was not altered.

Carcinogenesis, Mutagenesis, Impairment of Fertility

Rats treated with nicardipine in the diet (at concentrations calculated to provide daily dosage levels of 5, 15 or 45 mg/kg/day) for two years showed a dose-dependent increase in thyroid hyperplasia and neoplasia (follicular adenoma/carcinoma). One and three month studies in the rat have suggested that these results are linked to a nicardipine-induced reduction in plasma thyroxine (T4) levels with a consequent increase in plasma levels of thyroid stimulating hormone (TSH). Chronic elevation of TSH is known to cause hyperstimulation of the thyroid. In rats on an iodine deficient diet, nicardipine administration for one month was associated with thyroid hyperplasia that was prevented by T4 supplementation. Mice treated with nicardipine in the diet (at concentrations calculated to provide daily dosage levels of up to 100 mg/kg/day) for up to 18 months showed no evidence of neoplasia of any tissue and no evidence of thyroid changes. There was no evidence of thyroid pathology in dogs treated with up to 25 mg nicardipine/kg/day for one year and no evidence of effects of nicardipine on thyroid function (plasma T4 and TSH) in man.

There was no evidence of a mutagenic potential of nicardipine in a battery of genotoxicity tests conducted on microbial indicator organisms, in micronucleus tests in mice and hamsters, or in a sister chromatid exchange study in hamsters.

No impairment of fertility was seen in male or female rats administered nicardipine at oral doses as high as 100 mg/kg/day (50 times the 40 mg TID maximum recommended antianginal or antihypertensive dose in man, assuming a patient weight of 60 kg).

Pregnancy Pregnancy Category C

Nicardipine was embryocidal when administered orally to pregnant Japanese White rabbits, during organogenesis, at 150 mg/kg/day (a dose associated with marked body weight gain suppression in the treated doe) but not at 50 mg/kg/day (25 times the maximum recommended antianginal or antihypertensive dose in man). No adverse effects on the fetus were observed when New Zealand albino rabbits were treated, during organogenesis, with up to 100 mg nicardipine/kg/day (a dose associated with significant mortality in the treated doe). In pregnant rats administered nicardipine orally at up to 100 mg/kg/day (50 times the maximum recommended human dose) there was no evidence of embryolethality or teratogenicity. However, dystocia, reduced birth weights, reduced neonatal survival and reduced neonatal weight gain were noted. There are no adequate and well-controlled studies in pregnant women. CARDENE® should be used during pregnancy only if the potential benefit justifies the potential risk to the fetus.

Nursing Mothers

Studies in rats have shown significant concentrations of CARDENE in maternal milk following oral administration. For this reason it is recommended that women who wish to breast-feed should not take this drug.

Pediatric Use

Safety and efficacy in patients under the age of 18 have not been established.

Use in the Elderly

Pharmacokinetic parameters did not differ between elderly hypertensive patients ($\geq$65 years) and healthy controls after one week of CARDENE treatment at 20 mg TID. Plasma CARDENE concentrations in elderly hypertensive patients were similar to plasma concentrations in healthy young adult subjects when CARDENE was administered at doses of 10, 20 and 30 mg TID, suggesting that the pharmacokinetics of CARDENE are similar in young and elderly hypertensive patients. No significant differences in responses to CARDENE have been observed in elderly patients and the general adult population of patients who participated in clinical studies.

ADVERSE REACTIONS

In multiple-dose U.S. and foreign controlled short-term (up to three months) studies 1,910 patients received CARDENE alone or in combination with other drugs. In these studies adverse events were reported spontaneously; adverse experiences were generally not serious but occasionally required dosage adjustment and about 10% of patients left the studies prematurely because of them. Peak responses were not observed to be associated with adverse effects during clinical trials, but physicians should be aware that adverse effects associated with decreases in blood pressure (tachycardia, hypotension, etc.) could occur around the time of the peak effect. Most adverse effects were expected consequences of the vasodilator effects of CARDENE.

Angina

The incidence rates of adverse effects in anginal patients were derived from multicenter, controlled clinical trials. Following are the rates of adverse effects for CARDENE (N=520) and placebo (N=310), respectively, that occurred in 0.4% of patients or more. These represent events considered probably drug-related by the investigator (except for certain cardiovascular events which were recorded in a different category). Where the frequency of adverse effects for CARDENE and placebo is similar, causal relationship is uncertain. The only dose-related effects were pedal edema and increased angina.

Percent of Patients with Adverse Effects in Controlled Studies
(Incidence of discontinuations shown in parentheses)

Adverse Experience	CARDENE (N=520)		PLACEBO (N=310)	
Pedal Edema	7.1	(0)	0.3	(0)
Dizziness	6.9	(1.2)	0.6	(0)
Headache	6.4	(0.6)	2.6	(0)
Asthenia	5.8	(0.4)	1.0	(0)
Flushing	5.6	(0.4)	4.2	(1.9)
Increased Angina	5.6	(3.5)	0.0	(0)
Palpitations	3.3	(0.4)	0.3	(0)
Nausea	1.9	(0)	0.6	(0.3)
Dyspepsia	1.5	(0.6)	0.6	(0)
Dry Mouth	1.4	(0)	1.0	(0)
Somnolence	1.4	(0)	1.0	(0)
Rash	1.2	(0.2)	0.6	(0)
Tachycardia	1.2	(0.2)	0.0	(0)
Myalgia	1.0	(0)	0.0	(0)
Other edema	1.0	(0.2)	0.3	(0)
Paresthesia	0.8	(0.6)	0.0	(0)
Sustained Tachycardia	0.8	(0.2)	0.0	(0)
Syncope	0.6	(0)	0.6	(0)
Constipation	0.6	(0.6)	0.0	(0)
Dyspnea	0.6	(0)	0.0	(0)
Abnormal ECG	0.6	(0)	0.0	(0)
Malaise	0.6	(0)	0.0	(0)
Nervousness	0.6	(0)	0.3	(0)
Tremor	0.6	(0)	0.0	(0)

In addition, adverse events were observed which are not readily distinguishable from the natural history of the atherosclerotic vascular disease in these patients. Adverse events in this category each occurred in <0.4% of patients receiving CARDENE and included myocardial infarction, atrial fibrillation, exertional hypotension, pericarditis, heart block, cerebral ischemia and ventricular tachycardia. It is possible that some of these events were drug-related.

Hypertension

The incidence rates of adverse effects in hypertensive patients were derived from multicenter, controlled clinical trials. Following are the rates of adverse effects for CARDENE (N = 1390) and placebo (N = 211), respectively, that occurred in 0.4% of patients or more. These represent events considered probably drug-related by the investigator. Where the frequency of adverse effects for CARDENE and placebo is similar, causal relationship is uncertain. The only dose-related effect was pedal edema.

Percent of Patients with Adverse Effects in Controlled Studies
(Incidence of discontinuations shown in parentheses)

Adverse Experience	CARDENE (N = 1390)		PLACEBO (N = 211)	
Flushing	9.7	(2.1)	2.8	(0)
Headache	8.2	(2.6)	4.7	(0)
Pedal Edema	8.0	(1.8)	0.9	(0)
Asthenia	4.2	(1.7)	0.5	(0)
Palpitations	4.1	(1.0)	0.0	(0)
Dizziness	4.0	(1.8)	0.0	(0)
Tachycardia	3.4	(1.2)	0.5	(0)
Nausea	2.2	(0.9)	0.9	(0)
Somnolence	1.1	(0.1)	0.0	(0)
Dyspepsia	0.8	(0.3)	0.5	(0)
Insomnia	0.6	(0.1)	0.0	(0)
Malaise	0.6	(0.1)	0.0	(0)
Other edema	0.6	(0.3)	1.4	(0)
Abnormal dreams	0.4	(0)	0.0	(0)
Dry mouth	0.4	(0.1)	0.0	(0)
Nocturia	0.4	(0)	0.0	(0)
Rash	0.4	(0.4)	0.0	(0)
Vomiting	0.4	(0.4)	0.0	(0)

Rare Events

The following rare adverse events have been reported in clinical trials or the literature:

Body as a Whole: infection, allergic reaction
Cardiovascular: hypotension, postural hypotension, atypical chest pain, peripheral vascular disorder, ventricular extrasystoles, ventricular tachycardia
Digestive: sore throat, abnormal liver chemistries
Musculoskeletal: arthralgia
Nervous: hot flashes, vertigo, hyperkinesia, impotence, depression, confusion, anxiety
Respiratory: rhinitis, sinusitis
Special Senses: tinnitus, abnormal vision, blurred vision
Urogenital: increased urinary frequency

OVERDOSAGE

Overdosage with a 600 mg single dose (15 to 30 times normal clinical dose) has been reported. Marked hypotension (blood pressure unobtainable) and bradycardia (heart rate 20 bpm in normal sinus rhythm) occurred, along with drowsiness, confusion and slurred speech. Supportive treatment with a vasopressor resulted in gradual improvement with normal vital signs approximately 9 hours post treatment.

Based on results obtained in laboratory animals, overdosage may cause systemic hypotension, bradycardia (following initial tachycardia) and progressive atrio-ventricular conduction block. Reversible hepatic function abnormalities and sporadic focal hepatic necrosis were noted in some animal species receiving very large doses of nicardipine.

For treatment of overdose standard measures (for example, evacuation of gastric contents, elevation of extremities, attention to circulating fluid volume and urine output) including monitoring of cardiac and respiratory functions should be implemented. The patient should be positioned so as to avoid cerebral anoxia. Frequent blood pressure determinations are essential. Vasopressors are clinically indicated for patients exhibiting profound hypotension. Intravenous calcium gluconate may help reverse the effects of calcium entry blockade.

DOSAGE AND ADMINISTRATION

Angina

The dose should be individually titrated for each patient beginning with 20 mg three times daily. Doses in the range of 20-40 mg three times a day have been shown to be effective. At least three days should be allowed before increasing the CARDENE dose to ensure achievement of steady state plasma drug concentrations.

Concomitant Use With Other Antianginal Agents
1. Sublingual NTG may be taken as required to abort acute anginal attacks during CARDENE therapy.
2. Prophylactic Nitrate Therapy - CARDENE may be safely coadministered with short- and long-acting nitrates.
3. Beta-blockers - CARDENE may be safely coadministered with beta-blockers. (See DRUG INTERACTIONS.)

Hypertension

The dose of CARDENE should be individually adjusted according to the blood pressure response beginning with 20 mg three times daily. The effective doses in clinical trials have ranged from 20 mg to 40 mg three times daily. The maximum blood pressure lowering effect occurs approximately 1-2 hours after dosing. To assess the adequacy of blood pressure response, the blood pressure should be measured at trough (8 hours after dosing). Because of the prominent peak effects of nicardipine, blood pressure should be measured 1-2 hours after dosing, particularly during initiation of therapy. (See PRECAUTIONS: Blood Pressures, INDICATIONS and CLINICAL PHARMACOLOGY - Peak/Trough Effects in Hypertension.) At least three days should be allowed before increasing the CARDENE dose to ensure achievement of steady state plasma drug concentrations.

Concomitant use with other Antihypertensive Agents
1. Diuretics - CARDENE may be safely coadministered with thiazide diuretics.
2. Beta-blockers - CARDENE may be safely coadministered with beta-blockers. (See DRUG INTERACTIONS.)

Special Patient Populations

Renal Insufficiency - although there is no evidence that CARDENE impairs renal function, careful dose titration beginning with 20 mg TID is advised. (See PRECAUTIONS.)

Hepatic Insufficiency - CARDENE should be administered cautiously in patients with severely impaired hepatic function. A suggested starting dose of 20 mg twice a day is advised with individual titration based on clinical findings maintaining the twice a day schedule. (See PRECAUTIONS.)

Congestive Heart Failure - Caution is advised when titrating CARDENE dosage in patients with congestive heart failure. (See WARNINGS.)

SYNTEX

SYNTEX LABORATORIES, INC.
PALO ALTO, CA 94304

02-2437-42-01

CYTOVENE®
(ganciclovir sodium)
Sterile Powder

FOR INTRAVENOUS INFUSION ONLY

DESCRIPTION

THE CLINICAL TOXICITY OF **CYTOVENE** INCLUDES GRANULOCYTOPENIA AND THROMBOCYTOPENIA. IN ANIMAL STUDIES **CYTOVENE** WAS CARCINOGENIC, TERATOGENIC, AND CAUSED ASPERMATOGENESIS. **CYTOVENE** IS INDICATED FOR USE *ONLY* IN IMMUNOCOMPROMISED PATIENTS WITH CYTOMEGALOVIRUS (CMV) RETINITIS.

CYTOVENE is the brand name for ganciclovir sodium, an antiviral drug active against cytomegalovirus. Reconstituted CYTOVENE Sterile Powder is for intravenous administration only. Each vial of CYTOVENE Sterile Powder contains the equivalent of 500 mg ganciclovir as the sodium salt (46 mg sodium). All doses in this insert are specified in terms of ganciclovir. The chemical name of ganciclovir sodium is 9-(1,3-dihydroxy-2-propoxymethyl) guanine, monosodium salt, and it has the following structure:

CYTOVENE is manufactured as a sterile lyophilized powder. Reconstitution with 10 mL of Sterile Water for Injection, USP, yields a solution with pH 11 and a ganciclovir concentration of approximately 50 mg/mL. Further dilution in an appropriate intravenous solution must be performed before infusion (see DOSAGE AND ADMINISTRATION).

CLINICAL PHARMACOLOGY

Virology

Ganciclovir is a synthetic nucleoside analogue of 2'-deoxyguanosine that inhibits replication of herpesviruses both *in vitro* and *in vivo*. Sensitive human viruses include cytomegalovirus (CMV), herpes simplex virus -1 and -2 (HSV-1, HSV-2), Epstein-Barr virus (EBV) and varicella zoster virus (VZV). Clinical studies have been limited to assessment of efficacy in patients with CMV infection.

Median effective inhibitory doses (ED_{50}) of ganciclovir for human CMV isolates tested *in vitro* in several cell lines ranged from 0.2 to 3.0 μg/mL. The relationship between *in vitro* sensitivity of CMV to ganciclovir and clinical response has not been established. CYTOVENE inhibits mammalian cell proliferation *in vitro* at higher concentrations (10 to 60 μg/mL) with bone marrow colony forming cells being the most sensitive ($ID_{50} \geq 10$ μg/mL) of those cell types tested.

Available evidence indicates that upon entry into host cells, cytomegaloviruses induce one or more cellular kinases that phosphorylate ganciclovir to its triphosphate. It has been shown that there is approximately a 10-fold greater concentration of ganciclovir-triphosphate in CMV-infected cells than in uninfected cells, indicating a preferential phosphorylation of ganciclovir in virus-infected cells. *In vitro*, ganciclovir-triphosphate is catabolized slowly, with 60 to 70% of the original level remaining in the infected cells 18 hours after removal of ganciclovir from the extracellular medium.[1] The antiviral activity of ganciclovir-triphosphate is believed to be the result of inhibition of viral DNA synthesis by two known modes: (1) competitive inhibition of viral DNA polymerases (2) direct incorporation into viral DNA, resulting in eventual termination of viral DNA elongation. The cellular DNA polymerase alpha is also inhibited, but at a higher concentration than required for viral DNA polymerase.

Ganciclovir has shown antiviral activity *in vivo* in several animal CMV infection models. Both normal and immunosuppressed mice had reduced titers of murine CMV when treated with ganciclovir at 5 to 50 mg/kg/day.[2] Normal mice had increased survival as well, when treated with doses of 3 mg/kg/day. Immunosuppressed mice did not show increased survival until they received doses of at least 10 mg/kg/day.[3] In guinea pigs infected with cavian CMV and treated with ganciclovir at 50 mg/kg/day for 7 days, viral titers in the salivary glands were reduced approximately 50% at day 28 post-infection as compared to sham-treated controls.[4]

Of 314 immunocompromised patients enrolled in an open label study of the treatment of life- or sight-threatening CMV disease, 121 patients were identified who had a positive culture for CMV within 7 days prior to treatment and had sequential viral cultures after treatment with CYTOVENE.[5] Post-treatment virologic response was defined as conversion to culture negativity, or a greater than 100-fold decrease in CMV infectious units, as shown in the following table:

Virologic Response

Culture Source	No. Patients Cultured	No. (%) Patients Responding	Median Days to Response
Urine	107	93 (87)	8
Blood	41	34 (83)	8
Throat	21	19 (90)	7
Semen	6	6 (100)	15

Emergence of viral resistance has been reported based on *in vitro* sensitivity testing of CMV isolates from patients receiving CYTOVENE treatment.[6] The prevalence of resistant isolates is unknown, and there is a possibility that some patients may be infected with strains of CMV resistant to ganciclovir. Therefore, the possibility of viral resistance should be considered in patients who show poor clinical response or experience persistent viral excretion during therapy.

Pharmacokinetics

The pharmacokinetics of CYTOVENE have been evaluated in immunocompromised patients with serious CMV disease. Twenty-two such patients with normal renal function, enrolled in open-label treatment at different study centers, received 5 mg/kg doses of CYTOVENE, each dose infused intravenously over one hour. The plasma level of ganciclovir at the end of the first one hour infusion (Cmax) was 8.3 ± 4.0 μg/mL (mean $\pm$ SD) and the plasma level 11 hours after the start of infusion (Cmin) was 0.56 ± 0.66 μg/mL. The plasma half-life was 2.9 ± 1.3 hours and the systemic clearance was 3.64 ± 1.86 mL/kg/min (approximately 250 mL/min/1.73M[2]). Dose-independent kinetics were demonstrated over the range of 1.6 to 5.0 mg/kg. Multiple-dose kinetics were measured in eight patients with normal renal function who received CYTOVENE* (ganciclovir sodium) Sterile Powder, 5 mg/kg twice daily for 12-14 days. After the first dose and after multiple dosing, plasma levels of ganciclovir at the end of infusion were 7.1 μg/mL (3.1 to 14.0 μg/mL) and 9.5 μg/mL (2.7 to 24.2 μg/mL), respectively. At 7 hours after infusion, plasma levels after the first dose were 0.85 μg/mL (0.2 to 1.8 μg/mL) and were 1.2 μg/mL (0.6 to 1.8 μg/mL) after multiple dosing.

Renal excretion of unchanged drug by glomerular filtration is the major route of elimination of CYTOVENE. In patients with normal renal function, more than 90% of the administered CYTOVENE was recovered unmetabolized in the urine. The pharmacokinetic analysis in 10 patients with renal impairment showed that in 4 patients with mild impairment (creatinine clearance 50 to 79 mL/min/1.73M[2]) the systemic clearance of CYTOVENE was 128 ± 63 mL/min/1.73M[2], and the plasma half-life was 4.6 ± 1.4 hours. In 3 patients with moderate impairment (creatinine clearance 25 to 49 mL/min/1.73M[2]) the systemic clearance of CYTOVENE was 57 ± 8 mL/min/1.73M[2], and the plasma half-life was 4.4 ± 0.4 hours. In 3 patients with severe impairment (creatinine clearance less than 25 mL/min/1.73M[2]) the systemic clearance was 30 ± 13 mL/min/1.73M[2], and the plasma half-life was 10.7 ± 5.7 hours. There was positive correlation between systemic clearance of CYTOVENE and creatinine clearance (r = 0.90).

Data from 4 patients with severe renal impairment showed that hemodialysis reduced plasma drug levels by approximately 50%.

BECAUSE THE MAJOR EXCRETION PATHWAY FOR CYTOVENE* IS RENAL, DOSAGE MUST BE REDUCED ACCORDING TO CREATININE CLEARANCE. FOR DOSING INSTRUCTIONS IN RENAL IMPAIRMENT, REFER TO THE SECTION ON DOSAGE AND ADMINISTRATION.

There is limited evidence to suggest that ganciclovir crosses the blood-brain barrier. Cerebrospinal fluid (CSF) concentrations have been measured in three patients who received 2.5 mg/kg ganciclovir intravenously q8 or q12 hours. The results are shown in the following table:

CSF Concentrations[7,8]

Patient	CSF Conc. (μg/mL)	Plasma Conc. (μg/mL)	Hr after dose	CSF/Plasma Ratio
1	0.62	0.92*	5.67	.67
	0.68	2.20*	3.5	.31
	0.51	1.96*	2.75	.26
2	0.50	2.05*	0.25	.24
3	0.31	0.44	5.5	.70

*Estimation (model-predicted values)

Binding of CYTOVENE to plasma proteins is 1-2%. Drug interactions involving binding site displacement are not expected

INDICATIONS AND USAGE

CYTOVENE is indicated for the treatment of CMV retinitis in immunocompromised individuals, including patients with acquired immunodeficiency syndrome (AIDS). SAFETY AND EFFICACY OF **CYTOVENE** HAVE NOT BEEN ESTABLISHED FOR CONGENITAL OR NEONATAL CMV DISEASE; NOR FOR TREATMENT OF OTHER CMV INFECTIONS (E.G., PNEUMONITIS, COLITIS); NOR FOR USE IN NON-IMMUNOCOMPROMISED INDIVIDUALS.

The diagnosis of CMV retinitis is ophthalmologic and should be made by indirect ophthalmoscopy. Other conditions in the differential diagnosis of CMV retinitis include candidiasis, toxoplasmosis, histoplasmosis, retinal scars, and cotton wool spots, any of which may produce a retinal appearance similar to CMV. For this reason it is essential that the diagnosis of familiar be established by an ophthalmologist familiar with the retinal presentation of these conditions. The diagnosis of CMV retinitis may be supported by culture of CMV from urine, blood, throat, or other sites, but a negative CMV culture does not rule out CMV retinitis.

In most studies conducted with CYTOVENE, treatment was begun with a BID dosage regimen (5 mg/kg/dose) for the first 2 to 3 weeks, followed by a once-daily regimen (maintenance treatment) to maintain viral suppression. Patients who experienced progression of retinitis while receiving maintenance treatment were retreated with the BID regimen (see DOSAGE AND ADMINISTRATION).

In a retrospective, non-randomized, single-center analysis[9,10] of 41 patients with AIDS and CMV retinitis, treatment with CYTOVENE resulted in a significant delay in median time to first retinitis progression compared to untreated controls (71 days from diagnosis versus 29 days from diagnosis). Patients in this series received induction treatment of CYTOVENE 5 mg/kg BID for 14-21 days followed by maintenance treatment with either 5 mg/kg once per day, seven days per week or 6 mg/kg once per day, five days each week.

CONTRAINDICATIONS

CYTOVENE is contraindicated in patients with hypersensitivity to ganciclovir or acyclovir.

WARNINGS

Approximately 40% of 522 immunocompromised patients who received intravenous CYTOVENE developed granulocytopenia (neutropenia, i.e., neutrophil count less than 1,000 cells/mm[3]). CYTOVENE should, therefore, be used with caution in patients with pre-existing cytopenias, or with a history of cytopenic reactions to other drugs, chemicals or irradiation. Granulocytopenia usually occurs during the first or second week of treatment, but may occur at any time during treatment. Cell counts usually begin to recover within 3 to 7 days of discontinuing drug. *CYTOVENE should not be administered if the absolute neutrophil count is less than 500 cells/mm[3] or the platelet count is less than 25,000/mm[3].*

Thrombocytopenia (platelet count <50,000/mm[3]) was observed in approximately 20% of the same 522 patients treated with CYTOVENE. Patients with iatrogenic immunosuppression were more likely to develop thrombocytopenia than patients with AIDS (46% versus 14% of cases).

Animal data indicate that administration of CYTOVENE causes inhibition of spermatogenesis and subsequent infertility. These effects were reversible at lower doses and irreversible at higher doses (see Carcinogenesis, Mutagenesis, Impairment of Fertility section in PRECAUTIONS). Although data in humans have not been obtained regarding this effect, *it is considered probable that intravenous CYTOVENE at the recommended doses causes temporary or permanent inhibition of spermatogenesis. Animal data also indicate that suppression of fertility in females may occur.*

Because of the mutagenic potential of CYTOVENE, women of childbearing potential should be advised to use effective contraception during treatment. Similarly, male patients should be advised to practice barrier contraception during and for at least 90 days following treatment with CYTOVENE.

PRECAUTIONS

General

In clinical studies with CYTOVENE, the maximum single dose administered was 6 mg/kg by intravenous infusion over one hour. It is likely that larger doses, or more rapid infusions, would result in increased toxicity.

Administration of CYTOVENE by intravenous infusion should be accompanied by adequate hydration, since CYTOVENE is excreted by the kidneys and normal clearance depends on adequate renal function. **IF RENAL FUNCTION IS IMPAIRED, DOSAGE ADJUSTMENTS ARE REQUIRED.** Such adjustments should be based on measured or estimated creatinine clearance (see DOSAGE AND ADMINISTRATION).

Initially reconstituted CYTOVENE solutions have a high pH (pH 11). Despite further dilution in intravenous fluids, phlebitis and/or pain may occur at the site of intravenous infusion. Care must be taken to infuse solutions containing CYTOVENE only into veins with adequate blood flow to permit rapid dilution and distribution (see DOSAGE AND ADMINISTRATION).

Information for Patients

CYTOVENE® (ganciclovir sodium) Sterile Powder is not a cure for CMV retinitis, and immunocompromised patients may continue to experience progression of retinitis during or following treatment. Patients should be advised to have ophthalmologic follow-up examinations at a minimum of every six weeks while being treated with CYTOVENE. (Many patients will require more frequent follow-up.) They should be informed that the major toxicities of ganciclovir are granulocytopenia and thrombocytopenia and that dose modifications may be required, including possible discontinuation. The importance of close monitoring of blood counts while on therapy should be emphasized.

Patients with AIDS may be receiving zidovudine (Retrovir). They should be counseled that treatment with zidovudine or CYTOVENE, and especially the combination, can result in severe granulocytopenia. Therefore, it is recommended that the two drugs not be given concomitantly.

Patients should be advised that CYTOVENE has caused decreased sperm production in animals and may cause infertility in humans. Women of childbearing potential should be advised that CYTOVENE causes birth defects in animals and should not be used during pregnancy. Women of childbearing potential should be advised to use effective contraception during CYTOVENE treatment. Similarly, men should be advised to practice barrier contraception during and for at least 90 days following CYTOVENE treatment.

Patients should be advised that CYTOVENE causes tumors in animals. Although there is no information from human studies, CYTOVENE should be considered a potential carcinogen.

Laboratory Testing

Due to the frequency of granulocytopenia and thrombocytopenia in patients receiving CYTOVENE (see ADVERSE REACTIONS), it is recommended that neutrophil counts and platelet counts be performed every two days during BID dosing of CYTOVENE and at least weekly thereafter. Neutrophil counts should be monitored daily in patients in whom CYTOVENE or other nucleoside analogues have previously resulted in leukopenia, or in whom neutrophil counts are less than 1,000 cells/mm[3] at the beginning of treatment. Because dosing must be modified in patients with renal impairment, patients should have serum creatinine or creatinine clearance monitored at least once every two weeks.

Drug Interactions

It is possible that probenecid, as well as other drugs that inhibit renal tubular secretion or resorption, may reduce renal clearance of CYTOVENE. It is also possible that drugs that inhibit replication of rapidly dividing cell populations such as bone marrow, spermatogonia, and germinal layers of skin and gastrointestinal mucosa may have additive toxicity when administered concomitantly with CYTOVENE. Therefore, drugs such as dapsone, pentamidine, flucytosine, vincristine, vinblastine, adriamycin, amphotericin B, trimethoprim/sulfa combinations or other nucleoside analogues, should be considered for concomitant use with CYTOVENE only if the potential benefits are judged to outweigh the risks.

Patients with AIDS may be receiving, or have received, treatment with zidovudine (Retrovir). *Because both zidovudine and CYTOVENE can cause granulocytopenia, it is recommended that these two drugs not be given concomitantly.* Data from a small number of patients indicate that treatment with ganciclovir plus zidovudine at the recommended doses is not tolerated.

Generalized seizures have been reported in six patients who received CYTOVENE and imipenem-cilastatin. These drugs should not be used concomitantly with CYTOVENE unless the potential benefits outweigh the risks.

Carcinogenesis, Mutagenesis, Impairment of Fertility

Ganciclovir was carcinogenic in the mouse after daily oral doses of 20 and 1000 mg/kg/day. The principally affected tissues at the dose of 1000 mg/kg/day were the preputial gland in males, forestomach (nonglandular mucosa) in males and females, and reproductive tissues and liver in females. At doses of 20 mg/kg/day, slightly increased tumor incidences occurred in the preputial and harderian glands in males, forestomach in males and females, and liver in females. All ganciclovir-induced tumors were of epithelial or vascular origin, except for histiocytic sarcoma of the liver. No carcinogenic effect occurred at the dose of 1 mg/kg/day. The preputial and clitoral glands, forestomach, and harderian glands of mice do not have human counterparts. However, CYTOVENE should be considered a potential carcinogen in humans.

Ganciclovir was mutagenic in mouse lymphoma cells and caused chromosomal damage *in vitro* in human lymphocytes and *in vivo* in mice.

Ganciclovir caused decreased mating behavior, decreased fertility, and increased embryolethality in female mice at doses approximately equivalent to the recommended human dose (calculated on the basis of body surface area). Ganciclovir caused decreased fertility in male mice and hypospermatogenesis in rats and dogs at doses equivalent to or less than the recommended human dose.

Pregnancy: Category C

CYTOVENE has been shown to be teratogenic in rabbits and embryotoxic in mice when given in doses approximately equivalent to the recommended human dose (calculated on the basis of body surface area). The adverse effects observed in mice were maternal/fetal toxicity and embryolethality. In rabbits, the effects were: fetal growth retardation, embryolethality, teratogenicity, and/or maternal toxicity. Teratogenic changes included cleft palate, anophthalmia/microphthalmia, aplastic organs (kidney and pancreas), hydrocephaly, and brachygnathia.

It is therefore expected that CYTOVENE may be teratogenic and/or embryotoxic at the dose levels recommended for human use. There are no adequate and well-controlled studies in pregnant women. CYTOVENE should be used during pregnancy only if the potential benefit justifies the potential risk to the fetus.

Nursing Mothers

It is not known if CYTOVENE is excreted in human milk. Carcinogenicity and teratogenicity occurred in animals treated with ganciclovir. Because many drugs are excreted in human milk and because of the potential for serious adverse reactions from ganciclovir in nursing infants, mothers should be instructed to discontinue nursing if they are receiving CYTOVENE. The minimum interval before nursing can safely be resumed after the last dose of CYTOVENE is unknown.

Daily intravenous doses of 90 mg/kg administered to female mice prior to mating, during gestation, and during lactation caused hypoplasia of the testes and seminal vesicles in the month-old male offspring, as well as pathologic changes in the non-glandular region of the stomach.

Pediatric Use

THE USE OF *CYTOVENE* IN CHILDREN WARRANTS EXTREME CAUTION DUE TO THE PROBABILITY OF LONG-TERM CARCINOGENICITY AND REPRODUCTIVE TOXICITY. ADMINISTRATION TO CHILDREN SHOULD BE UNDERTAKEN ONLY AFTER CAREFUL EVALUATION AND ONLY IF THE POTENTIAL BENEFITS OF TREATMENT OUTWEIGH THE RISKS.

There has been very limited clinical experience in treating cytomegalovirus retinitis in patients under the age of 12 years. Two children (ages 9 and 5 years) showed improvement or stabilization of retinitis for 23 and 9 months, respectively. These children received induction treatment with 2.5 mg/kg TID followed by maintenance therapy with 6-6.5 mg/kg once per day, five to seven days per week. When retinitis progressed during once daily maintenance therapy, both children were treated with the 5 mg/kg BID regimen. Two other children (ages 2.5 and 4 years) who received similar induction regimens showed only partial or no response to treatment. Another child, a six year old with T-cell dysfunction, showed stabilization of retinitis for 3 months while receiving continuous infusions of CYTOVENE at doses of 2-5 mg/kg/24 hours. Continuous infusion treatment was discontinued due to granulocytopenia. Pharmacokinetic data have not been obtained in pediatric patients.

Adverse events reported in 120 immunocompromised children with serious CMV infections receiving ganciclovir were similar to those reported in adults. Granulocytopenia (17%) and thrombocytopenia (10%) were the most common adverse events reported.

Use in Patients with Renal Impairment

CYTOVENE should be used with caution in patients with impaired renal function because the plasma half-life and peak plasma levels of CYTOVENE will be increased due to reduced renal clearance (see DOSAGE AND ADMINISTRATION).

Data from 4 patients indicate that CYTOVENE plasma levels are reduced approximately 50% following hemodialysis.

Use in the Elderly

No studies of the efficacy or safety of CYTOVENE in elderly patients have been conducted. Since elderly individuals frequently have reduced glomerular filtration, particular attention should be paid to assessing renal function before and during CYTOVENE administration (see DOSAGE AND ADMINISTRATION).

ADVERSE REACTIONS

During clinical trials, CYTOVENE* (ganciclovir sodium) Sterile Powder was withdrawn or interrupted in approximately 32% of patients because of adverse events. In some instances treatment was restarted and the reappearance of adverse events again necessitated withdrawal or interruption.

The most frequent adverse events seen in patients treated with CYTOVENE involved the hematopoietic system. Granulocytopenia (defined as an absolute neutrophil count less than 1,000 cells/mm³) occurred in approximately 40% and thrombocytopenia (defined as a platelet count below 50,000/mm³) occurred in approximately 20% of the patients. In most cases, withdrawal of CYTOVENE resulted in increased neutrophil or platelet counts.

While granulocytopenia was generally reversible with discontinuation of treatment, some patients experienced irreversible neutropenia or died with severe bacterial or fungal infections during neutropenic episodes.

Adverse events other than granulocytopenia and thrombocytopenia were reported as "probably related", "probably not related", and "unknown" in relationship to CYTOVENE therapy. Evaluation of these reports was difficult because of the protean manifestations of the underlying disease, and because most patients received numerous concomitant medications.

Retinal detachments have been observed in patients with CMV retinitis both before and after initiation of CYTOVENE therapy. The relationship of retinal detachments to CYTOVENE therapy is unknown. Patients with CMV retinitis should have frequent ophthalmologic evaluations to monitor the status of their retinitis and detect any other retinal lesions.

Other than leukopenia and thrombocytopenia, the most frequent adverse events observed in over 5,000 patients who received CYTOVENE were anemia, fever, rash, and abnormal liver function values, each of which was reported in approximately 2% of treated patients. Adverse events that were thought to be possibly related to drug and occurred in 1% or fewer patients who received CYTOVENE were:

Body as a Whole: chills, edema, infections, malaise

Cardiovascular System: arrhythmia, hypertension, hypotension

Central Nervous System: abnormal thoughts or dreams, ataxia, coma, confusion, dizziness, headache, nervousness, paresthesia, psychosis, somnolence, tremor. (Overall, neurologic system events occurred in 5% of patients.)

Digestive System: nausea, vomiting, anorexia, diarrhea, hemorrhage, abdominal pain

Hematologic System: eosinophilia

Laboratory Abnormalities: decrease in blood glucose

Respiratory System: dyspnea

Skin and Appendages: alopecia, pruritus, urticaria

Urogenital System: hematuria, increased serum creatinine, increased blood urea nitrogen (BUN)

Injection Site: inflammation, pain, phlebitis

OVERDOSAGE

Overdosage with CYTOVENE has been reported in five patients. In three of these patients, no adverse events were observed after the overdosage. (The doses received were: 7 doses of 22 mg/kg over a 3-day period, 9 mg/kg BID for 3 days, and 2 doses of 500 mg given to a 21 month old child.)

Neutropenia was reported following overdoses in two patients: one who had a history of bone marrow suppression prior to treatment and who received CYTOVENE 5 mg/kg BID for 14 days followed by treatment with 8 mg/kg given as single daily doses for 4 days, and one patient who received a single dose of 1,675 mg (approximately 24 mg/kg). In both cases the neutropenia was reversible (17 days and 1 day, respectively), following discontinuation of CYTOVENE.

Single intravenous doses of ganciclovir given to mice and dogs caused mortality at high dosages. The median lethal acute intravenous dose of ganciclovir was 900 mg/kg in mice and between 150 and 500 mg/kg in dogs. Toxic manifestations observed in mice and dogs given very high single doses of CYTOVENE (500 mg/kg) included emesis, hypersalivation, anorexia, bloody diarrhea, inactivity, cytopenia, elevated blood urea nitrogen, elevated liver function test results, testicular atrophy and death.

Hemodialysis and hydration may be of benefit in reducing drug plasma levels in patients who receive an overdosage of CYTOVENE.

DOSAGE AND ADMINISTRATION

CAUTION – DO NOT ADMINISTER CYTOVENE BY RAPID OR BOLUS INTRAVENOUS INJECTION. THE TOXICITY OF CYTOVENE MAY BE INCREASED AS A RESULT OF EXCESSIVE PLASMA LEVELS.

CAUTION – INTRAMUSCULAR OR SUBCUTANEOUS INJECTION OF RECONSTITUTED CYTOVENE MAY RESULT IN SEVERE TISSUE IRRITATION DUE TO HIGH PH (11).

Dosage
THE RECOMMENDED DOSAGE, FREQUENCY, OR INFUSION RATES SHOULD NOT BE EXCEEDED.

Induction Treatment. The recommended initial dose of CYTOVENE for patients with normal renal function is 5 mg/kg (given intravenously at a constant rate over 1 hour) every 12 hours for 14-21 days.

Maintenance Treatment. Following induction treatment the recommended dose of CYTOVENE is 5 mg/kg given as an intravenous infusion over one hour once per day on seven days each week, or 6 mg/kg once per day on five days each week. Patients who experience progression of retinitis while receiving maintenance therapy may be retreated with the BID regimen.

Patients should have frequent hematologic monitoring throughout treatment. CYTOVENE should not be administered if the neutrophil count falls below 500 cells/mm³ or the platelet count falls below 25,000/mm³.

RENAL IMPAIRMENT
For patients with impairment of renal function, refer to the table below for recommended doses during the induction phase of treatment, and adjust the dosing interval as indicated.

Creatinine Clearance* (mL/min)	CYTOVENE Dose (mg/kg)	Dosing Interval (hours)
≥80	5.0	12
50-79	2.5	12
25-49	2.5	24
<25	1.25	24

*Creatinine clearance can be related to serum creatinine by the following formulae:

$$\text{Creatinine clearance for males} = \frac{(140 - \text{age[yrs]}) \, (\text{body wt [kg]})}{(72) \, (\text{serum creatinine [mg/dL]})}$$

Creatinine clearance for females = 0.85 × male value

The optimal maintenance dose for patients with renal impairment is not known. Physicians may elect to reduce the dose to 50% of the induction dose and monitor the patient for disease progression.

Only limited data are available on CYTOVENE® (ganciclovir sodium) Sterile Powder elimination in patients undergoing hemodialysis. Dosing for these patients should not exceed 1.25 mg/kg/24 hours. On days when hemodialysis is performed, the dose should be given shortly after the completion of the hemodialysis session, since hemodialysis has been shown to reduce plasma levels by approximately 50%. Neutrophil and platelet counts should be monitored daily.

PATIENT MONITORING

Due to the frequency of granulocytopenia and thrombocytopenia in patients receiving CYTOVENE (see ADVERSE REACTIONS), it is recommended that neutrophil counts and platelet counts be performed every two days during BID dosing of CYTOVENE and at least weekly thereafter. In patients in whom CYTOVENE or other nucleoside analogues have previously resulted in leukopenia, or in whom neutrophil counts are less than 1,000 cells/mm^3 at the beginning of treatment, neutrophil counts should be monitored daily. Because dosing must be modified in patients with renal impairment, all patients should have serum creatinine or creatinine clearance monitored at least once every two weeks.

REDUCTION OF DOSE

The most frequently reported adverse event following treatment with CYTOVENE is leukopenia/neutropenia, which occurs in approximately 40% of patients. Therefore, frequent white blood cell counts should be performed. Severe neutropenia (ANC less than 500/mm^3) or severe thrombocytopenia (platelets less than 25,000/mm^3) requires a dose interruption until evidence of marrow recovery is observed (ANC ≥ 750/mm^3).

Method of Preparation

Each 10 mL clear glass vial contains ganciclovir sodium equivalent to 500 mg of the free base form of CYTOVENE and 46 mg of sodium. The contents of the vial should be prepared for administration in the following manner:

1. Lyophilized CYTOVENE should be reconstituted by injecting 10 mL of Sterile Water for Injection, USP, into the vial.

DO NOT USE BACTERIOSTATIC WATER FOR INJECTION CONTAINING PARABENS. IT IS INCOMPATIBLE WITH CYTOVENE STERILE POWDER AND MAY CAUSE PRECIPITATION.

2. The vial should be shaken to dissolve the drug.

3. Reconstituted solution should be inspected visually for particulate matter and discoloration prior to proceeding with admixture preparation. If particulate matter or discoloration is observed, the vial should be discarded.

4. Reconstituted solution in the vial is stable at room temperature for 12 hours. It should not be refrigerated.

Admixture Preparation and Administration

Based on patient weight, the appropriate calculated dose volume should be removed from the vial (ganciclovir concentration 50 mg/mL) and added to an acceptable (see below) infusion fluid (typically 100 mL) for delivery over the course of one hour. Infusion concentrations greater than 10 mg/mL are not recommended. The following infusion fluids have been determined to be chemically and physically compatible with CYTOVENE: 0.9% Sodium Chloride, 5% Dextrose, Ringer's Injection, and Lactated Ringer's Injection, USP.

Note: Because non-bacteriostatic infusion fluid must be used with CYTOVENE, the infusion solution must be used within 24 hours of dilution to reduce the risk of bacterial contamination. The infusion solution should be refrigerated. Freezing is not recommended.

HANDLING AND DISPOSAL

Caution should be exercised in the handling and preparation of CYTOVENE solutions. CYTOVENE solutions are alkaline (pH 11). Avoid direct contact with the skin or mucous membranes. If such contact occurs, wash thoroughly with soap and water; rinse eyes thoroughly with plain water.

Because CYTOVENE shares some of the properties of anti-tumor agents (i.e., carcinogenicity and mutagenicity), consideration should be given to handling and disposal according to guidelines issued for antineoplastic drugs. Several guidelines on this subject have been published.[11-16]

There is no general agreement that all of the procedures recommended in the guidelines are necessary or appropriate.

HOW SUPPLIED

CYTOVENE® (ganciclovir sodium) Sterile Powder is supplied in 10 mL sterile vials, each containing ganciclovir sodium equivalent to 500 mg of ganciclovir, in cartons of 25 (NDC 0033-2903-48).

Store at room temperature. Avoid excessive heat, above 40°C (104°F).

CAUTION: Federal law prohibits dispensing without prescription.

REFERENCES

1. Smee D.F., Boehme R., Chernow M., et al: Intracellular metabolism and enzymatic phosphorylation of 9-(1,3-dihydroxy-2-propoxymethyl) guanine and acyclovir in herpes simplex virus-infected and uninfected cells. Biochemical Pharmacol 1985; 34:1049-1056.

2. Shanley J.D., Morningstar J., Jordan M.C.: Inhibition of murine cytomegalovirus lung infection and interstitial pneumonitis by acyclovir and 9-(1,3-dihydroxy-2-propoxymethyl) guanine. Antimicrob Agents Chemother 1985; 28: 172-175.

3. Wilson E.J., Medearis D.N. Jr., Hansen L.A., et al: 9-(1,3-dihydroxy-2-propoxymethyl) guanine prevents death but not immunity in murine cytomegalovirus-infected normal and immunosuppressed BALB/c mice. Antimicrob Agents Chemother 1987; 31:1017-1020.

4. Fong C.K.Y., Cohen S.D., McCormick S., Hsiung G.D.: Antiviral Effect of 9-(1,3-dihydroxy-2-propoxymethyl) guanine against cytomegalovirus infection in a guinea pig model. Antiviral Res 1987; 7: 11-23.

5. Buhles W.C., Mastre B.J., Tinker A.J., et al: Ganciclovir Treatment of Life-or Sight-Threatening Cytomegalovirus Infection: Experience in 314 Immunocompromised Patients. Rev Inf Dis 1988; 10:495-506.

6. Erice A., Chou S., Byron K.K., et al: Progressive disease due to ganciclovir-resistant cytomegalovirus in immunocompromised patients. N Eng J Med 1989; 320:289-293.

7. Fletcher C., Balfour H.: Evaluation of ganciclovir for cytomegalovirus disease. DICP, Ann Pharmacother 1989; 23:5-12.

8. Fletcher C., Sawchuk R., Chinnock B., et al: Human pharmacokinetics of the antiviral drug DHPG. Clin Pharmacol Ther 1986; 40: 281-286.

9. Jabs D., Enger E., Bartlett J.: Cytomegalovirus retinitis and acquired immunodeficiency syndrome. Arch Ophthalmol 1989; 107: 75-80.

10. Updated unpublished data on file with Syntex Corp.

11. Recommendations for the Safe Handling of Parenteral Antineoplastic Drugs. NIH Publication No. 83-2621. For sale by the Superintendent of Documents, U.S. Government Printing Office. Washington, D.C. 20402.

11. Recommendations for the Safe Handling of Parenteral Antineoplastic Drugs. NIH Publication No. 83-2621. For sale by the Superintendent of Documents, U.S. Government Printing Office, Washington, D.C. 20402.

12. AMA Council Report. Guidelines for Handling Parenteral Antineoplastics. *JAMA*, March 15, 1985.

13. National Study Commission on Cytotoxic Exposure-Recommendations for Handling Cytotoxic Agents. Available from Louis P. Jeffrey, Sc. D., Director of Pharmacy Services, Rhode Island Hospital, 593 Eddy Street, Providence, Rhode Island 02902.

14. Clinical Oncological Society of Australia: Guidelines and recommendations for safe handling of antineoplastic agents. *Med J Australia* 1:426-428 1983.

15. Jones R.B., et al. Safe handling of chemotherapeutic agents: A report from the Mount Sinai Medical Center, CA – *A Cancer Journal for Clinicians* Sept/Oct, 258-263 1983.

16. American Society of Hospital Pharmacists technical assistance bulletin on handling cytotoxic drugs in hospitals. *Am J Hosp Pharm* 42:131-137, 1985.

SYNTEX

Mfd. for Syntex Laboratories, Inc.
Palo Alto, CA 94304
Mfd. by Ben Venue Laboratories, Inc.
Bedford, Ohio 44146

02-2903-48-03
Revised August 1990

U.S. Patent No. 4,355,032; 4,507,305 and others.

FEMSTAT® PREFILL
(butoconazole nitrate)

Vaginal Cream 2%
Prefilled Applicator

DESCRIPTION

FEMSTAT Vaginal Cream contains butoconazole nitrate 2%, an imidazole derivative with antifungal activity. Its chemical name is (±)-1-[4-(p-Chlorophenyl)-2-[(2,6-dichlorophenyl) thio]butyl] imidazole mononitrate and it has the following chemical structure:

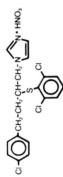

Butoconazole nitrate is a white to off-white crystalline powder with a molecular weight of 474.79. It is sparingly soluble in methanol; slightly soluble in chloroform, methylene chloride, acetone, and ethanol; very slightly soluble in ethyl acetate; and practically insoluble in water. It melts at about 159°C with decomposition.

FEMSTAT Vaginal Cream contains butoconazole nitrate 2% in a water-washable emollient cream of stearyl alcohol, propylene glycol, cetyl alcohol, sorbitan monostearate, glyceryl stearate (and) PEG-100 stearate, mineral oil, polysorbate 60, purified water, with methylparaben and propylparaben as preservatives.

CLINICAL PHARMACOLOGY

Butoconazole nitrate is an imidazole derivative that has fungicidal activity *in vitro* against *Candida, Trichophyton, Microsporum,* and *Epidermophyton.* It is also active against some gram positive bacteria. Clinically, it is highly effective against vaginal infections induced by strains of *Candida albicans, Candida tropicalis,* and other species of this genus.

The primary site of action of imidazoles appears to be the cell membrane. The permeability of the cell membrane is altered, resulting in a reduced osmotic resistance and viability of the fungus. The exact mechanism of antifungal activity of butoconazole nitrate is not known.

Following vaginal administration of butoconazole nitrate, 5.5% of the dose is absorbed on average. After vaginal administration peak plasma levels of the drug and its metabolites are attained at 24 hours and the plasma half-life is approximately 21-24 hours.

INDICATIONS AND USAGE

FEMSTAT Vaginal Cream is indicated for the local treatment of vulvovaginal mycotic infections caused by *Candida* species. The diagnosis should be confirmed by KOH smears and/or cultures.

FEMSTAT Vaginal Cream can be used in association with oral contraceptive and antibiotic therapy. FEMSTAT is effective in both non-pregnant and pregnant women but in pregnant women it should be used only during the second and third trimesters.

CONTRAINDICATIONS

FEMSTAT Vaginal Cream 2% is contraindicated in patients with a history of hypersensitivity to any of the components of the cream.

PRECAUTIONS

General:

If clinical symptoms persist, microbiological tests should be repeated to rule out other pathogens and to confirm the diagnosis.

If sensitization or irritation is reported during use, the treatment should be discontinued.

Information for the Patient:

The patient should be cautioned against premature discontinuation of the medication during menstruation or in response to relief of symptoms.

Carcinogenesis:

Long-term studies in animals have not been performed to evaluate the carcinogenic potential of this drug.

Mutagenesis:

Butoconazole nitrate was not mutagenic when tested on microbial indicator organisms.

Impairment of Fertility:

No impairment of fertility was seen in rabbits or rats administered butoconazole nitrate in oral doses up to 30 mg/kg/day or 100 mg/kg/day respectively.

Pregnancy:

Pregnancy Category C: In pregnant rats administered 6 mg/kg/day (3-7 times the human dose) butoconazole nitrate intravaginally during the period of organogenesis, there was an increase in resorption rate and decrease in litter size, but no teratogenicity. Butoconazole nitrate had no apparent adverse effect when administered orally to pregnant rats throughout organogenesis, at dose levels up to 50 mg/kg/day. Daily oral doses of 100, 300, or 750 mg/kg resulted in fetal malformations (abdominal wall defects, cleft palate), but maternal stress was evident at these higher dose levels. There were no adverse effects on litters of rabbits receiving butoconazole nitrate orally, even at maternally stressful dose levels (e.g., 150 mg/kg). There are no adequate and well-controlled studies in pregnant women during the first trimester.

Butoconazole nitrate, like other azole antimycotic agents, causes dystocia in rats when treatment is extended through parturition. However, this effect was not apparent in rabbits treated with as much as 100 mg/kg orally.

In clinical studies, over 200 pregnant patients have used butoconazole nitrate cream 2% for 3 or 6 days during the second or third trimester and the drug had no adverse effect on the course of pregnancy. Follow-up reports available on infants born to these women reveal no adverse effects or complications that were attributable to the drug.

Nursing Mothers:

It is not known whether this drug is excreted in human milk. Because many drugs are excreted in human milk, caution should be exercised when butoconazole nitrate is administered to a nursing woman.

Pediatric Use:

Safety and effectiveness in children have not been established.

ADVERSE REACTIONS

Of the 561 patients treated with butoconazole nitrate cream 2% for 3 or 6 days in controlled clinical trials, 13 (2.3%) reported complaints probably related to therapy. Vulvar/vaginal burning occurred in 2.3%, vulvar itching in 0.9%, and discharge, soreness, swelling, and itching of the fingers each occurred in 0.2%. Nine patients (1.6%) discontinued because of these complaints.

MARCH 1990

DOSAGE AND ADMINISTRATION

Non-pregnant Patients: The recommended dose is one applicatorful of cream (approximately 5 grams) intravaginally at bedtime for three days. Treatment can be extended for an additional three days if necessary.

Pregnant Patients (2nd and 3rd trimesters only): The recommended dose is one applicatorful of cream (approximately 5 grams) intravaginally at bedtime for six days.

HOW SUPPLIED

FEMSTAT® PREFILL (butoconazole nitrate) Vaginal Cream 2% is available in cartons containing 3 single dose prefilled disposable applicators (NDC 0033-2280-16).

Store at room temperature. Avoid excessive heat, above 40°C (104°F), and avoid freezing.

CAUTION: Federal law prohibits dispensing without prescription.

U.S. Patent Nos. 4,078,071 and 4,636,202

SYNTEX LABORATORIES, INC.
PALO ALTO, CA 94304

02-2280-16-03

PHYSICIAN LABELING

BREVICON® 21-DAY Tablets
(norethindrone and ethinyl estradiol)

BREVICON® 28-DAY Tablets
(norethindrone and ethinyl estradiol)

NORINYL® 1 + 35 21-DAY Tablets
(norethindrone and ethinyl estradiol)

NORINYL® 1 + 35 28-DAY Tablets
(norethindrone and ethinyl estradiol)

NORINYL® 1 + 50 21-DAY Tablets
(norethindrone and mestranol)

NORINYL® 1 + 50 28-DAY Tablets
(norethindrone and mestranol)

NOR-QD® Tablets
(norethindrone)

The inactive orange tablets in the 28-day regimens of BREVICON, NORINYL, NORINYL 1 + 35 and NORINYL 1 + 50 contain the following ingredients: FD&C Yellow No. 6, lactose, magnesium stearate, povidone, and starch.

The yellow-green TRI-NORINYL tablets contain the following inactive ingredients: D&C Green No. 5, D&C Yellow No. 10, lactose, magnesium stearate, povidone, and starch.

The blue TRI-NORINYL tablets contain the following inactive ingredients: FD&C Blue No. 1, lactose, magnesium stearate, povidone, and starch.

The inactive orange tablets in the 28-day regimen contain the following inactive ingredients: FD&C Yellow No. 6, lactose, magnesium stearate, povidone, and starch.

CLINICAL PHARMACOLOGY

Combination oral contraceptives act by suppression of gonadotrophins. Although the primary mechanism of this action is inhibition of ovulation, other alterations include changes in the cervical mucus (which increase the difficulty of sperm entry into the uterus) and the endometrium (which may reduce the likelihood of implantation).

INDICATIONS AND USAGE

Oral contraceptives are indicated for the prevention of pregnancy in women who elect to use these products as a method of contraception.

Oral contraceptives are highly effective. Table I lists the typical accidental pregnancy rates for users of combination oral contraceptives and other methods of contraception.[1] The efficacy of these contraceptive methods, except sterilization, depends upon the reliability with which they are used. Correct and consistent use of methods can result in lower failure rates.

TRI-NORINYL® 21-DAY Tablets
(norethindrone and ethinyl estradiol)

TRI-NORINYL® 28-DAY Tablets
(norethindrone and ethinyl estradiol)

ORAL CONTRACEPTIVE AGENTS

DESCRIPTION

BREVICON 21-DAY Tablets provide an oral contraceptive regimen consisting of 21 blue tablets containing norethindrone 0.5 mg and ethinyl estradiol 0.035 mg.

BREVICON 28-DAY Tablets provide a continuous oral contraceptive regimen consisting of 21 blue tablets containing norethindrone 0.5 mg and ethinyl estradiol 0.035 mg and 7 orange tablets containing inert ingredients.

NORINYL 1 + 35 21-DAY Tablets provide an oral contraceptive regimen consisting of 21 yellow-green tablets containing norethindrone 1 mg and ethinyl estradiol 0.035 mg.

NORINYL 1 + 35 28-DAY Tablets provide a continuous oral contraceptive regimen consisting of 21 yellow-green tablets containing norethindrone 1 mg and ethinyl estradiol 0.035 mg followed by 7 orange tablets containing inert ingredients.

NORINYL 1 + 50 21-DAY Tablets provide an oral contraceptive regimen consisting of 21 white tablets containing norethindrone 1 mg and mestranol 0.05 mg.

NORINYL 1 + 50 28-DAY Tablets provide a continuous oral contraceptive regimen consisting of 21 white tablets containing norethindrone 1 mg and mestranol 0.05 mg and 7 orange tablets containing inert ingredients.

NOR-QD Tablets provide a continuous oral contraceptive regimen of one yellow norethindrone 0.35 mg tablet daily.

TRI-NORINYL 21-DAY Tablets provide an oral contraceptive regimen of 7 blue tablets followed by 9 yellow-green tablets and 5 more blue tablets. Each blue tablet contains norethindrone 0.5 mg and ethinyl estradiol 0.035 mg and each yellow-green tablet contains norethindrone 1 mg and ethinyl estradiol 0.035 mg.

TRI-NORINYL 28-DAY Tablets provide a continuous oral contraceptive regimen of 7 blue tablets, 9 yellow-green tablets, 5 more blue tablets, and then 7 orange tablets. Each blue tablet contains norethindrone 0.5 mg and ethinyl estradiol 0.035 mg, each yellow-green tablet contains norethindrone 1 mg and ethinyl estradiol 0.035 mg, and each orange tablet contains inert ingredients.

Norethindrone is a potent progestational agent with the chemical name 17-Hydroxy-19-nor-17α-pregn-4-en-20-yn-3-one. Ethinyl estradiol is an estrogen with the chemical name 19-nor-17α-pregna-1,3,5(10)-trien-20-yne-3,17-diol. Mestranol is an estrogen with the chemical name 3-Methoxy-19-nor-17α-pregna-1,3,5(10)-trien-20-yn-17-ol. Their structural formulae follow:

NORETHINDRONE ETHINYL ESTRADIOL MESTRANOL

The blue BREVICON tablets contain the following inactive ingredients: FD&C Blue No. 1, lactose, magnesium stearate, povidone, and starch.

The yellow-green NORINYL 1 + 35 tablets contain the following inactive ingredients: D&C Green No. 5, D&C Yellow No. 10, lactose, magnesium stearate, povidone, and starch.

The white NORINYL 1 + 50 tablets contain the following inactive ingredients: lactose, magnesium stearate, povidone, and starch.

The yellow NOR-QD tablets contain the following inactive ingredients: D&C Yellow No. 10, FD&C Yellow No. 6, lactose, magnesium stearate, povidone, and starch.

TABLE I: LOWEST EXPECTED AND TYPICAL FAILURE RATES DURING THE FIRST YEAR OF CONTINUOUS USE OF A METHOD

% of Women Experiencing an Accidental Pregnancy in the First Year of Continuous Use

Method	Lowest Expected[a]	Typical[b]
(No Contraception)	(89)	(89)
Oral contraceptives combined	0.1	3
progestogen only	0.5	N/Ac
Diaphragm with spermicidal cream or jelly	3	18
Spermicides alone (foam, creams, jellies and vaginal suppositories)	3	21
Vaginal Sponge Nulliparous	5	18
Multiparous	>8	>28
IUD (medicated)	1	6d
Condom without spermicides	2	12
Periodic abstinence (all methods)	2–10	20
Female sterilization	0.2	0.4
Male sterilization	0.1	0.15

Adapted from J. Trussell and K. Kost, Table 11[1]

[a] The authors' best guess of the percentage of women expected to experience an accidental pregnancy among couples who initiate a method (not necessarily for the first time) and who use it consistently and correctly during the first year if they do not stop for any other reason.

[b] This term represents "typical" couples who initiate use of a method (not necessarily for the first time), who experience an accidental pregnancy during the first year if they do not stop use for any other reason. The authors derive these data largely from the National Surveys of Family Growth (NSFG), 1976 and 1982.

[c] N/A—Data not available from the NSFG, 1976 and 1982.

[d] Combined typical rate for both medicated and non-medicated IUD. The rate for medicated IUD alone is not available.

CONTRAINDICATIONS

Oral contraceptives should not be used in women who have the following conditions:

● Thrombophlebitis or thromboembolic disorders
● A past history of deep vein thrombophlebitis or thromboembolic disorders
● Cerebral vascular or coronary artery disease
● Known or suspected carcinoma of the breast
● Carcinoma of the endometrium, and known or suspected estrogen-dependent neoplasia
● Undiagnosed abnormal genital bleeding
● Cholestatic jaundice of pregnancy or jaundice with prior pill use
● Hepatic adenomas, carcinomas or benign liver tumors
● Known or suspected pregnancy

WARNINGS

Cigarette smoking increases the risk of serious cardiovascular side effects from oral contraceptive use. This risk increases with age and with heavy smoking (15 or more cigarettes per day) and is quite marked in women over 35 years of age. Women who use oral contraceptives should be strongly advised not to smoke.

The use of oral contraceptives is associated with increased risks of several serious conditions including myocardial infarction, thromboembolism, stroke, hepatic neoplasia and gallbladder disease, although the risk of serious morbidity and mortality increases significantly in the presence of other underlying risk factors such as hypertension, hyperlipidemias, hypercholesterolemia, obesity and diabetes.[2-5]

Practitioners prescribing oral contraceptives should be familiar with the following information relating to these risks.

The information contained in this package insert is principally based on studies carried out in patients who used oral contraceptives with formulations containing 0.05 mg or higher of estrogen.[6-11] The effects of long-term use with lower dose formulations of both estrogens and progestogens remain to be determined.

Throughout this labeling, epidemiological studies reported are of two types: retrospective or case control studies and prospective or cohort studies. Case control studies provide a measure of the relative risk of a disease. Relative risk, the *ratio* of the incidence of a disease among oral contraceptive users to that among non-users, cannot be assessed directly from case control studies, but the odds ratio obtained is a measure of relative risk. The relative risk does not provide information on the actual clinical occurrence of a disease. Cohort studies provide not only a measure of the relative risk but a measure of attributable risk, which is the *difference* in the incidence of disease between oral contraceptive users and non-users. The attributable risk does provide information about the actual occurrence of a disease in the population.[12,13]

1. THROMBOEMBOLIC DISORDERS AND OTHER VASCULAR PROBLEMS

a. Myocardial Infarction

An increased risk of myocardial infarction has been attributed to oral contraceptive use. This risk is primarily in smokers or women with other underlying risk factors for coronary artery disease such as hypertension, hypercholesterolemia, morbid obesity and diabetes.[2,5,13] The relative risk of heart attack for current oral contraceptive users has been estimated to be 2 to 6.[2,14-19] The risk is very low under the age of 30. However, there is the possibility of a risk of cardiovascular disease even in very young women who take oral contraceptives.

Smoking in combination with oral contraceptive use has been shown to contribute substantially to the incidence of myocardial infarctions in women 35 or older, with smoking accounting for the majority of excess cases.[20]

Mortality rates associated with circulatory disease have been shown to increase substantially in smokers over the age of 35 and non-smokers over the age of 40 among women who use oral contraceptives (see Table II).[16]

TABLE II: CIRCULATORY DISEASE MORTALITY RATES PER 100,000 WOMAN YEARS BY AGE, SMOKING STATUS AND ORAL CONTRACEPTIVE USE

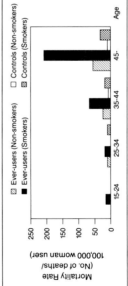

Mortality Rate (No. of deaths)/100,000 woman user)

Legend: Ever-users (Smokers) ; Ever-users (Non-smokers) ; Controls (Non-smokers) ; Controls (Smokers)

Age groups: 15-24, 25-34, 35-44, 45-

Adapted from P.M. Layde and V. Beral, Table V[16]

b. Thromboembolism

An increased risk of thromboembolic and thrombotic disease associated with the use of oral contraceptives is well established. Case control studies have found the relative risk of users compared to non-users to be 3 for the first episode of superficial venous thrombosis, 4 to 11 for deep vein thrombosis or pulmonary embolism, and 1.5 to 6 for women with predisposing conditions for venous thromboembolic disease.[12,13, 26-31] One cohort study has shown an increased risk of thromboembolism to be somewhat lower, about 3 for new

---

Because of these changes in practice and, also, because of some limited new data which suggest that the risk of cardiovascular disease with the use of oral contraceptives may now be less than previously observed,[78, 79] the Fertility and Maternal Health Drugs Advisory Committee was asked to review the topic in 1989. The Committee concluded that although cardiovascular disease risks may be increased with oral contraceptive use after age 40 in healthy non-smoking women (even with the newer low-dose formulations), there are greater potential health risks associated with pregnancy in older women and with the alternative surgical and medical procedures which may be necessary if such women do not have access to effective and acceptable means of contraception.

Therefore, the Committee recommended that the benefits of oral contraceptive use by healthy non-smoking women over 40 may outweigh the possible risks. Of course, older women, as all women who take oral contraceptives, should take the lowest possible dose formulation that is effective.[80]

TABLE III: ESTIMATED ANNUAL NUMBER OF BIRTH-RELATED OR METHOD-RELATED DEATHS ASSOCIATED WITH CONTROL OF FERTILITY PER 100,000 NONSTERILE WOMEN, BY FERTILITY CONTROL METHOD ACCORDING TO AGE

Method of control and outcome	15-19	20-24	25-29	30-34	35-39	40-44
No fertility control methods*	7.0	7.4	9.1	14.8	25.7	28.2
Oral contraceptives non-smoker**	0.3	0.5	0.9	1.9	13.8	31.6
Oral contraceptives smoker**	2.2	3.4	6.6	13.5	51.1	117.2
IUD**	0.8	0.8	1.0	1.0	1.4	1.4
Condom*	1.1	1.6	0.7	0.2	0.3	0.4
Diaphragm/Spermicide*	1.9	1.2	1.2	1.3	2.2	2.8
Periodic abstinence*	2.5	1.6	1.6	1.7	2.9	3.6

*Deaths are birth-related
**Deaths are method-related

Estimates adapted from H.W. Ory, Table 3[41]

3. CARCINOMA OF THE BREAST AND REPRODUCTIVE ORGANS

Numerous epidemiological studies have been performed on the incidence of breast, endometrial, ovarian and cervical cancer in women using oral contraceptives. The evidence in the literature suggests that use of oral contraceptives is not associated with an increase in the risk of developing breast cancer, regardless of the age and parity of first use or with most of the marketed brands and doses.[42, 43] The Cancer and Steroid Hormone study also showed no latent effect on the risk of breast cancer for at least a decade following long-term use.[43] A few studies have shown a slightly increased relative risk of developing breast cancer,[44-47] although the methodology of these studies, which included differences in examination of users and non-users and differences in age at start of use, has been questioned.[47-49] Some studies have reported an increased relative risk of developing breast cancer, particularly at a younger age. This increased relative risk appears to be related to duration of use.[81, 82]

Some studies suggest that oral contraceptive use has been associated with an increase in the risk of cervical intraepithelial neoplasia in some populations of women.[50-53] However, there continues to be controversy about the extent to which such findings may be due to differences in sexual behavior and other factors.

In spite of many studies of the relationship between oral contraceptive use and breast or cervical cancers, a cause and effect relationship has not been established.

4. HEPATIC NEOPLASIA

Benign hepatic adenomas are associated with oral contraceptive use although the incidence of benign tumors is rare in the United States. Indirect calculations have estimated the attributable risk to be in the range of 3.3 cases per 100,000 for users, a risk that increases after 4 or more years of use.[54] Rupture of rare, benign, hepatic adenomas may cause death through intra-abdominal hemorrhage.[55-56]

Studies in the United States and Britain have shown an increased risk of developing hepatocellular carcinoma in long-term (> 8 years) oral contraceptive users.[57-59] How-

cases (subjects with no past history of venous thrombosis or varicose veins) and about 4.5 for new cases requiring hospitalization.[32] The risk of thromboembolic disease due to oral contraceptives is not related to length of use and disappears after pill use is stopped.[12]

A 2- to 6-fold increase in relative risk of post-operative thromboembolic complications has been reported with the use of oral contraceptives.[18] If feasible, oral contraceptives should be discontinued at least 4 weeks prior to and for 2 weeks after elective surgery and during and following prolonged immobilization. Since the immediate postpartum period also is associated with an increased risk of thromboembolism, oral contraceptives should be started no earlier than 4 to 6 weeks after delivery in women who elect not to breast feed.[33]

c. Cerebrovascular diseases

An increase in both the relative and attributable risks of cerebrovascular events (thrombotic and hemorrhagic strokes) has been shown in users of oral contraceptives. In general, the risk is greatest among older (>35 years), hypertensive women who also smoke. Hypertension was found to be a risk factor for both users and non-users for both types of strokes while smoking interacted to increase the risk for hemorrhagic strokes.[34]

In a large study, the relative risk of thrombotic strokes has been shown to range from 3 for normotensive users to 14 for users with severe hypertension.[35] The relative risk of hemorrhagic stroke is reported to be 1.2 for non-smokers who used oral contraceptives, 2.6 for smokers who did not use oral contraceptives, 7.6 for smokers who used oral contraceptives, 1.8 for normotensive users and 25.7 for users with severe hypertension.[35] The attributable risk also is greater in women 35 or older and among smokers.[13]

d. Dose-related risk of vascular disease from oral contraceptives

A positive association has been observed between the amount of estrogen and progestogen in oral contraceptives and the risk of vascular disease.[36-38] A decline in serum high density lipoproteins (HDL) has been reported with some progestational agents.[22-24] A decline in serum high density lipoproteins has been associated with an increased incidence of ischemic heart disease.[39] Because estrogens increase HDL cholesterol, the net effect of an oral contraceptive depends on a balance achieved between doses of estrogen and progestogen and the nature and absolute amount of progestogens used in the contraceptives. The amount of both hormones should be considered in the choice of an oral contraceptive.[37]

Minimizing exposure to estrogen and progestogen is in keeping with good principles of therapeutics. For any particular estrogen/progestogen combination, the dosage regimen prescribed should be one which contains the least amount of estrogen and progestogen that is compatible with a low failure rate and the needs of the individual patient. New acceptors of oral contraceptive agents should be started on preparations containing the lowest estrogen content that produces satisfactory results for the individual.

e. Persistence of risk of vascular disease

There are three studies which have shown persistence of risk of vascular disease for ever-users of oral contraceptives.[17, 34, 40] In a study in the United States, the risk of developing myocardial infarction after discontinuing oral contraceptives persists for at least 9 years for women 40-49 years who had used oral contraceptives for 5 or more years, but this increased risk was not demonstrated in other age groups.[17] In another study in Great Britain, the risk of developing cerebrovascular disease persisted for at least 6 years after discontinuation of oral contraceptives, although excess risk was very small.[40] Subarachnoid hemorrhage also has a significantly increased relative risk after termination of use of oral contraceptives.[34] However, these studies were performed with oral contraceptive formulations containing 0.05 mg or higher of estrogen.

2. ESTIMATES OF MORTALITY FROM CONTRACEPTIVE USE

One study gathered data from a variety of sources which have estimated the mortality rates associated with different methods of contraception at different ages (see Table III).[41] These estimates include the combined risk of death associated with contraceptive methods plus the risk attributable to pregnancy in the event of method failure. Each method of contraception has its specific benefits and risks. The study concluded that with the exception of oral contraceptive users 35 and older who smoke and 40 and older who do not smoke, mortality associated with all methods of birth control is low and below that associated with childbirth. The observation of a possible increase in risk of mortality with age for oral contraceptive users is based on data gathered in the 1970's—but not reported in the U.S. until 1983.[16, 41] However, current clinical practice involves the use of lower estrogen dose formulations combined with careful restriction of oral contraceptive use to women who do not have the various risk factors listed in this labeling.

ever, these cancers are extremely rare in the United States and the attributable risk (the excess incidence) of liver cancers in oral contraceptive users is less than 1 per 1,000,000 users.

5. OCULAR LESIONS

There have been clinical case reports of retinal thrombosis associated with the use of oral contraceptives. Oral contraceptives should be discontinued if there is unexplained partial or complete loss of vision; onset of proptosis or diplopia; papilledema; or retinal vascular lesions. Appropriate diagnostic and therapeutic measures should be undertaken immediately.

6. ORAL CONTRACEPTIVE USE BEFORE OR DURING EARLY PREGNANCY

Extensive epidemiological studies have revealed no increased risk of birth defects in women who have used oral contraceptives prior to pregnancy.[60-62] More recent studies do not suggest a teratogenic effect, particularly insofar as cardiac anomalies and limb reduction defects are concerned, when taken inadvertently during early pregnancy.[60, 61, 63, 64]

The administration of oral contraceptives to induce withdrawal bleeding should not be used as a test for pregnancy. Oral contraceptives should not be used during pregnancy to treat threatened or habitual abortion.

It is recommended that for any patient who has missed 2 consecutive periods, pregnancy should be ruled out before continuing oral contraceptive use. If the patient has not adhered to the prescribed schedule, the possibility of pregnancy should be considered at the time of the first missed period. Oral contraceptive use should be discontinued if pregnancy is confirmed.

7. GALLBLADDER DISEASE

Earlier studies have reported an increased lifetime relative risk of gallbladder surgery in users of oral contraceptives and estrogens.[65-66] More recent studies, however, have shown that the relative risk of developing gallbladder disease among oral contraceptive users may be minimal.[67] The recent findings of minimal risk may be related to the use of oral contraceptive formulations containing lower hormonal doses of estrogens and progestogens.[68]

8. CARBOHYDRATE AND LIPID METABOLIC EFFECTS

Oral contraceptives have been shown to impair oral glucose tolerance.[69] Oral contraceptives containing greater than 0.075 mg of estrogen cause glucose intolerance with impaired insulin secretion, while lower doses of estrogen may produce less glucose intolerance.[70] Progestogens increase insulin secretion and create insulin resistance, this effect varying with different progestational agents.[25, 71] However, in the non-diabetic woman, oral contraceptives appear to have no effect on fasting blood glucose.[69] Because of these demonstrated effects, prediabetic and diabetic women should be carefully observed while taking oral contraceptives.

Some women may develop persistent hypertriglyceridemia while on the pill.[72] As discussed earlier (see WARNINGS, sections 1a. and 1d.), changes in serum triglycerides and lipoprotein levels have been reported in oral contraceptive users.[23]

9. ELEVATED BLOOD PRESSURE

An increase in blood pressure has been reported in women taking oral contraceptives. The incidence of risk also was reported to increase with continued use and among older women.[66] Data from the Royal College of General Practitioners and subsequent randomized trials have shown that the incidence of hypertension increases with increasing concentrations of progestogens.

Women with a history of hypertension or hypertension-related diseases or renal disease should be encouraged to use another method of contraception. If women elect to use oral contraceptives, they should be monitored closely and if significant elevation of blood pressure occurs oral contraceptives should be discontinued. For most women, elevated blood pressure will return to normal after stopping oral contraceptives and there is no difference in the occurrence of hypertension among ever- and never-users.[73-75]

10. HEADACHE

The onset or exacerbation of migraine or development of headache with a new pattern which is recurrent, persistent or severe requires discontinuation of oral contraceptives and evaluation of the cause.

11. BLEEDING IRREGULARITIES

Breakthrough bleeding and spotting are sometimes encountered in patients on oral contraceptives, especially during the first 3 months of use. Non-hormonal causes should be considered and adequate diagnostic measures taken to rule out malignancy or pregnancy in the event of breakthrough bleeding, as in the case of any abnormal vaginal bleeding. If pathology has been excluded, time or a change to another formula-

Effects on menses:
• Increased menstrual cycle regularity
• Decreased blood loss and decreased incidence of iron deficiency anemia
• Decreased incidence of dysmenorrhea

Effects related to inhibition of ovulation:
• Decreased incidence of functional ovarian cysts
• Decreased incidence of ectopic pregnancies

Effects from long-term use:
• Decreased incidence of fibroadenomas and fibrocystic disease of the breast
• Decreased incidence of acute pelvic inflammatory disease
• Decreased incidence of endometrial cancer
• Decreased incidence of ovarian cancer

DOSAGE AND ADMINISTRATION

To achieve maximum contraceptive effectiveness, oral contraceptives must be taken exactly as described and at intervals not exceeding 24 hours.

BREVICON, NORINYL 1 + 35, NORINYL 1 + 50

21-Day Schedule: For the initial cycle of therapy the first tablet may be taken on Day 5 of the menstrual cycle, counting the first day of menstrual flow as Day 1 (DAY 5 START), or the first tablet may be taken on the first Sunday after menstrual flow begins (SUNDAY START). For SUNDAY START when menstrual flow begins on Sunday, the first tablet is taken on that day. With either DAY 5 START or SUNDAY START, 1 tablet is taken each day at the same time for 21 days. No tablets are taken for 7 days, then, whether bleeding has stopped or not, a new course is started of 1 tablet a day for 21 days. This institutes a 3 weeks on, 1 week off dosage regimen.

28-Day Schedule: For the initial cycle of therapy the first tablet may be taken on Day 5 of the menstrual cycle, counting the first day of menstrual flow as Day 1 (DAY 5 START), or the first tablet may be taken on the first Sunday after menstrual flow begins (SUNDAY START). For SUNDAY START when menstrual flow begins on Sunday, the first tablet is taken on that day. With either DAY 5 START or SUNDAY START, 1 white, yellow-green, or blue tablet is taken each day at the same time for 21 days. Then the orange tablets are taken, 1 each evening at bedtime for 7 days. After all 28 tablets have been taken, whether bleeding has stopped or not, repeat the same dosage schedule beginning on the following day.

NOR-QD (norethindrone) is administered as a continuous daily dosage regimen starting on the first day of menstruation, i.e., 1 tablet each day, every day. Tablets should be taken at the same time each day and continued daily, without interruption, whether bleeding occurs or not. This is especially important for patients new to progestogen-only oral contraception. The patient should be advised that if prolonged bleeding occurs, she should consult her physician.

TRI-NORINYL

21-Day Regimen Dosage Schedule: The first blue tablet is taken on the first Sunday after menstrual flow begins. If menstrual flow begins on Sunday, the first blue tablet is taken on that day. One blue tablet is taken each evening at bedtime for 7 days, then one yellow-green tablet each evening for 9 days, then one blue tablet each evening for 5 days. No tablets are taken for 7 days; then, whether bleeding has stopped or not, a new sequence of tablets is started for 21 days. This institutes a three weeks on, one week off dosage regimen.

28-Day Regimen Dosage Schedule: The first blue tablet is taken on the first Sunday after menstrual flow begins. If menstrual flow begins on Sunday, the first blue tablet is taken on that day. One blue tablet is taken each evening at bedtime for 7 days, then one yellow-green tablet each evening for 9 days, then one blue tablet each evening for 5 days, then one orange (inert) tablet each evening for 7 days. After all 28 tablets have been taken, whether bleeding has stopped or not, the same dosage schedule is repeated beginning on the following day.

INSTRUCTIONS TO PATIENTS

• To achieve maximum contraceptive effectiveness, the oral contraceptive pill must be taken exactly as directed and at intervals not exceeding 24 hours.
• Important: Women should be instructed to use an additional method of protection until after the first 7 days of administration in the initial cycle.
• Due to the normally increased risk of thromboembolism occurring postpartum, women should be instructed not to initiate treatment with oral contraceptives earlier than 4 weeks after a full-term delivery. If pregnancy is terminated in the first 12 weeks, the patient should be instructed to start oral contraceptives immediately or within 7 days. If pregnancy is terminated after 12 weeks, the patient should be instructed to start oral contraceptives after 2 weeks.[33, 77]
• If spotting or breakthrough bleeding should occur, the patient should continue the

---

tion may solve the problem. In the event of amenorrhea, pregnancy should be ruled out.

Some women may encounter post-pill amenorrhea or oligomenorrhea, especially when such a condition was pre-existent.

PRECAUTIONS

1. PHYSICAL EXAMINATION AND FOLLOW-UP

A complete medical history and physical examination should be taken prior to the initiation or reinstitution of oral contraceptives and at least annually during use of oral contraceptives. These physical examinations should include special reference to blood pressure, breasts, abdomen and pelvic organs, including cervical cytology and relevant laboratory tests. In case of undiagnosed, persistent or recurrent abnormal vaginal bleeding, appropriate diagnostic measures should be conducted to rule out malignancy. Women with a strong family history of breast cancer or who have breast nodules should be monitored with particular care.

2. LIPID DISORDERS

Women who are being treated for hyperlipidemias should be followed closely if they elect to use oral contraceptives. Some progestogens may elevate LDL levels and may render the control of hyperlipidemias more difficult.

3. LIVER FUNCTION

If jaundice develops in any woman receiving oral contraceptives the medication should be discontinued. Steroid hormones may be poorly metabolized in patients with impaired liver function.

4. FLUID RETENTION

Oral contraceptives may cause some degree of fluid retention. They should be prescribed with caution, and only with careful monitoring, in patients with conditions which might be aggravated by fluid retention.

5. EMOTIONAL DISORDERS

Women with a history of depression should be carefully observed and the drug discontinued if depression recurs to a serious degree.

6. CONTACT LENSES

Contact lens wearers who develop visual changes or changes in lens tolerance should be assessed by an ophthalmologist.

7. DRUG INTERACTIONS

Reduced efficacy and increased incidence of breakthrough bleeding and menstrual irregularities have been associated with concomitant use of rifampin. A similar association though less marked, has been suggested with barbiturates, phenylbutazone, phenytoin sodium, and possibly with griseofulvin, ampicillin and tetracyclines.[76]

8. INTERACTIONS WITH LABORATORY TESTS

Certain endocrine and liver function tests and blood components may be affected by oral contraceptives:

a. Increased prothrombin and factors VII, VIII, IX, and X; decreased antithrombin 3; increased norepinephrine-induced platelet aggregability.

b. Increased thyroid binding globulin (TBG) leading to increased circulating total thyroid hormone, as measured by protein-bound iodine (PBI), T4 by column or by radioimmunoassay. Free T3 resin uptake is decreased, reflecting the elevated TBG. Free T4 concentration is unaltered.

c. Other binding proteins may be elevated in serum.

d. Sex steroid binding globulins are increased and result in elevated levels of total circulating sex steroids and corticoids; however, free or biologically active levels remain unchanged.

e. Triglycerides may be increased.

f. Glucose tolerance may be decreased.

g. Serum folate levels may be depressed by oral contraceptive therapy. This may be of clinical significance if a woman becomes pregnant shortly after discontinuing oral contraceptives.

9. CARCINOGENESIS

See WARNINGS section.

10. PREGNANCY

Pregnancy Category X. See CONTRAINDICATIONS and WARNINGS sections.

11. NURSING MOTHERS

Small amounts of oral contraceptive steroids have been identified in the milk of nursing mothers and a few adverse effects on the child have been reported, including jaundice and breast enlargement. In addition, oral contraceptives given in the postpartum period may interfere with lactation by decreasing the quantity and quality of breast milk. If possible, the nursing mother should be advised not to use oral contraceptives but to use other forms of contraception until she has completely weaned her child.

See **PATIENT LABELING.**

INFORMATION FOR THE PATIENT

ADVERSE REACTIONS

An increased risk of the following serious adverse reactions has been associated with the use of oral contraceptives (see **WARNINGS** section):

- Thrombophlebitis
- Arterial thromboembolism
- Pulmonary embolism
- Myocardial infarction
- Cerebral hemorrhage
- Cerebral thrombosis
- Hypertension
- Gallbladder disease
- Hepatic adenomas, carcinomas or benign liver tumors

There is evidence of an association between the following conditions and the use of oral contraceptives, although additional confirmatory studies are needed:

- Mesenteric thrombosis
- Retinal thrombosis

The following adverse reactions have been reported in patients receiving oral contraceptives and are believed to be drug-related:

- Nausea
- Vomiting
- Gastrointestinal symptoms (such as abdominal cramps and bloating)
- Breakthrough bleeding
- Spotting
- Change in menstrual flow
- Amenorrhea
- Temporary infertility after discontinuation of treatment
- Edema
- Melasma which may persist
- Breast changes: tenderness, enlargement, secretion
- Change in weight (increase or decrease)
- Change in cervical erosion and secretion
- Diminution in lactation when given immediately postpartum
- Cholestatic jaundice
- Migraine
- Rash (allergic)
- Mental depression
- Reduced tolerance to carbohydrates
- Vaginal candidiasis
- Change in corneal curvature (steepening)
- Intolerance to contact lenses

The following adverse reactions have been reported in users of oral contraceptives and the association has been neither confirmed nor refuted:

- Pre-menstrual syndrome
- Cataracts
- Changes in appetite
- Cystitis-like syndrome
- Headache
- Nervousness
- Dizziness
- Hirsutism
- Loss of scalp hair
- Erythema multiforme
- Erythema nodosum
- Hemorrhagic eruption
- Vaginitis
- Porphyria
- Impaired renal function
- Hemolytic uremic syndrome
- Budd-Chiari syndrome
- Acne
- Changes in libido
- Colitis

OVERDOSAGE

Serious ill effects have not been reported following acute ingestion of large doses of oral contraceptives by young children. Overdosage may cause nausea, and withdrawal bleeding may occur in females.

NON-CONTRACEPTIVE HEALTH BENEFITS

The following non-contraceptive health benefits related to the use of oral contraceptives are supported by epidemiological studies which largely utilized oral contraceptive formulations containing estrogen doses exceeding 0.035 mg of ethinyl estradiol or 0.05 mg of mestranol.[6-11]

---

medication according to the schedule. Should spotting or breakthrough bleeding persist, the patient should notify her physician.

- If the patient misses 1 pill, she should be instructed to take it as soon as she remembers and then take the next pill at the regular time. If the patient has missed 2 pills, she should take 1 of the missed pills as soon as she remembers and discard the other missed pill. She should then take her next pill at the regular time. Furthermore, she should use an additional method of contraception in addition to taking her pills for the remainder of the cycle.
- If the patient has missed more than 2 pills, she should be instructed to discontinue taking the remaining pills and to use an alternative method of contraception until pregnancy has been ruled out.
- Use of oral contraceptives in the event of a missed menstrual period:
  1. If the patient has not adhered to the prescribed dosage regimen, the possibility of pregnancy should be considered after the first missed period and oral contraceptives should be withheld until pregnancy has been ruled out.
  2. If the patient has adhered to the prescribed regimen and misses 2 consecutive periods, pregnancy should be ruled out before continuing the contraceptive regimen.

HOW SUPPLIED

BREVICON® 21-DAY Tablets and BREVICON® 28-DAY Tablets (norethindrone and ethinyl estradiol), NORINYL® 1 + 35 21-DAY Tablets and NORINYL® 1 + 35 28-DAY Tablets (norethindrone and ethinyl estradiol), and NORINYL® 1 + 50 21-DAY Tablets and NORINYL® 1 + 50 28-DAY Tablets (norethindrone and mestranol) are available in 21-pill or 28-pill blister cards with a WALLETTE® pill dispenser. Each 28-pill card contains 7 orange inert pills.

NOR-QD® (norethindrone) tablets are available in 42-tablet dispensers.

TRI-NORINYL® 21-DAY Tablets and TRI-NORINYL® 28-DAY Tablets (norethindrone and ethinyl estradiol) are available in 21-pill or 28-pill blister cards with a WALLETTE® pill dispenser. Each 28-pill card contains 7 orange inert pills.

CAUTION: Federal law prohibits dispensing without prescription.

REFERENCES

1. Trussell, J., et al.: *Stud Fam Plann* 18(5):237–283, 1987. **2.** Mann, J., et al.: *Br Med J* 2(5956):241–245, 1975. **3.** Knopp, R.H.: *J Reprod Med* 31(9):913–921, 1986. **4.** Mann, J.I., et al.: *Br Med J* 2:445–447, 1976. **5.** Ory, H.: *JAMA* 237:2619–2622, 1977. **6.** The Cancer and Steroid Hormone Study of the Centers for Disease Control: *JAMA* 249(2):1596–1599, 1983. **7.** The Cancer and Steroid Hormone Study of the Centers for Disease Control: *JAMA* 257(6):796–800, 1987. **8.** Ory, H.W.: *JAMA* 228(1):68–69, 1974. **9.** Ory, H.W., et al.: *N Engl J Med* 294:419–422, 1976. **10.** Ory, H.W.: *Fam Plann Perspect* 14:182–184, 1982. **11.** Ory, H.W., et al.: *Making Choices*, New York, The Alan Guttmacher Institute, 1983. **12.** Stadel, B.: *N Engl J Med* 305(11):612–618, 1981. **13.** Stadel, B.: *N Engl J Med* 305(12):672–677, 1981. **14.** Adam, S., et al.: *Br J Obstet Gynaecol* 88:838–845, 1981. **15.** Mann, J., et al.: *Br Med J* 2(5965):245–248, 1975. **16.** Royal College of General Practitioners' Oral Contraceptive Study: *Lancet* 1:541–546, 1981. **17.** Slone, D., et al.: *N Engl J Med* 305(8):420–424, 1981. **18.** Vessey, M.P.: *Br J Fam Plann* 6 (supplement): 1–12, 1980. **19.** Russell-Briefel, R., et al.: *Prev Med* 15:352–362, 1986. **20.** Goldbaum, G., et al.: *JAMA* 258(10):1339–1342, 1987. **21.** LaRosa, J.C.: *J Reprod Med* 31(9):906–912, 1986. **22.** Krauss, R.M., et al.: *Am J Obstet Gynecol* 145:446–452, 1983. **23.** Wahl, P., et al.: *N Engl J Med* 308(15):862–867, 1983. **24.** Wynn, V., et al.: *Am J Obstet Gynecol* 142(6):766–771, 1982. **25.** Wynn, V., et al.: *J Reprod Med* 31(9):892–897, 1986. **26.** Inman, W.H., et al.: *Br Med J* 2(5599):193–199, 1968. **27.** Maguire, M.G., et al.: *Am J Epidemiol* 110(2):188–195, 1979. **28.** Petitti, D., et al.: *JAMA* 242(11):1150–1154, 1979. **29.** Vessey, M.P., et al.: *Br Med J* 2(5599):199–205, 1968. **30.** Vessey, M.P., et al.: *Br Med J* 2(5658):651–657, 1969. **31.** Porter, J.B., et al.: *Obstet Gynecol* 59(3):299–302, 1982. **32.** Vessey, M.P. et al.: *J Biosoc Sci* 8:373–427, 1976. **33.** Mishell, D.R., et al.: *Reproductive Endocrinology*, Philadelphia, F.A. Davis Co., 1979. **34.** Petitti, D.B., et al.: *Lancet* 2:234–236, 1978. **35.** Collaborative Group for the Study of Stroke in Young Women: *JAMA* 231(7):718–722, 1975. **36.** Inman, W.H., et al.: *Br Med J* 2:203–209, 1970. **37.** Meade, T.W., et al.: *Br Med J* 280(6224):1157–1161, 1980. **38.** Kay, C.R.: *Am J Obstet Gynecol* 142(6):762–765, 1982. **39.** Gordon, T., et al.: *Am J Med* 62:707–714, 1977. **40.** Royal College of General Practitioners' Oral Contraception Study: *J Coll Gen Pract* 33:75–82, 1983. **41.** Ory, H.W.: *Fam Plann Perspect* 15(2):57–63, 1983. **42.** Paul, C., et al.: *Br Med J* 293:723–725, 1986. **43.** The Cancer and Steroid Hormone Study of the Centers for Disease Control: *N Engl J Med* 315(7):405–411, 1986. **44.** Pike, M.C., et al.: *Lancet* 2:926–929, 1983. **45.** Miller, D.R., et al.: *Obstet Gynecol* 68:863–868, 1986. **46.** Olsson, H., et al.: *Lancet* 2:748–749, 1985. **47.** McPherson, K., et al.: *Br J Cancer* 56:653–660, 1987. **48.** Huggins, G.R., et al.: *Fertil Steril* 47(5):733–761, 1987. **49.** McPherson, K., et al.: *Br Med J* 293:709–710, 1986. **50.** Ory, H., et al.: *Am J Obstet Gynecol* 124(6):573–577, 1976. **51.** Vessey, M.P., et al.: *Lancet* 2:930, 1983. **52.** Brinton, L.A., et al.: *Int J Cancer* 38:339–344, 1986. **53.** WHO Collaborative Study of Neoplasia and Steroid Contraceptives: *Br**

Med J 290:961–965, 1985. **54.** Rooks, J.B., et al.: JAMA 242(7):644–648, 1979. **55.** Bein, N.N., et al.: Br J Surg 64:433–435, 1977. **56.** Klatskin, G.: Gastroenterology 73:386–394, 1977. **57.** Henderson, B.E., et al.: Br J Cancer 48:437–440, 1983. **58.** Neuberger J., et al.: Br Med J 292:1355–1357, 1986. **59.** Forman, D., et al.: Br Med J 292:1357–1361, 1986. **60.** Harlap, S., et al.: Obstet Gynecol 55(4):447–452, 1980. **61.** Savolainen, E., et al.: Am J Obstet Gynecol 140(5):521–524, 1981. **62.** Janerich, D.T., et al.: Am J Epidemiol 112(1):73–79, 1980. **63.** Ferencz, C., et al.: Teratology 21:225–239, 1980. **64.** Rothman, K.J., et al.: Am J Epidemiol 109(4):433–439, 1979. **65.** Boston Collaborative Drug Surveillance Program: Lancet 1:1399–1404, 1973. **66.** Royal College of General Practitioners: Oral contraceptives and health, New York, Pittman, 1974. **67.** Rome Group for the Epidemiology and Prevention of Cholelithiasis: Am J Epidemiol 119(5):796–805, 1984. **68.** Strom, B.L., et al.: Clin Pharmacol Ther 39(3):335–341, 1986. **69.** Perlman, J.A., et al.: J Chronic Dis 38(10):857–864, 1985. **70.** Wynn, V., et al.: Lancet 1:1045–1049, 1979. **71.** Wynn, V.: Progesterone and Progestin, New York, Raven Press, 1983. **72.** Wynn, V., et al.: Lancet 2:720–723, 1966. **73.** Fisch, I.R., et al.: JAMA 237(23):2499–2503, 1977. **74.** Laragh, J.H.: Am J Obstet Gynecol 126(1):141–147, 1976. **75.** Ramcharan, S., et al.: Pharmacology of Steroid Contraceptive Drugs, New York, Raven Press, 1977. **76.** Stockley, I.: Pharm J 216:140–143, 1976. **77.** Dickey, R: Managing Contraceptive Pill Patients, Oklahoma, Creative Infomatics Inc. 1984. **78.** Porter J.B., Hunter J., Jick H., et al: Obstet Gynecol 1985;66:1–4. **79.** Porter J.B., Hershel J., Walker A.M.: Obstet Gynecol 1987:70:29–32. **80.** Fertility and Maternal Health Drugs Advisory Committee, F.D.A., October, 1989. **81.** Schiesselman J., Stadel B.V., Murray F., Lai S.: Breast cancer in relation to early use of oral contraceptives. JAMA 1988;259:1828–1833. **82.** Hennekens C.H., Speizer FE., Lipnick R.J., Rosner B., Bain C., Belanger C., Stampfer M.J., Willett W., Peto R.: A case-control study of oral contraceptive use and breast cancer. JNCI 1984:72:39–42.

DETAILED PATIENT LABELING

INTRODUCTION

Any woman who considers using oral contraceptives ("birth control pills" or "the pill") should understand the benefits and risks of using this form of birth control. This leaflet will give you much of the information you will need to make this decision and also will help you determine if you are at risk of developing any of the serious side effects of the pill. It will tell you how to use the pill properly so that it will be as effective as possible. However, this leaflet is not a replacement for a careful discussion between you and your health care provider. You should discuss the information provided in this leaflet with him or her, both when you first start taking the pill and during your regular visits. You also should follow the advice of your health care provider with regard to regular check-ups while you are on the pill.

EFFECTIVENESS OF ORAL CONTRACEPTIVES

Oral contraceptives are used to prevent pregnancy and are more effective than other non-surgical methods of birth control. When they are taken correctly, without missing any pills, the chance of becoming pregnant is less than 1% (1 pregnancy per 100 women per year of use). Typical failure rates are actually 3% per year. The chance of becoming pregnant increases with each missed pill during a menstrual cycle.

In comparison, typical failure rates for other non-surgical methods of birth control during the first year are as follows:

IUD: 6%
Diaphragm with spermicides: 18%
Spermicides alone: 21%
Vaginal sponge: 18 to 30%
Condom alone: 12%
Periodic abstinence: 20%
No methods: 89%

WHO SHOULD NOT TAKE ORAL CONTRACEPTIVES

Cigarette smoking increases the risk of serious cardiovascular side effects from oral contraceptive use. This risk increases with age and with heavy smoking (15 or more cigarettes per day) and is quite marked in women over 35 years of age. Women who use oral contraceptives are strongly advised not to smoke.

Some women should not use the pill. For example, you should not take the pill if you are pregnant or think you may be pregnant. You also should not use the pill if you have any of the following conditions:

● A history of heart attack or stroke
● Blood clots in the legs (thrombophlebitis), brain (stroke), lungs (pulmonary embo-

---

5. Cancer of the breast and reproductive organs

There is, at present, no confirmed evidence that oral contraceptives increase the risk of cancer of the reproductive organs in women. Several studies have found no overall increase in the risk of developing breast cancer. However, women who use oral contraceptives and have a strong family history of breast cancer or who have breast nodules or abnormal mammograms should be followed closely by their doctors. Some studies have reported an increase in the risk of developing breast cancer, particularly at a younger age. This increased risk appears to be related to duration of use.

Some studies have found an increase in the incidence of cancer of the cervix in women who use oral contraceptives. However, this finding may be related to factors other than the use of oral contraceptives.

ESTIMATED RISK OF DEATH FROM A BIRTH CONTROL METHOD OR PREGNANCY

All methods of birth control and pregnancy are associated with a risk of developing certain diseases which may lead to disability or death. An estimate of the number of deaths associated with different methods of birth control and pregnancy has been calculated and is shown in the following table:

ESTIMATED ANNUAL NUMBER OF BIRTH-RELATED OR METHOD-RELATED DEATHS ASSOCIATED WITH CONTROL OF FERTILITY PER 100,000 NON-STERILE WOMEN, BY FERTILITY CONTROL METHOD ACCORDING TO AGE

Method of control and outcome	15-19	20-24	25-29	30-34	35-39	40-44
No fertility control methods*	7.0	7.4	9.1	14.8	25.7	28.2
Oral contraceptives non-smoker**	0.3	0.5	0.9	1.9	13.8	31.6
Oral contraceptives smoker**	2.2	3.4	6.6	13.5	51.1	117.2
IUD**	0.8	0.8	1.0	1.0	1.4	1.4
Condom*	1.1	1.6	0.7	0.2	0.3	0.4
Diaphragm/Spermicide*	1.9	1.2	1.2	1.3	2.2	2.8
Periodic abstinence*	2.5	1.6	1.6	1.7	2.9	3.6

* Deaths are birth-related
** Deaths are method-related

In the above table, the risk of death from any birth control method is less than the risk of childbirth except for oral contraceptive users over the age of 35 who smoke and pill users over the age of 40 even if they do not smoke. It can be seen from the table that for women aged 15 to 39 the risk of death is highest with pregnancy (7–26 deaths per 100,000 women, depending on age). Among pill users who do not smoke the risk of death is always lower than that associated with pregnancy for any age group, although over the age of 40 the risk increases to 32 deaths per 100,000 women compared to 28 associated with pregnancy at that age. However, for pill users who smoke and are over the age of 35 the estimated number of deaths exceeds those for other methods of birth control. If a woman is over the age of 40 and smokes, her estimated risk of death is 4 times higher (117/100,000 women) than the estimated risk associated with pregnancy (28/100,000 women) in that age group.

The suggestion that women over 40 who don't smoke should not take oral contraceptives is based on information from older high-dose pills and on less selective use of pills than is practiced today. An Advisory Committee of the FDA discussed this issue in 1989 and recommended that the benefits of oral contraceptive use by healthy, non-smoking women over 40 years of age may outweigh the possible risks. However, all women, especially older women, are cautioned to use the lowest dose pill that is effective.

WARNING SIGNALS

If any of these adverse effects occur while you are taking oral contraceptives, call your doctor immediately:

● Sharp chest pain, coughing of blood or sudden shortness of breath (indicating a possible clot in the lung)
● Pain in the calf (indicating a possible clot in the leg)

lism) or eyes
- A history of blood clots in the deep veins of your legs
- Chest pain (angina pectoris)
- Known or suspected breast cancer or cancer of the lining of the uterus, cervix or vagina
- Unexplained vaginal bleeding (until a diagnosis is reached by your doctor)
- Yellowing of the whites of the eyes or of the skin (jaundice) during pregnancy or during previous use of the pill
- Liver tumor (benign or cancerous)
- Known or suspected pregnancy

Tell your health care provider if you have ever had any of these conditions. Your health care provider can recommend a safer method of birth control.

OTHER CONSIDERATIONS BEFORE TAKING ORAL CONTRACEPTIVES

Tell your health care provider if you have or have had:
- Breast nodules, fibrocystic disease of the breast, an abnormal breast x-ray or mammogram
- Diabetes
- Elevated cholesterol or triglycerides
- High blood pressure
- Migraine or other headaches or epilepsy
- Mental depression
- Gallbladder, heart or kidney disease
- History of scanty or irregular menstrual periods

Women with any of these conditions should be checked often by their health care provider if they choose to use oral contraceptives.

Also, be sure to inform your doctor or health care provider if you smoke or are on any medications.

RISKS OF TAKING ORAL CONTRACEPTIVES

1. Risk of developing blood clots

Blood clots and blockage of blood vessels are the most serious side effects of taking oral contraceptives. In particular, a clot in the legs can cause thrombophlebitis and a clot that travels to the lungs can cause a sudden blocking of the vessel carrying blood to the lungs. Rarely, clots occur in the blood vessels of the eye and may cause blindness, double vision, or impaired vision.

If you take oral contraceptives and need elective surgery, need to stay in bed for a prolonged illness or have recently delivered a baby, you may be at risk of developing blood clots. You should consult your doctor about stopping oral contraceptives three to four weeks before surgery and not taking oral contraceptives for two weeks after surgery or during bed rest. You should also not take oral contraceptives soon after delivery of a baby. It is advisable to wait for at least four weeks after delivery if you are not breast feeding. If you are breast feeding, you should wait until you have weaned your child before using the pill (see GENERAL PRECAUTIONS, While Breast Feeding).

2. Heart attacks and strokes

Oral contraceptives may increase the tendency to develop strokes (stoppage or rupture of blood vessels in the brain) and angina pectoris and heart attacks (blockage of blood vessels in the heart). Any of these conditions can cause death or temporary or permanent disability.

Smoking greatly increases the possibility of suffering heart attacks and strokes. Furthermore, smoking and the use of oral contraceptives greatly increase the chances of developing and dying of heart disease.

3. Gallbladder disease

Oral contraceptive users may have a greater risk than non-users of having gallbladder disease, although this risk may be related to pills containing high doses of estrogen.

4. Liver tumors

In rare cases, oral contraceptives can cause benign but dangerous liver tumors. These benign liver tumors can rupture and cause fatal internal bleeding. In addition, a possible but not definite association has been found with the pill and liver cancers in 2 studies in which a few women who developed these very rare cancers were found to have used oral contraceptives for long periods. However, liver cancers are extremely rare.

- Crushing chest pain or heaviness in the chest (indicating a possible heart attack)
- Sudden severe headache or vomiting, dizziness or fainting, disturbances of vision or speech, weakness or numbness in an arm or leg (indicating a possible stroke)
- Sudden partial or complete loss of vision (indicating a possible clot in the eye)
- Breast lumps (indicating possible breast cancer or fibrocystic disease of the breast: ask your doctor or health care provider to show you how to examine your breasts)
- Severe pain or tenderness in the stomach area (indicating a possible ruptured liver tumor)
- Difficulty in sleeping, weakness, lack of energy, fatigue or change in mood (possibly indicating severe depression)
- Jaundice or a yellowing of the skin or eyeballs, accompanied frequently by fever, fatigue, loss of appetite, dark colored urine or light colored bowel movements (indicating possible liver problems)

SIDE EFFECTS OF ORAL CONTRACEPTIVES

1. Vaginal bleeding

Irregular vaginal bleeding or spotting may occur while you are taking the pill. Irregular bleeding may vary from slight staining between menstrual periods to breakthrough bleeding which is a flow much like a regular period. Irregular bleeding occurs most often during the first few months of oral contraceptive use but may also occur after you have been taking the pill for some time. Such bleeding may be temporary and usually does not indicate any serious problem. It is important to continue taking your pills on schedule. If the bleeding occurs in more than 1 cycle or lasts for more than a few days, talk to your doctor or health care provider.

2. Contact lenses

If you wear contact lenses and notice a change in vision or an inability to wear your lenses, contact your doctor or health care provider.

3. Fluid retention

Oral contraceptives may cause edema (fluid retention) with swelling of the fingers or ankles and may raise your blood pressure. If you experience fluid retention, contact your doctor or health care provider.

4. Melasma (Mask of Pregnancy)

A spotty darkening of the skin is possible, particularly of the face.

5. Other side effects

Other side effects may include change in appetite, headache, nervousness, depression, dizziness, loss of scalp hair, rash and vaginal infections.

If any of these side effects occur, contact your doctor or health care provider.

GENERAL PRECAUTIONS

1. Missed periods and use of oral contraceptives before or during early pregnancy

At times you may not menstruate regularly after you have completed taking a cycle of pills. If you have taken your pills regularly and miss 1 menstrual period, continue taking your pills for the next cycle but be sure to inform your health care provider before doing so. If you have not taken the pills daily as instructed and miss 1 menstrual period, or if you miss 2 consecutive menstrual periods, you may be pregnant. You should stop taking oral contraceptives until you are sure you are not pregnant and continue to use another method of contraception.

There is no conclusive evidence that oral contraceptive use is associated with an increase in birth defects when taken inadvertently during early pregnancy. Previously, a few studies had reported that oral contraceptives might be associated with birth defects but these studies have not been confirmed. Nevertheless, oral contraceptives or any other drugs should not be used during pregnancy unless clearly necessary and prescribed by your doctor. You should check with your doctor about risks to your unborn child from any medication taken during pregnancy.

2. While breast feeding

If you are breast feeding, consult your doctor before starting oral contraceptives. Some of the drug will be passed on to the child in the milk. A few adverse effects on the child have been reported, including yellowing of the skin (jaundice) and breast enlargement. In addition, oral contraceptives may decrease the amount and quality of your milk. If possible, use another method of contraception while breast feeding. You should consider starting oral contraceptives only after you have weaned your child completely.

3. Laboratory tests

If you are scheduled for any laboratory tests, tell your doctor you are taking birth control pills. Certain blood tests may be affected by birth control pills.

4. Drug interactions

Certain drugs may interact with birth control pills to make them less effective in preventing pregnancy or cause an increase in breakthrough bleeding. Such drugs include rifampin; drugs used for epilepsy such as barbiturates (for example phenobarbital) and phenytoin (Dilantin is one brand of this drug); phenylbutazone (Butazolidin is one brand of this drug) and possibly certain antibiotics. You may need to use additional contraception when you take oral contraceptives less effective.

HOW TO TAKE ORAL CONTRACEPTIVES

1. General instructions

● You must take your pill every day according to the instructions. Oral contraceptives are most effective if taken no more than 24 hours apart. Take your pill at the same time every day so that you are less likely to forget to take it. You will then maintain the proper amount of drug in your body.

● If you are scheduled for surgery or you need prolonged bed rest you should advise your doctor that you are on the pill and stop taking the pill 4 weeks before surgery to avoid an increased risk of blood clots. It also is advisable not to start oral contraceptives sooner than 4 weeks after delivery of a baby.

● When you first begin to use the pill, you should use an additional method of protection until you have taken your first 7 pills.

Your physician has prescribed one of the following dosage schedules. Please follow the instructions appropriate for your schedule.

● 21-Day Schedule for BREVICON® (norethindrone and ethinyl estradiol), NORINYL® 1 + 35 (norethindrone and ethinyl estradiol), NORINYL® 1 + 50 (norethindrone and mestranol) Tablets: You may start taking the pill on Day 5 of your menstrual cycle or on Sunday. To start on Day 5, count the first day of menstrual flow as Day 1 and take the first pill on Day 5 of the menstrual cycle whether or not the flow has stopped. To start on Sunday, take the first pill on the first Sunday after your menstrual period begins. If it begins on Sunday, take the first pill that day. Whether you start on Day 5 or on Sunday, take another pill at the same time each day, preferably at bedtime, for 21 days. Then wait for 7 days, during which time a menstrual period usually occurs, and begin taking 1 pill every day on the eighth day after you took your last pill, whether or not the menstrual flow has stopped. This cycle of 21 days on pills and 7 days off pills is repeated until the time for your visit with your physician or health care provider.

● 28-Day Schedule for BREVICON, NORINYL 1 + 35, NORINYL 1 + 50 Tablets: You may start taking the pill on Day 5 of your menstrual cycle or on Sunday. To start on Day 5, count the first day of menstrual flow as Day 1 and take the first white, yellow-green, or blue pill on Day 5 of the menstrual cycle whether or not the flow has stopped. To start on Sunday, take the first white, yellow-green, or blue pill on the first Sunday after your menstrual period begins. If it begins on Sunday, take the first pill that day. Whether you start on Day 5 or on Sunday, follow the sequence around the card and continue taking another pill at the same time each day, preferably at bedtime, for 21 days. Then take an orange pill from the bottom of the card each day for 7 days and expect a menstrual period during this week. The orange pills contain no active drug and are included simply for your convenience—to eliminate the need for counting days. After all 28 pills have been taken, whether bleeding has stopped or not, take the first white, yellow-green, or blue pill of the next cycle without any interruption. With the 28-day package, pills are taken every day with no gap between cycles until the time for your visit with your physician or health care provider.

● NOR-QD® (norethindrone) Tablets 0.35 mg Schedule: Take the first pill on the first day of the menstrual flow, and take another pill each day, every day until the time for your visit with your physician or health care provider. The pill should be taken at the same time of day, preferably at bedtime, and continued daily without interruption whether bleeding occurs or not. If prolonged bleeding occurs, you should consult your physician.

● 21-Day Schedule for TRI-NORINYL® (norethindrone and ethinyl estradiol) Tablets: Take the first blue pill on the first Sunday after menstrual flow begins. If menstrual flow begins on Sunday, take the first blue pill on that day. Take 1 blue pill the same time each day, preferably at bedtime, for the first 7 days, 1 yellow-green pill daily for the next 9 days, and then 1 blue pill each day for 5 days. Wait for 7 days, during which time a menstrual period usually occurs, then begin a new cycle of pills on the eighth day after you took your last pill, whether or not the menstrual flow has stopped. This cycle of 21 days on pills and 7 days off pills is repeated until the time for your visit with your

tives, especially if you had irregular menstrual cycles before you used oral contraceptives. It may be advisable to postpone conception until you begin menstruating regularly once you have stopped taking the pill and desire pregnancy.

There does not appear to be any increase in birth defects in newborn babies when pregnancy occurs soon after stopping the pill.

6. Overdosage

Serious ill effects have not been reported following ingestion of large doses of oral contraceptives by young children. Overdosage may cause nausea and withdrawal bleeding in females. In case of overdosage, contact your health care provider or pharmacist.

7. Other information

Your health care provider will take a medical and family history and will examine you before prescribing oral contraceptives. You should be reexamined at least once a year. Be sure to inform your health care provider if there is a family history of any of the conditions listed previously in this leaflet. Be sure to keep all appointments with your health care provider because this is a time to determine if there are early signs of side effects from oral contraceptive use.

Do not use the drug for any condition other than the one for which it was prescribed. This drug has been prescribed specifically for you; do not give it to others who may want birth control pills.

If you want more information about birth control pills, ask your doctor or health care provider. They have a more technical leaflet called PHYSICIAN LABELING which you may wish to read.

NON-CONTRACEPTIVE HEALTH BENEFITS

In addition to preventing pregnancy, use of oral contraceptives may provide certain non-contraceptive health benefits:

● Menstrual cycles may become more regular
● Blood flow during menstruation may be lighter and less iron may be lost. Therefore, anemia due to iron deficiency is less likely to occur
● Pain or other symptoms during menstruation may be encountered less frequently
● Ectopic (tubal) pregnancy may occur less frequently
● Non-cancerous cysts or lumps in the breast may occur less frequently
● Acute pelvic inflammatory disease may occur less frequently
● Oral contraceptive use may provide some protection against developing two forms of cancer: cancer of the ovaries and cancer of the lining of the uterus

BRIEF SUMMARY
PATIENT PACKAGE INSERT

Oral contraceptives, also known as "birth control pills" or "the pill," are taken to prevent pregnancy and, when taken correctly, have a failure rate of about 1% per year when used without missing any pills. The typical failure rate of large numbers of pill users is less than 3% per year when women who miss pills are included. For most women, oral contraceptives are also free of serious or unpleasant side effects. However, forgetting to take oral contraceptives considerably increases the chances of pregnancy.

For the majority of women, oral contraceptives can be taken safely, but there are some women who are at high risk of developing certain serious diseases that can be life-threatening or may cause temporary or permanent disability. The risks associated with taking oral contraceptives increase significantly if you:

● Smoke
● Have high blood pressure, diabetes or high cholesterol
● Have or have had clotting disorders, heart attack, stroke, angina pectoris, cancer of the breast or sex organs, jaundice or malignant or benign liver tumors

You should not take the pill if you suspect you are pregnant or have unexplained vaginal bleeding.

Cigarette smoking increases the risk of serious cardiovascular side effects from oral contraceptive use. This risk increases with age and with heavy smoking (15 or more cigarettes per day) and is quite marked in women over 35 years of age. Women who use oral contraceptives are strongly advised not to smoke.

physician or health care provider.
- 28-Day Schedule for TRI-NORINYL Tablets: Take the first blue pill on the first Sunday after menstrual flow begins. If menstrual flow begins on Sunday, take the first blue pill on that day. Take 1 blue pill the same time each day, preferably at bedtime, for the first 7 days. 1 yellow-green pill daily for the next 9 days, and then 1 blue pill each day for 5 days. Take 1 orange pill daily for the next 7 days and expect a menstrual period during this week. The orange pills contain no active drug and are included simply for your convenience—to eliminate the need for counting days. After all 28 pills have been taken, whether bleeding has stopped or not, take the first blue pill of the next cycle without any interruption. With the 28-day package, a pill is taken every day with no gap between cycles until the time for your visit with your physician or health care provider.

2. Missed periods/breakthrough bleeding

At times, there may be no menstrual period after you complete a cycle of pills. If you miss 1 menstrual period but have taken the pills *exactly as you were supposed to*, continue as usual into the next cycle. If you have not taken the pills correctly, and have missed a menstrual period, *you may be pregnant* and you should stop taking oral contraceptives until your doctor determines whether or not you are pregnant. Until you can get to your doctor, use another form of contraception. If you miss 2 consecutive menstrual periods, you should stop taking the pills until it is determined that you are not pregnant.

Even if spotting or breakthrough bleeding should occur, continue the medication according to the schedule. Should spotting or breakthrough bleeding persist, you should notify your physician.

3. If you forget to take your pill

If you miss only 1 pill in a cycle, the chance of becoming pregnant is small. Take the missed pill as soon as you realize that you have forgotten it. Since the risk of pregnancy increases with each additional pill you skip, it is very important that you take each pill according to schedule.

If you miss 2 pills in a row, you should take 1 of the missed pills as soon as you remember, discard the other missed pill and take your regular pill for that day at the proper time. Furthermore, you should use an additional method of contraception in addition to taking your pills for the remainder of the cycle. If more than 2 pills in a row have been missed, discontinue taking your pills immediately and use an additional method of contraception until you have a period or your doctor determines that you are not pregnant. Missing orange pills in the 28-day schedule does not increase your chances of becoming pregnant.

4. Pregnancy due to pill failure

When taken correctly, the incidence of pill failure resulting in pregnancy is approximately 1% (i.e., 1 pregnancy per 100 women per year). If failure occurs, the risk to the fetus is minimal. The typical failure rate of large numbers of pill users is less than 3% when women who miss pills are included. If you become pregnant, you should discuss your pregnancy with your doctor.

5. Pregnancy after stopping the pill

There may be some delay in becoming pregnant after you stop using oral contracep-

Most side effects of the pill are not serious. The most common such effects are nausea, vomiting, bleeding between menstrual periods, weight gain, breast tenderness and difficulty wearing contact lenses. These side effects, especially nausea and vomiting, may subside within the first 3 months of use.

The serious side effects of the pill occur very infrequently, especially if you are in good health and are young. However, you should know that the following medical conditions have been associated with or made worse by the pill:

1. Blood clots in the legs (thrombophlebitis) or lungs (pulmonary embolism), stoppage or rupture of a blood vessel in the brain (stroke), blockage of blood vessels in the heart (heart attack or angina pectoris), eye or other organs of the body. As mentioned above, smoking increases the risk of heart attacks and strokes and subsequent serious medical consequences.
2. Liver tumors, which may rupture and cause severe bleeding. A possible but not definite association has been found with the pill and liver cancer. However, liver cancers are extremely rare.
3. High blood pressure, although blood pressure usually returns to normal when the pill is stopped.

The symptoms associated with these serious side effects are discussed in the detailed leaflet given to you with your supply of pills. Notify your doctor or health care provider if you notice any unusual physical disturbances while taking the pill. In addition, drugs such as rifampin, as well as some anti-convulsants and some antibiotics, may decrease oral contraceptive effectiveness.

Studies to date of women taking the pill have not shown an increase in the incidence of cancer of the breast or cervix. There is, however, insufficient evidence to rule out the possibility that the pill may cause such cancers. Some studies have reported an increase in the risk of developing breast cancer, particularly at a younger age. This increased risk appears to be related to duration of use.

Taking the pill may provide some important non-contraceptive health benefits. These include less painful menstruation, less menstrual blood loss and anemia, fewer acute pelvic infections and fewer cancers of the ovary and the lining of the uterus.

Be sure to discuss any medical condition you may have with your health care provider. Your health care provider will take a medical and family history before prescribing oral contraceptives and will examine you. You should be reexamined at least once a year while taking oral contraceptives. The detailed patient information leaflet gives you further the information which you should read and discuss with your health care provider.

 SYNTEX

SYNTEX (F.P.) INC.
HUMACAO, PR 00661

REVISED MARCH 1990
814-H2218-90

©1990 SYNTEX (F.P.) INC.

Easterbrook, Gregg   WZ100
Surgeon Koop   E13s

Easterbrook, Gregg
AUTHOR
Surgeon Koop   WZ100
TITLE
8339   E13s

DATE DUE

JAN 2 3 1992	BORROWER'S NAME
FEB 4 1992	1991
	CmFreese 2E
	Melissa Kugler Educ

8339